U-TURN FOR CHRIST 2

THE RIPPLE EFFECT OF GOD'S GRACE

GERRY BROWN

U-Turn For Christ 2: The Ripple Effect of God's Grace
By Gerry Brown

We would especially like to thank Nancy Aguilar for her editorial skill. Her expertise made this book possible. Special thanks as well to Miriam Rogers for her meticulous proofreading of every line, every page.

Cover design by John Shaffer

© 2015 Published by U-Turn For Christ
20170 Patterson Ave., Perris, CA 92570
Web site: www.uturnforchrist.com
E-mail: info@uturnforchrist.com
(951) 943-7097

ISBN: 978-1-59751-934-2

Translational emendations, amplifications, and paraphrases are by the author.

Printed in the United States of America.

TABLE OF CONTENTS

FOREWORD

On a sweltering summer day in June of 2013, I walked onto the grounds of the U-Turn For Christ ranch for the first time. A festive celebration surrounded me, with a decorated stage featuring live bands, guitar-strumming singers, and passionate speakers from around the world. A friendly crowd milled about, and a long line of men, women, and children waited to fill their plates with pulled pork, potato salad, baked beans, and an impressive spread of desserts.

What was this joy-filled event? It was the annual U-Turn For Christ Pig Roast in Perris, California, where U-Turn pastors and alumni gather each year to celebrate God's victory in their lives.

As I searched the crowd for Cathy Rich, the overseer of this project, a complete stranger walked up to me and said, "Hello Nancy, how are you doing?" I was taken aback at first—until I learned that Cathy had shown this U-Turn staff member my Facebook picture and said, "Find this girl!" I eventually connected with Cathy, and we spent the next few hours talking about the vision for *U-Turn For Christ 2*.

Cathy asked me to pick someone to interview from the list of prospective stories, and I randomly chose Anthony Dowdy. After lunch, we met up with Anthony in Pastor Gerry Brown's office. I pulled out my questions, Cathy pressed the record button, and for the next hour, Anthony shared how God had transformed his destructive life of drugs and crime into one of grace and service. I'd never heard anything quite like it, yet it was only the first of many miraculous stories to come.

When I returned home to Seattle, Anthony and I had a couple more conversations by phone, and then I wrote out his story. Weeks later I received the heartbreaking news that Anthony had died suddenly. I grieved for his family and the numerous friends he left behind. Though I'd only known him a short time, his life had touched mine deeply, and I realized that God had planned all along that his story was to be written first.

These stories were pieced together with much prayer, and the entire project was a blessing for all involved. In the process of many phone interviews, emails, and texts back and forth, I had the privilege of meeting fourteen of the most humble and courageous people I've ever known. Besides drug and alcohol addiction, they have dealt with real-life struggles that are familiar to us all—fear, depression, pride, selfishness, grief, confusion, and loneliness.

The men and women on these pages are my new heroes, and the lessons they share have brought me to my knees again and again. My heartfelt thanks to each one of you for inspiring us all to live our lives for the only One who really matters.

Nancy Aguilar
Editor
Seattle, Washington

INTRODUCTION

Now to Him who is able to do exceedingly abundantly above all that we ask or think, according to the power that works in us, to Him be glory in the church by Christ Jesus to all generations, forever and ever. Amen.

EPHESIANS 3:20-21

THE RIPPLE EFFECT

Throw a pebble into a tranquil lake and right away you'll observe an inevitable ripple effect spreading across the surface of the water.

Years ago the Lord gave this vision to my wife, Peggy, illustrating a powerful truth about the impact that our lives have on one another. In the same way that a dropped pebble ripples across the entire surface of water, our lives will produce a ripple effect, good or bad, on others.

Often those addicted to drugs or alcohol will generate a ripple effect, although they are usually too self-absorbed to notice or care. At times it may look like they are hurling boulders into the water, causing those who love them to be tossed about or even brought under by the impact of their actions. Some ripples last long and go deep, like a child losing a parent who has overdosed and died, or a mother burying her son who drank while driving.

Equally, this ripple effect works both ways. Restored lives can also have a tremendous impact. Some who arrive at U-Turn For Christ may begin the program with a trail of destruction behind them, but when they decide to turn from their addictions and live for Jesus, they start influencing others for the Lord. Like ripples on water, I have witnessed God move in hundreds of lives over the years, including those whose stories you are about to read.

We serve an incredible God, who can take individuals from any background, any ethnic culture, any status in life, and give them victory over the sin of addiction. This truth is at the heart of *U-Turn For Christ 2: The Ripple Effect of God's Grace*, a compilation of real life stories from men and women who came to U-Turn For Christ after hitting rock bottom. With no hope and nowhere else to go, each person was introduced to the One who can turn a disastrous existence into a dynamic life of living for God. And their testimonies are all very personal to Peggy and me. Surrendered to Him, they are now being used around the world to touch others for the Lord Jesus Christ.

As you journey through these stories, I pray that your life will be touched as well. May you recognize God's endless grace poured out for you, and may you be assured that when you place your trust in Jesus Christ, He will be there, waiting to begin the ripple effect of His love in your life too.

CHAPTER 1

If anyone is in Christ, he is a new creation; old things have passed away; behold, all things have become new.

2 CORINTHIANS 5:17

PASTOR RON BROWN
An Ocean of Mercy

Life couldn't get much better for high school linebacker, Ron Brown. A blue chip player recruited by colleges across the country, Ron accepted a full-ride scholarship to USC, the most prestigious football program in the world. With his heart set on the NFL, Ron's dream of becoming a professional player was almost within reach. That is, until the accident.

"Your neck is broken," the doctor said. "I'm sorry to tell you this, but you'll never play football again," At that moment, Ron had nothing left to live for.

This is Ron's story.

Some might say I lived a charmed life. The oldest of fifteen children, I had ten brothers and four sisters who all adored me. We were raised in a loving home with deeply religious parents, and on Sunday mornings our family filled an entire pew at St. Pius V Catholic Church. Our parents taught us to love the Lord, and every night Dad led us in evening prayers. I attended Catholic schools and breezed through all my classes with good grades.

Growing up, my life revolved around one thing—football. I was pretty good at it too. On the first Christmas I could walk, I received a child-sized football with little football pads and a kid's helmet. My brothers received the same gift when they were toddlers, and as soon as they'd strap on their new gear, we'd head for the backyard and scrimmage together. As we got older I coached all my brothers, teaching them everything I knew about the game, and eventually they all loved it as much as I did.

THE PHONE CALL

During my senior year, I was elected captain of the Mater Dei High School football team in Santa Ana, California, where I played defense as a middle linebacker and also defensive tackle. I saw a lot of minutes on the field, leading our team to win the CIF championship and capturing the attention of numerous college coaches. Several of them wined and dined me during football recruiting season, hoping I'd sign a contract. But I held out, waiting to hear from one particular coach from USC. Finally, he called. "Hello, Ron?"

"Yes, this is Ron."

"John McKay here."

My thoughts raced. *John McKay? It's him!*

"Say, Ron, the coaches here at USC want to talk to you about playing football for the Trojans next year." Excited and nervous, I accepted the coach's invitation to dinner and we arranged a time and place. A few days later my dad and I drove to a fancy restaurant in Los Angeles, where Coach McKay, Coach Coury, and another colleague joined us. After dinner, Coach McKay offered the scholarship. I looked over at Dad, who was beaming. "If it's okay with you, Coach, I'd like to talk it over with my parents," I said.

Coach McKay nodded and smiled. "Of course."

So many things attracted me to USC. Besides their excellent academic reputation, they had a powerhouse football team of national prominence in the late '60s, when OJ Simpson played on the team. In addition, my beloved uncle, Dick Coury, had just been hired as Coach McKay's assistant. While coaching Mater Dei through its championship season, Uncle Dick was handpicked for the USC position. So after talking to my parents, they gave their blessing on my choice and I accepted Coach McKay's offer. Soon my dream-come-true future began to sink in.

Meanwhile, as big man on campus at Mater Dei, I reveled in the glory. All the attention I received as a football hero went straight to my head so much so that pride consumed my heart. When football season was over, I celebrated my good fortune with friends by drinking beer—lots of beer. In three months' time, from January to March, I became a full-fledged teenage alcoholic. The sad part was that I knew better. My parents had taught me that drunkenness is a sin, and yet I was often the instigator, encouraging my friends to drink often. Proverbs 23:21 says it well:

"For the drunkard...will come to poverty."

Looking back, it's clear that drinking eventually led to my poverty of mind, body, and spirit.

THE DIVE

The summer after high school graduation, my friends and I spent as much time together as possible before leaving for college. Some-

11

times we'd meet at my girlfriend's house in Newport Beach on the Back Bay. Her house faced a canal that goes out to the ocean, and we'd hang out on her twenty-foot-high dock—the perfect spot for diving. One hot July day, two of my buddies joined me there, and we spent the morning diving off the dock and swimming back to shore. In between dives, one friend and I drank a few beers. We broke for lunch around noon and drank more beer.

By the time we arrived at the dock later that afternoon, I was drunk and forgot to check the tide before diving into the water. When I dove in, I knew immediately something was wrong. My extended hands hit the sandy ocean floor abruptly, lessening the blow, right before the top of my head slammed into the sand. I felt my neck and back compress, and then a sudden pain shot through my body. At the same time, a silent prayer rose from deep within me: *Lord, please don't let this injury be permanent!* Without knowing it, I had landed in three feet of water, after a twenty-foot fall. Yet God had mercy on me. I surfaced right away and swam back to shore on my own.

Witnessing the dive, my friends ran out to meet me. "Wow, that hurt!" Stumbling onto shore and holding my head, I said, "I think I'd better go home now." One of my friends—the one who hadn't been drinking—took me home and left me in the care of my brother Billy, who immediately drove me to Hoag Hospital in Newport Beach. My dad met us there, and after the ER doctor ordered x-rays, we all waited in the lobby for the results. Finally the doctor reappeared. "Your x-rays are inconclusive," he said. "I don't see any injury, so you can go home."

Dad wasn't happy with the doctor's vague report. "Something's not right with you, Ron, I just know it. First thing tomorrow I'm taking you to a specialist." I spent a fitful night lying on a mattress at home, with my dad and brothers checking on me around the clock. The next day Dad and Billy drove me to Los Angeles, where I saw an orthopedist. More x-rays revealed three fractured thoracic vertebrae, and another thoracic vertebrae that had separated.

"Your neck is broken," the orthopedist said, "and we're going to admit you to the hospital for a month of neck traction. The doctor went on to explain that he didn't want to risk surgery because it might cause further injury. Then came the worst news of all—my football career was over. I was shaken to the core, and my emotions spiraled big time.

What now? I wondered. *There's nothing left for me! What's the sense of living?*

Word of my accident reached the USC football department, and the coaches all surprised me with a visit to the hospital. "We're going to miss having you on the team, Ron," Coach McKay said, "but USC is still honoring your scholarship. You can sign up for classes whenever you're ready." His generous offer touched my heart.

A month later I came home from the hospital with a plaster body cast, extending from the top of my head down to my waist. Then I received a phone call from Mater Dei, inviting me to help coach football at the high school. With some of my brothers now on the team, spending time out on the field again was an unexpected blessing. By the end of football season, my body cast was removed and replaced with a neck brace. Six months later, the neck brace came off and miraculously, I had no residual symptoms—not even a stiff neck!

FINDING MY WAY

Free of cumbersome devices, I finally enrolled at USC in February of 1967; however, I soon discovered that I didn't like college. Without football, I felt aimless, so I spent a lot of time smoking marijuana and drinking heavily. By the end of my first year at USC, I realized I couldn't handle being there any longer so I dropped out. That summer, at the height of the Vietnam war, I received a draft notice from the U.S. Army and was summoned to L.A. for an interview. I went to the interview but because of my injury, they rejected me.

Unsure of what to do next, I asked a friend to catch a flight with me to Hawaii, hoping we'd find work on the islands. We ended up on Oahu in the North Shore area—a surfer's paradise. The year was 1969, and the North Shore was still recovering from a hurricane that had struck the previous year, when fifty-foot waves knocked homes off their foundations. We ran into a work crew that was jacking up fallen houses and moving them onto concrete foundations. The crew needed help and we were hired.

While living in North Shore, I embraced the hippie lifestyle, identifying with Timothy Leary's slogan of that era: "Turn on, tune in, drop out." Searching for enlightenment, I investigated gurus, yogis, Eastern mysticism, Hinduism, Buddhism, and Tao. Drugs were everywhere and I experimented with LSD, mescaline, peyote, and anything else that was available. I eventually lost touch with my family, even my parents. My mom—a faithful prayer warrior for all her children—began asking everyone she knew to pray for me.

After living for about a year on the islands, I returned to Southern California in the early '70s. My family was overjoyed to see me again, especially Mom. True to my new hippie image, I wandered back and forth between my parents' home in Norco and my friends' homes in Newport Beach. I loved reconnecting with my siblings again and was surprised to see how much they had all grown up while I was gone.

I learned that my brother Gerry, now a high school senior, was captain of the Norco High School football team. He was playing linebacker too, just like I did. One Friday night when I was home, hanging out in the kitchen with the family, Mom made tacos for dinner and she set out all the toppings on the kitchen counter. Gerry stood at the counter with his back to me, fixing his tacos first because he had to leave for a game. As I watched Gerry, looking so fine in his blue and white football jersey, I suddenly had a flashback of myself at that age, and an unexpected anger welled up inside of me. I quietly walked up behind Gerry and kicked him as hard as I could, right in the butt. Gerry caught himself before hitting the counter, his tacos went flying, and he spun around to face me. But I escaped out the back door and started running down the street. Gerry chased after me, and my brother Dave ran after him. "Hold on, Gerry!" Dave shouted. Gerry stopped.

"Try to understand Ron's frustration," Dave said. "Remember, he doesn't really know what he's doing right now."

"Yeah, okay…you're right," Gerry conceded. He turned around and headed home. Back in the kitchen, Gerry swept up the mess, fixed a new plate of tacos, and moved on.

LOVED ANYWAY

At times like that, when I hurt in ways that I couldn't even understand myself, my family kept loving me whether I deserved it or not. They were like the Lord Himself to me, helping me realize that I was loved simply because I was Ron—not because of football or anything I had accomplished. And in the years ahead, I would eventually realize that God's love and kindness was even more amazing, that He loved me before I even acknowledged Him, as it says in Titus 3:4-5:

> "But when the kindness and love of God our Savior appeared,
> He saved us, not because of righteous things we had done,
> but because of His mercy." (NIV)

Though my behavior was sometimes unpredictable, thankfully I never lost my sense of humor, and my antics as the family jokester helped us all through these challenging times. A few years after my accident, our parents took some of the kids to Louisville, Kentucky for a summer vacation. The older kids stayed home and my sister

Debbie, who was then a senior in high school, was left in charge. I happened to be at the house too, though I still came and went as I pleased. My siblings who were at home either had summer jobs or sports practice that they couldn't miss.

One day Debbie announced, "I want everybody in the kitchen in half an hour for lunch." She fixed some sandwiches and thirty minutes later, my brothers and sisters came in and sat down at the kitchen table. I swung the back door open and walked in holding a couple of our chickens and pulling Gerry's dwarf pony, Smokey, by the reins. I looked at Debbie innocently. "What? You said you wanted *everybody* in here," I explained, "and these guys don't want to miss lunch either!" The kids all roared with laughter.

"Get those animals out of here—now!" Debbie said, trying to stifle a grin. To this day, we still joke about the pony and chickens having lunch with us in the kitchen.

WANDERINGS

I continued bumming around from place to place, living a life of vagrancy. Once while staying in Newport Beach, I wandered into a Calvary Chapel commune called Mansion Messiah. I walked into the living room, where a group of long-haired, barefoot young people sat on the floor cross-legged in a circle. They must have been in the middle of a church service because they were all singing and praying together. I figured it was some kind of hippie gathering—a real "happening"—so I sat down and joined the circle, waiting for them to pass a hash pipe around. Of course, they didn't pass a pipe but I was entertained, and after their service ended I stood up and left.

Sometimes I ended up in places I wasn't supposed to be, like private residences. Perhaps all the drugs had taken away my inhibitions, because if someone left their front door open, I'd walk in and make myself at home. When the resident came home, I'd be sitting there on the couch, minding my own business. Needless to say, I scared the heck out of people, and it wasn't long before I was arrested for breaking and entering. Honestly, I meant no harm; in fact, I didn't even realize I had done anything wrong.

After that arrest, I stayed in jail for a couple of weeks, until a judge issued a court order to move me to a halfway house for mental patients. According to Gerry, I "zoned out" during this time and often disengaged from conversations. I understood what people said, but I was so out of it that I didn't care what I said back. If someone said, "How are you doing, Ron?" I might answer, "Black widow," or if someone asked, "What time is it?" I might say, "Purple haze." Though my family visited me, it was difficult for them to see me that way. Meanwhile, my mother continued her vigil of prayer.

Gerry believes that God's hand of mercy sustained me during those days of wandering. He had plans for my life that no one could have imagined, preserving me for a future of service. Jeremiah 29:11 describes those plans, not only for me, but for all who trust Him:

> "'For I know the plans I have for you,' declares the Lord, 'plans to prosper you and not to harm you, plans to give you hope and a future.'" (NIV)

As a hippie, I wasn't thinking much about my future—I simply lived from day to day.

Over the next five years, I moved in and out of mental rehab facilities, where psychiatrists evaluated me and prescribed medication. Some places had lock-down units with padded walls and straightjackets, but thankfully I wasn't violent so I was placed in unlocked rooms. Most facilities were bleak, sterile-looking, and depressing. My days often consisted of watching TV and waiting for the next meal.

After my required five-year stint in rehab, I wanted an adventure. Without any illegal drugs or alcohol in rehab, my mind was clearer, and

I hitchhiked through California, Oregon, Washington, Arizona, and New Mexico. I hung out with fellow hippies in Haight-Ashbury and even landed a job running carnival rides in Albuquerque. Wherever I traveled, I'd stay in communes along the way, and if beer was available, I'd help myself, although I felt I was no longer addicted.

SCHOOL AGAIN

After a year on the road, I made my way back to Southern California and moved in with my parents. Now thirty-three years of age, I went back to college again, enrolling at Riverside Community College. Each subject sounded fascinating and I wanted to study them all: theology, science, history, astrology, and whatever else interested me. I would pick one subject, take every class available, and then move on to a new subject. For instance, I started out taking introductory auto mechanics and finished all the automotive courses offered through advanced body shop. In addition to academics, I joined the cross-country and track teams, and even earned a letter. I also played rugby and worked part-time at the college bookstore.

While I was in school, my brother Gerry arrived home from the Navy and began taking classes too. Whenever we'd see each other on campus, Gerry would say, "Come on out to the car, Ron," and we'd head for the parking lot to smoke a joint. A savvy businessman by now, my brother hired me to clean carpets and install flooring for a couple of his new businesses. After Gerry finished his AA degree, I stayed on and eventually accumulated 400 credits—more than any student had ever earned at Riverside City College. I finally graduated, five years later, with three associate degrees.

CHURCH REVISITED

After Gerry's marriage to Peggy, they both became addicted to crystal meth. Their addiction launched yet another business venture for Gerry—drug dealing. They eventually lost everything and split up for several months. Then in 1989, Gerry and Peggy gave their lives to the Lord, and God healed their addictions and restored their marriage. (Read their story in Gerry's book, *U-Turn For Christ*). One Sunday morning I knocked on Gerry's door, hoping to hang out and smoke some weed together. Gerry opened the door and seemed especially glad to see me. "Hey, Ron, come in for a minute." I followed him inside, where Peggy and their two children were waiting by the door, all dressed up and ready to go somewhere. "We're on our way to church," Gerry said. "Will you come with us?"

"Uh, no, thanks, I'll pass." I said and quickly left. But I noticed something different at Gerry's house over the next few months—a new topic of conversation I'd never heard there before. Instead of talking about drugs and making money, Gerry talked about the Lord. He also kept inviting me to church, and for a while I continued to say no. But as the old saying goes, "If you hang around the barber shop long enough, you're bound to get a hair cut." So I eventually gave in and went with Gerry's family to Calvary Chapel Hemet, where I was introduced to Christianity.

Amazed at how his own life and marriage had been restored, Gerry began reaching out to others who were caught in the cycle of addiction, helping them find the same healing that God had given him. His desire to help other addicts led him to open the first U-Turn For Christ ranch in Perris, California, in 1993.

MOVING TO THE RANCH

At this time I still lived with my parents and worked for Gerry, whose carpet and flooring businesses were up and running again. Then in 1994 Gerry invited me to move out to the ranch so he could have more input in my life. "Just come out here with me and see how it goes," he said, and so I did. I moved into the Fourth Street house, which was the ministry home for those in Phase 2 of the program at U-Turn For Christ. Although I wasn't officially part of Phase 2,

I realized later that I actually went through the program without knowing it, and perhaps that's what Gerry had in mind all along. When I arrived at the ranch, I agreed to abide by the same rules, go to the same Bible studies, and take part in the same activities as everyone else. But unfortunately, whenever I had the opportunity, I would sneak off to drink. Still, God got a hold of me there, and it all started when one of my housemates asked me to listen to him say his memory verse. "Sure, go for it!" I told him.

Then this big, burly guy recited Romans 6:23:

> "For the wages of sin is death, but the gift of God is eternal life in Christ Jesus our Lord."

I'd heard the verse before, but in that moment, the words pierced my heart—"for the wages of sin…the gift of God…eternal life." Suddenly I sensed the Lord saying, "Ron, are you ready to ask for forgiveness and accept My gift?"

Without hesitation, I prayed, *Yes, Lord, I'm ready!* God continued speaking to me through the men I lived with at the ranch. Many were much harder cases than me—felons and social outcasts who'd spent years in prison before ending up at U-Turn For Christ. Yet there they were, reciting God's Word, believing it with all their hearts, and being transformed before my eyes.

All the religious teaching I had received in church and school, all the fervent prayers of my mom, and all the mercy God had shown me through the years had brought me to this place, where Romans 6:23 became personal and I truly believed it. The knowledge in my head finally connected with the Lord's presence in my heart, and I knew that He was forming a new creation inside of me.

GROWING

I started reading my Bible seriously for the first time in my life and had many questions about Scriptures that I didn't understand.

Unlike my most difficult college courses, which I had always managed to ace, I'd get stumped by something I read in the Bible and would dig for answers until the Lord gave me understanding. I figured if I was going to believe what it says, I needed to make sure it was God's Word and not just someone's opinion. Romans 10:17 says,

"Faith comes by hearing, and hearing by the Word of God."

That's exactly how it happened for me—my faith was born as I listened to a recovering addict share God's Word.

The Lord gave me the opportunity to acknowledge my faith publicly the following year at a Harvest Crusade. Thousands filled the stands at Anaheim Stadium that night to hear Pastor Greg Laurie share the gospel, and I joined the crowd which gathered afterwards down on the stadium field, where I made a commitment to follow Christ. Later, Gerry baptized me in Lake Perris near the ranch.

Through these experiences, the spiritual influence of my mom and dad reawakened in me, yet it was still only the beginning of what the Lord was doing. Besides teaching us about God, my parents also instilled in their children a desire to share His love with the poor. My mom especially had a heart for missions and a willingness to give of herself to those in need. Her example paved the way for God's next incredible plan for my life.

THE PHILIPPINES

In 1997 Gerry received an invitation to a pastors conference in the Philippines. Deeply moved by the desperate needs he saw there, Gerry recruited me to accompany him on a second trip to San Joaquin a few months later. We brought a team with us to dig a well to provide clean water for the town. Later we built a house for orphaned children and made additional trips to build a church—Calvary Chapel U-Turn For Christ, San Joaquin. Then in the year 2000 we went back to build a house for the pastor. On that particular trip, I noticed a young woman sitting in church one Sunday morning with her twelve-year-old brother, Rogie. I knew Rogie—he and his buddies were all in the youth group, and they played on the streets near the church. But that was the first time I saw Rogie's sister, and she was beautiful.

The next day our construction crew was back on the job, and I saw her again, this time serving drinks at a little stand that had been set up outside her parents' store nearby. The refreshment she served was called *halo-halo*, a traditional Filipino cold treat made with jackfruit, ice cream and shaved ice. When our crew saw Rogie's sister with *halo-halos*, we all made our way over to the stand for a break. "Hi, I'm Tess," she said, introducing herself. She smiled and laughed as she conversed with all of us, and I loved the sound of her laughter. Right away I was attracted to her.

The next Sunday when I saw Tess again at church, we were formally introduced, and after that we talked after service each week. I found out that she worked in Manila but was staying in San Joaquin with her family. I eventually asked Tess's father, Ramon, as well as our pastor, for permission to take Tess out, and six months later, I got down on one knee and proposed. It all happened very quickly, but we both felt it was God's will for us to be married, and I then moved permanently to the Philippines. The following year, on February 15, 2002, Tess and I were married at our church in San Joaquin with Gerry officiating.

MY LIFE TODAY

After serving as the senior teaching pastor since 2003, I now oversee the administrative needs at Calvary Chapel U-Turn For Christ San Joaquin. Tess helps in children's ministry and is a wonderful mother to our four sons—Gerry, age eleven; Bart, eight; Ron James (RJ), six; and Gabriel, who is a toddler. My older sons do well in school and they love learning the Bible. More than anything, I pray that my boys will all walk close to the Lord, follow His example, and grow in their understanding of His Word.

Besides my work in San Joaquin, I also oversee the U
Christ School of Ministry in Eastern Samar. Started in   , ᴜᴇ
School of Ministry equips Filipino men to teach the Word of God.
Pastor Joshua Bahado, a graduate of the school, currently serves
as the director. There are now eight U-Turn For Christ churches
planted throughout the Philippines, all served by pastors who graduated from our School of Ministry. Each pastor also teaches in the
school and mentors students.

The U-Turn For Christ School of Ministry is a two-year program of
biblical studies that culminates in an internship at one of the U-Turn
churches in the Philippines. The internship begins with a student
serving as a pastor's assistant for a year. Later he travels to a village
that doesn't have a Bible-teaching church and starts a Bible study
there. Our goal is for every village in Samar to have access to a Bible-
teaching church. There's still much work to be done, but we're gain-
ing on it. As overseer of the school, I travel from church to church
to encourage and teach the pastors. I love watching new students
develop as they pursue their studies and apply what they've learned.

One of my favorite Scriptures is Matthew 20:16:

> "The last will be first, and the first last. For many are called,
> but few are chosen."

I believe this verse shows that we are a new and chosen generation
of believers, significant because of the salvation we have received
through Jesus Christ. Whatever place He sets us in, and whatever
job He gives us to do, we can be assured that He has chosen it for us.
It's humbling to be chosen! Because it's not by works we have done
or possessions we have gained or places we have established—it's
only by the cross of Jesus that we are given this privilege.

My life was once empty in so many ways. I searched everywhere to
find meaning—in football, alcohol, drugs, and Eastern religions. I
was such a lost soul, and it's only by God's mercy that I have held on.

His blessing has been abundant in my life, allowing me to be married to my beautiful wife and becoming a father. God has made my life full and complete, and all I can do now is thank Him.

· · · · · ⟲ · · · · · ·

Tess, RJ, Gerry, Ron, Gabriel, and Bart

Lord, we come before You to thank you for Pastor Ron. He is such a blessing to the work that You have called us to do. His love for his wife and family set such an example for others to follow, and his testimony is an inspiration to many in how You have touched his life in such a miraculous way. And now You are using him to be a blessing to thousands of people all over the world.

Thank you for Your compassion and how You are using him to train up and encourage pastors in the Philippines to lead their churches with the same compassion. May You continue to use him for Your glory. In Jesus' name, Amen.

U-TURN FOR CHRIST SAN JOAQUIN, PHILIPPINES
Pastor Ron & Tess Brown
Brgy. San Joaquin, Tinambacan Dist., Calbayog City, W. Samar 6710
email: bwy92506@yahoo.com
website: www.uturnforchrist.com/locations/international

Blessed is the man who endures temptation; for when he has been approved, he will receive the crown of life which the Lord has promised to those who love Him.

JAMES 1:12

PASTOR ANTHONY DOWDY
A Legacy of Grace

When Anthony's wife dropped off divorce papers at Donovan State Prison, Anthony flipped out. Maribel had threatened divorce before, but he'd never taken her seriously.

Now, the thought of losing her and their three daughters was more than he could bear. Planning to end his life, Anthony climbed the stairs to the second tier of the prison and peered over the ledge, ready to jump. Life as an addict had finally taken its toll.

This is Anthony's story.

The year I turned five, my world fell apart. My only sibling, Bobby, who was just three years old, became sick and died from an enlarged heart. Not long after that, my parents divorced. I don't remember much about my brother's death—or the divorce—but Dad got custody of me and whisked me off to live with him in St. Louis, Missouri. In my young mind I wondered, *What's going on?* I felt confused, I missed my mom, and all I wanted was for my parents to be together.

But while in Missouri, Dad remarried. For some reason we moved around so much that I never finished a full year at the same school. Typically in the summers, I'd stay with my mom in California, and then I'd go back to Missouri in September to start school again. When I was nine, my mom had another child, my half-brother, Daniel. I loved spending the summers at Mom's because she would let me do whatever I wanted, unlike my dad, who had tons of rules. Dad insisted that I stay in school, go to church, and do what's right.

Although it was hard to get away with stuff at my dad's, I learned to sneak around behind his back as I got older. By the time I turned thirteen, I was smoking cigarettes and using marijuana. Eventually Dad got suspicious and I remember one day he called me into the kitchen. He looked me straight in the eye—while I was stoned—and said, "Are you smoking pot?"

"No!" I lied.

Dad got quiet and his expression became serious. I could tell he was very angry, and my step mom, who was also in the kitchen, suddenly grabbed me and pulled me toward her. In that moment, Dad raised his fist and swung at me. Fortunately, he missed and hit the refrigerator instead, leaving a huge dent. I was stunned. *Yikes!* I thought. *That could have been my jaw!* Dad had punched so hard that a plastic shelf inside the freezer broke into pieces. I think more than anything else, Dad was trying to scare me. And he did. After that day, I chose to live with my mom.

The day Mom picked me up, we started smoking cigarettes together in the car—something I could have never done with Dad! In time, as teenagers do, I stopped listening to my mom altogether and started getting into a lot of trouble. I hung out with the wrong crowd and we got high together by "huffing"—inhaling glue, gas, or paint in a bread bag. As a result, I missed a lot of school and didn't care much about anything except getting high with my friends. After my sophomore year, I dropped out of Buena Park High. Because I'd messed up in school and had been caught drinking, smoking pot, and taking PCP, I entered a court-ordered Job Corps program in Utah at the age of eighteen.

TROUBLE AHEAD

While attending Job Corps, I got busted for possession and being under the influence of LSD. The court sent me back to California, to the Irvine Musick Facility—aka Camp Snoopy—where low-risk offenders serve their court-appointed time working in a farm-like environment. Camp Snoopy had structure. We woke up early, worked all day, and then kicked back in the evening, playing pool or watching TV. I was assigned to a work crew with three guys, and we did cleanup up at a nearby park. Ironically, we ended up finding a drug contact at the park who dropped off heroin for us, so I'd get high when I was supposed to be working.

After my release from Camp Snoopy a year later, I continued with the same drug use rather than incorporating the good habits I had just learned. It's like the Bible says, when we obey our sin nature, we become a slave to it.

> "Do you not know that to whom you present yourselves slaves to obey, you are that one's slaves whom you obey, whether of sin leading to death, or of obedience leading to righteousness?" (Romans 6:16)

Camp Snoopy presented an opportunity for me to be free from the slavery of drugs, but I chose instead to cross the line and keep using. Over the next couple of years, I ended up bouncing in and out of county jail for various drug-related charges.

MARIBEL

At age twenty-one I worked as a janitor at a medical clinic where I made a friend named Jerry. My friend lived in a nice neighborhood in Norwalk, and when we weren't working, we'd hang out at his house playing basketball, drinking, or getting high. One summer afternoon as I drove up to Jerry's house, I saw a beautiful young girl walking out the front door onto the porch. Even now, I remember that moment vividly—her long black hair was tied up in pigtails, and she wore a white T-shirt and gray pants. *Wow,* I thought, *she's cute!* Then right away I realized, *Nah, she's too young.* Jerry came out of the house next and I pulled him aside. "Hey, man," I said, "who's that?"

"That's my cousin, Maribel. She's here from Mexico on a student visa."

"How old is she?" I said.

"Almost eighteen."

"Really?" I smiled. "Well then, hook a brother up!"

Maribel spoke only a few words of English, and I didn't know much Spanish, so it was a little hard to communicate at first. But we had fun together—dancing in the clubs, going out to eat, and relaxing at the beach. A year later on September 23, 1988, we were married, and the following year, Ashlie, our first daughter, was born. I continued drinking and getting high, even though it saddened my wife and it took me away from my little girl. Maribel thought I would change, but I didn't. And when Ashlie was three months old, I drove a friend's car while drunk and rear-ended another car. Afraid of getting caught and facing the consequences of driving under the influence, I jumped out of the car and ran home. I confessed to Maribel

28

and we packed up everything and took off for my uncle's home in Missouri, where the police never caught up with me. One good thing that came from our move was that my dad got to meet Maribel and his new granddaughter.

Six months later Maribel received a letter from her mom in Tijuana. Her mom wasn't feeling well and she'd been diagnosed with breast cancer. Maribel wanted to help her, so we moved to Tijuana to live with my mother-in-law. I found a custodial job at a hotel in San Diego, crossing the border every day to get to work and back home. In the years that followed, we added two more daughters to our family, Cynthia in 1991 and Jamie in 1992. Even though I loved being a dad to our daughters, I was still getting in trouble and was arrested again for being under the influence of marijuana. Before sentencing, the judge told me he'd drop all the charges if I would enlist in the service—all I had to do was sign the papers. I said I would, but I never followed through, so in the end I was sentenced to the county prison for a year.

SMUGGLING

After my release from prison, I got lucky and landed a maintenance job at the California-Mexico border as part of a government program for parolees on probation. This new job offered me another chance to do something right for my family, yet I still caved in to the temptations that came my way. It didn't take long before some locals from Mexico approached me asking, "Hey, do you want to make some money?" They offered me $1,300 to $2,500 a head to smuggle illegals across the border. With a wife and three kids to support, I felt the offer was too hard to resist. It was a dangerous risk but I took it, and pretty soon I got really good at it. When my contacts heard how good I was, they started sending more illegals my way.

Sometimes I would make the illegals cross the border on foot, pick them up on the other side, and load them in my car. Other times I'd put them in my trunk and drive across. Though arrested fifteen times, I was never convicted because the Border Patrol was unable to produce enough evidence against me. It was only a matter of time before the border officials got to know me well—too well. "Mr. Dowdy," they'd say, "How are you? What are you doing here, Mr. Dowdy?"

Whenever they caught me smuggling an illegal, I'd lie, saying, "This car doesn't really belong to me—I was just driving it" or "I didn't know that person was in the car." It was often like playing a cat-and-mouse game with the Border Patrol.

One night before reaching the checkpoint with a car full of illegals, I made a quick stop at a park along the way. It was completely dark outside, and I got out of the car and opened the trunk. When I looked up, there was a shotgun in my face. Then I heard a male voice: "Back up, open your pockets, and take off your shoes." Fearing for my life, I did everything exactly as he said. "Now turn around," he continued, "and walk away." As I turned, the door slammed and the car sped off with the illegals. Even though I'd lost my car, my money, and my shoes, I felt happy to be alive! Barefoot, I ran back to a main road and called for help.

That night should have scared me enough to stop smuggling, but then a friend showed me how to smuggle marijuana from Mexico into the States. I paid someone to install false walls and floors in my car, and then I packed the hidden compartments full of marijuana. Sometimes I smuggled at night, sometimes in broad daylight. I always felt nervous, but I got an adrenaline rush whenever I made it across the border. I smuggled drugs many times before getting caught in 1993, when I was convicted and sent to Donovan State Prison. After serving my time, I got out and did it all over again. It became a never-ending cycle of temptation and sin.

Apparently I earned a reputation for myself, because in the mid-'90s I made the headlines twice in a local San Diego newspaper:

"International Smuggler Anthony Dowdy Apprehended Again." When I saw my name in print, I proudly cut out the articles to show them off. But when Maribel saw them, she became upset. "This isn't anything to be proud of!" she scolded. "You've brought shame to our family." Then she tore up the articles and threw them in the trash.

"Wait—what are you doing?" I yelled. "I wanted to save those in a scrapbook for the girls. This is my legacy!" I was so lost, refusing to see the true condition of my heart. King Solomon once wrote,

> "There is a way that seems right to a man, but its end is the way of death." (Proverbs 14:12)

ARREST FOR ATTEMPTED MURDER

During the time I was smuggling, we lived with my mother-in-law so Maribel could help take care of her. Sadly, the turmoil in our lives spilled over to Maribel's mom, who hated watching her daughter and granddaughters suffer because of my lifestyle. She began telling Maribel that I was no good, and though perhaps it was true, it was hard for Maribel to hear this over and over while she was trying to hold our marriage together.

One day I left the house to get high and when I returned a few hours later, I was shocked to see Maribel sitting in a police car in the driveway. The police officer wouldn't let me talk to her, but he told me that an ambulance had just left taking Maribel's mom to the hospital. Little by little, the story came out. Maribel had been at home alone with her mom, and they had argued—first about money, then about me. As Maribel's mom carried on, the argument escalated and Maribel's emotions snapped. She yanked the electric cord from a blender and wrapped the cord around her mom's neck, choking her. As her mom struggled to pull away, they got into a fistfight. Maribel's mom escaped and ran out the front door, screaming for help, but Maribel grabbed a knife and ran after her.

Once outside, Maribel sat on top of her mom and pinned her to the ground, holding the knife up over her mom in one hand. Just then, the neighbors showed up and pulled Maribel off. Someone called the police, and I arrived as the ambulance rushed her mom to the hospital.

Maribel's mom came home a few days later, and thankfully she was okay. But the police arrested Maribel for assault and attempted murder. Hoping to get Maribel out of jail by posting bail, I left the girls with a drug dealer and tried to smuggle some marijuana across the border, but I got caught and was thrown back in prison.

My mom found out what had happened and decided to drive to Tijuana to look for the girls. The drug dealer lived in our neighborhood, and when my mom drove by, the girls just happened to be playing outside. By God's grace, they saw my mom and ran up to her. Then Mom took the girls back to her home in Sun City, California. Three months later, Maribel's brother generously posted the $5,000 bail for her release. Maribel's charges were dropped and she went to pick up the girls from my mom.

By this time, my mom realized the extent of our dangerous lifestyle, and she was very reluctant to give Ashlie, Cynthia, and Jamie back. She sat Maribel down and had a long talk with her. "If you ever make a mistake like this again," she said, "I'll take the girls away." Even though my mom was firm, she was also loving toward Maribel and the girls, taking them all in to live with her and later helping them find their own place in Lake Elsinore. Mom, Maribel, and the girls all grew close through this difficult time.

My mom's kindness and patience reminds me of how the Lord treats us when we stray from Him. Romans 2:4 (NLT) says,

> "Don't you see how wonderfully kind, tolerant, and patient God is with you? Does this mean nothing to you? Can't you see that His kindness is intended to turn you from your sin?"

To this day, I've never forgotten my mom's help, and I try to pass on that same grace she showed to my family, recognizing that it may lead others to the Lord.

After her discharge from the hospital, Maribel's mom lived only a few more months before passing away. Though her mom didn't press charges, Maribel experienced a lot of guilt and wondered if the assault had contributed to her mom's death. Later, the autopsy report revealed that the actual cause of death was breast cancer.

DEFYING DEATH

After all that Maribel had been through, she was pretty upset when she found out that I had left the girls with a drug dealer. She'd had enough. Sick and tired of my risky behaviors, she wanted a divorce. Even when she said this, I thought, *Yeah, right, you haven't done it yet.* I'd been drinking and smoking pot since we first met, and she had always forgiven me and given me chance after chance. But not this time. Just shy of our tenth anniversary in 1997, she filed for divorce.

Maribel dropped off the divorce papers at the prison. When I found out that our marriage was over, I was devastated. Not only was I serving my third sentence for smuggling pot, I was also losing my family! *This can't be happening,* I thought. Sitting in my prison cell with lots of time to think, I felt hopeless and looked for a way out. I decided to do a swan dive from the second tier of the prison yard, thinking I would land on my head and die instantly. So several days later, ready to carry out my plan, I climbed the stairs and leaned over the bannister facing the yard. Peering over the ledge, I thought, *I'm too scared to do this!* Then someone saw me up there and hit the alarm.

With the loud noise blaring in my ears, I panicked, grabbed hold of the bannister, and tried to lower myself as far as I could before falling. Meanwhile, everyone in the prison yard stopped in their tracks and sat on the ground. The gates bolted shut and the yard closed down. Correctional officers rushed up the stairs, and when I saw them lunge to grab me, I let go of the bannister and fell. A powerful jolt surged through my body as I hit the ground. I didn't die instantly as planned but only broke my left arm, dislocated my collarbone, and banged my head badly. I was lifted onto a stretcher and taken to the ER infirmary, where they put a cast on my arm and bandaged me up.

Bruised and broken, they transferred me to the psych ward for evaluation, and it was there that I met a wonderful volunteer named John Conway. John was in his sixties, white, about six feet tall, with tattoos all over his body. Serving a life sentence for murder, John looked like a bully—definitely someone you didn't want to mess with. But as I got to know him, I found that he was soft-spoken and kind. Once again, the Lord brought someone to show His grace to me. John started hanging out with me and sharing the gospel. Remembering what I learned in Sunday school as a child, I saw how the Lord was using those early lessons to prepare my heart. I listened intently to John's words: "Just pray, just trust Him." In my despair I finally prayed, *Lord, if You're real, You've got to show me! Jesus, please come into my heart.*

In the days that followed, John encouraged me to read the Bible. "Take your time," he said, "don't try to figure out everything all at once." It turned out to be great advice.

In addition to John, a psychiatrist and a psychologist were assigned to work with me in the psych ward. I didn't think I needed either one of them, but as it turned out, they became instrumental in my healing. My psychologist was an older gentleman, and I sensed right away that there was something different about him, even in the way he carried himself. After talking with him several times, he commented on how he noticed a change in my attitude. Then he hesitated for a moment and asked, "How can I help you, Anthony?"

"Well...I...what I really want is to walk closer with the Lord," I replied. "I want to learn more about Him."

"Let's go in here," the psychologist said, walking into his office. Then, closing the door behind us, he motioned for me to sit in a chair.

"I could get into a lot of trouble for this," he said as he pulled out a Bible from his desk, "but I want you to know that I'm a Christian too."

I tripped out and thought, *How cool is that!* Next he asked me what I wanted to do when I got out of prison.

That was a good question! He said if I wanted to walk closer with Jesus, I would need to change my lifestyle, and he suggested that I consider going to a place where I could be discipled in my faith.

"That's just what I want!" I exclaimed. "Can you help me with that?"

"Yes," he smiled. "I'll look into it for you."

Following that session, I started praying for God to show me where He wanted me to go after my release. I really wanted to change and make a true commitment to follow Jesus. The next time I met with the psychologist, he gave me some pamphlets from Christian rehab programs, including one from U-Turn For Christ. That was exactly what I needed—a U-turn from the lifestyle I was living to a life lived for Jesus Christ. I read every single pamphlet, but I didn't know which one to choose, so I never followed through with any of them.

After three months in the psych ward, I returned to the general prison population where I spent another year incarcerated. Although I had lost touch with Maribel and the girls, Maribel surprised me with a visit as the time drew closer to my release date. She said she still loved me and that she never really wanted a divorce. She encouraged me by saying that I needed to get my life together and start taking responsibility for the kids. And then she topped it all off with, "I've accepted the Lord, Anthony, and I want to follow Him now."

Really? I thought. I couldn't believe it. I was so excited.

"Me too!" I blurted out.

Maribel looked skeptical. "Yeah, right."

"I'm serious. I'm really serious!"

It took a lot of convincing, but Maribel finally believed me. She went on to share that the Lord had spoken to her about giving me one more chance. She had prayed, *All right, Lord, but only if You deal with Anthony, because I can't.*

As we continued talking, she told me that she had gone to a Somebody Loves You Christian outreach where she prayed to accept Jesus as her Savior. Since then, she and the girls had been attending Calvary Chapel Lake Elsinore. There she got to know Pastor John Duncan and eventually told him about me. Pastor John informed her that there was a ranch called U-Turn For Christ that might help me. When Maribel said this, I suddenly remembered that my psychologist had mentioned U-Turn For Christ's treatment program. I was blown away because in my heart I knew it was a confirmation from God. *Okay, Lord,* I prayed, *that's where I'm going.*

I'll never forget the day I was released from prison—Saturday, February 3, 1999. With my gate money I bought a bus ticket and rode all the way from San Diego to Lake Elsinore. I had one thing on my mind: seeing Maribel and the girls. When I reached their apartment late that night, I knocked on the door, hoping Maribel would answer. She opened it partway, looking surprised.

"May I come in?" I said.

"No way, you can't be here!" Maribel laughed, surprised and glad to see me at the same time. "Okay, fine. But you'll have to sleep on the floor. And be quiet—the girls are asleep!"

She let me in and made a bed for me on the living room floor. When the girls woke up the next morning, they were excited to see me. So much time had passed. By now Ashlie was nine, Cynthia was seven, and Jamie was six. They had grown so much! As Maribel and the girls were accustomed to doing on Sunday mornings, they went to Calvary Chapel Lake Elsinore, and I attended my first church service as a free man. Maribel introduced me to Pastor John, who graciously told me that the church wanted to sponsor me for the two-month program at U-Turn For Christ. Before I could change my mind, an elder from the church drove me to the ranch that afternoon.

LIFE AT THE RANCH

It wasn't long before I thought, *Oh no, I'm being told what to do again, just like in prison.* God started revealing my prideful nature and how much I needed a lesson in humility. Even though I had accepted the Lord, I hadn't fully surrendered to Him. It wasn't until I began reading the Bible faithfully every day that the Word of God started penetrating my heart. Every morning we would open up the book of Proverbs for our devotional time, and then after breakfast we'd go to work. Then each night after the workday was over and we ate dinner, someone would come in and teach a Bible study. We were encouraged to have our own personal Bible reading and prayer time before we went to sleep. I learned so much about God's Word every day, yet I still had a lot to learn.

One time I flippantly told the overseer at the ranch, "I can do your job better than you." Pastor Gerry Brown heard about it and said four words to me: "Go dig a hole."

Let me explain. Digging a hole makes no sense in and of itself. But Pastor Gerry shares that when the ranch first started, God gave him the idea. The depth and length of the hole is based upon the size of the shovel, which is five feet. So I had to dig a hole five feet wide by five feet deep. Digging that first foot, I was mad and I thought, *This is a lot of work for nothing!* But as I continued digging the second foot, I did a lot of thinking and that led to praying. It sort of broke me down and softened and humbled me. It opened me up to receive and hear from God. As I reflected on what I said to the overseer, I realized, *What do I know about overseeing the ranch anyway? And what makes me think I can do it better than him?* By the third foot, God revealed how proud I was. I was sorry for what I said, and I asked God for His forgiveness. When I reached the fourth foot, I was so happy that God had forgiven me! I knew He would help me with my pride issue.

God says in Hebrews 13:5-6,

> "'I will never leave you nor forsake you.' So we may boldly say: 'The LORD is my helper.'"

Also, Paul assures us in Philippians 1:6 that we can be…

> "confident of this very thing, that He who has begun a good work in you will complete it until the day of Jesus Christ."

Finally, when I made it to the fifth and last foot, I was ready to bury my sin of pride and walk away. It was a great lesson but one that I never wanted to have to do again! After digging my hole, I apologized to the overseer. Slowly but surely, I was learning the Christlike attribute of humility.

Throughout my time on the ranch, I watched Pastor Gerry Brown's example of what grace looks like. I soon learned the source of his grace, meekness, and humility as he began reading Scriptures to us about ministering to others, like in James 5:20:

> "Let him know that he who turns a sinner from the error of his way will save a soul from death and cover a multitude of sins."

ANTHONY DOWDY: *A Legacy of Grace*

He also read 1 Peter 4:10:

> "As each has received a gift, use it to serve one another, as good stewards of God's grace." (ESV)

And 1 Corinthians 10:24:

> "Let no one seek his own, but each one the other's well-being."

I saw Pastor Gerry live these out with some of the guys who were prideful and walked away from the ranch—sometimes three, four, or even five times. He didn't condemn or forget about them; he showed them grace.

One day Pastor Gerry put me to the test and said, "Hey, Anthony, I want you to go out and look for so-and-so. See if you can find him and bring him back to the ranch."

Really? I thought. *But I don't want him to come back. He's a jerk!* I reasoned that those who left the ranch should either return on their own or not come back at all. It was a great lesson from Pastor Gerry, learning how to show God's grace to others. And later on, that same grace would be extended to me too, when I deserved a lengthy imprisonment but received forgiveness instead.

ACCOUNTABILITY DEFINED

As much as I wanted to be delivered from my flesh, changes in my heart came slowly. I hung out with some real knuckleheads when I first got to the ranch. By "knuckleheads" I mean guys who didn't take the program at U-Turn For Christ seriously. Some of these men had been admitted by court order and simply didn't want to be there. They'd goof around or sneak off to get beer or to smoke. God is so good because He spoke to my heart and said, "Anthony, this isn't why you're here." So I separated myself from them and started hanging out with guys who were serious about their relationship with the Lord.

The serious guys were tight. I could see that they loved each other like brothers and held each other accountable. By surrounding myself with these godly men, I built close relationships with them. We woke up early to eat and pray together, and we went to sleep the same way—praying together. Sometimes a few of us continued praying even after the lights went out. We prayed for each other, for the new brothers coming in, and for those who were sick when they were kicking the dope.

Before coming to the ranch, I prayed only for myself, that I would be healthy and things would go well for me. But at the ranch I learned to pray for others, and when I prayed this way God filled me with a peace and contentment that I didn't have before. I loved listening to all the guys pray, and I saw 1 Corinthians 12:25 come alive because we all had "the same care for one another." As I learned how to apply God's Word in my life, I finally started changing.

I experienced wonderful fellowship at the ranch, especially with Mario Rocha, who now serves as the associate pastor there. Mario and I overcame struggles together, like when we both quit smoking. After Mario quit, someone who had gone through the program called me aside and said, "I saw Mario smoking again." At the time, I had graduated from the program and was serving as an overseer. Because Mario and I were friends, I didn't quite know how to handle the situation, so I prayed, *Lord, what should I do?* And the Lord reminded me of some of the Scriptures that helped me overcome my own smoking and drug use. God's Word has a lot to say about keeping ourselves pure from habits like that:

> "I beseech you therefore, brethren, by the mercies of God, that you present your bodies a living sacrifice, holy, acceptable to God, which is your reasonable service. And do not be conformed to this world, but be transformed by the renewing of your mind, that you may prove what is that good and acceptable and perfect will of God." (Romans 12:1-2)

"But put on the Lord Jesus Christ, and make no provision for the flesh, to fulfill its lusts." (Romans 13:14)

"All things are lawful for me, but all things are not helpful. All things are lawful for me, but I will not be brought under the power of any." (1 Corinthians 6:12)

"Therefore, having these promises, beloved, let us cleanse ourselves from all filthiness of the flesh and spirit, perfecting holiness in the fear of God." (2 Corinthians 7:1)

After reading the Word and praying, I decided to meet up with Mario at Starbucks. We ordered our coffee drinks, started talking, and I casually asked if he was still smoking. Right away he got upset. "No! Why?"

"Because a guy at the ranch said he saw you smoking."

"He's lying!" Mario insisted. "It's a setup."

"Okay, All right. That's all I need to know. I'll go talk to him." I headed back to the men's house to deal with the young man. On my way there, Pastor Mario called and said, "Don't do anything. I lied. I really did smoke." The next day Mario told me he was sorry for lying and thankful that I held him accountable.

"I still have to discipline you," I said. Then I prayed, *Lord, what am I supposed to do? He's a pastor!* Finally, I came up with something. "Write a 1,500-word essay about Exodus 20:16: 'You shall not bear false witness.'"

"Come on," Mario said. "That's nothing."

"Make it 5,000 words then."

"That's all? No, I'm digging a hole too."

"Okay, you're digging too," I agreed. Afterward, I wasn't sure if Mario would be out to get me for disciplining him. But because of my concern for him and his truthfulness about the whole thing, we grew to be close brothers in the Lord, and today we're the best of friends.

Accountability with one another is so important. Though it isn't always easy, Mario and I have learned to be open and honest with each other, which is essential in the process of accountability. Ecclesiastes 4:9-10 describes accountability this way:

> "Two are better than one, because they have a good reward for their labor. For if they fall, one will lift up his companion. But woe to him who is alone when he falls, for he has no one to help him up."

Discipleship—or helping each other grow in our walk with the Lord—is huge at U-Turn For Christ. The staff constantly pours the Word of God into the men and women's lives. Whatever the situation, everything always comes back to the Word. Even with little struggles, like sneaking cigarettes, we always say that God has called us to be holy, to separate ourselves from the things of the world, and to present our bodies as a living sacrifice, holy and acceptable to God. Through discipleship, men and women learn what becoming a living sacrifice means.

After living at the ranch several months, I felt ready to start a new life with Maribel and the girls. From Maribel's perspective, she could see how much I had changed and that I was serious about living for the Lord. So together we decided to renew our wedding vows. As we planned for that day, Pastor Gerry counseled us, taught us scriptures about marriage, and agreed to officiate.

At last on September 11, 1999, our girls, my mom, and my brother gathered at the ranch to witness our vows and celebrate with us. I never thought God would bring us back together, but I'm so grateful He did. Pastor Gerry allowed Maribel and the girls to live with me at one of the houses on the ranch while I served in the ministry.

Titus 3:4-7 reads,

> "But when the kindness and the love of God our Savior toward man appeared, not by works of righteousness which we have done, but according to His mercy He saved us, through the washing of regeneration and renewing of the Holy Spirit, whom He poured out on us abundantly through Jesus Christ our Savior, that having been justified by His grace we should become heirs according to the hope of eternal life."

The Lord washed me and poured out His Holy Spirit upon me, and I became an heir of His wonderful grace. Because of His goodness in restoring our marriage and family, I felt so happy I could not imagine leaving or forsaking Him.

BACKSLIDING AND REPENTANCE

Everything was going great until one day when I had an overwhelming desire to use drugs again. Impulsively, I left the ranch, taking the van that Pastor Gerry loaned me for ministry. Despite my parole conditions that required me to stay 1,000 feet from the border, I drove to Tijuana, sold the van, and spent the money on "speedballs," a combination of cocaine and heroin. When I took the first hit, I felt remorseful right away. Still, I kept taking hits and getting high. The next morning I called the ranch and talked to the overseer, shamefully admitting to him what I had done. "Can I come back?" I asked. "I'm blowing it!"

"Quit playing around," he said. "Get back here now!" But I didn't listen. I stayed in Mexico five more weeks, calling the overseer every day while getting high at the same time. I thought it would be fun and exciting, but no matter how many times I took a hit, it was never the same fun as it used to be. A part of me wanted to get high—my flesh—yet a part of me didn't want to, because the Holy Spirit was living inside of me now, convicting me of sin. I learned the hard way that once I gave my life to Jesus, I couldn't go back to doing the sinful things I'd done before. I would still be tempted, but as a true child of God, I would be miserable if I gave in to that temptation.

Finally realizing my helpless, sinful state, I stopped taking the drugs and surrendered to the Lord. I found a ride back to the ranch and was ready to face whatever consequences awaited me. Not only had I relapsed into drugs, I had violated my parole and I deserved to go back to prison.

When Pastor Gerry saw I was back he said, "Go dig a hole." And it was a hard hole to dig because the ground was like a rock! I remember feeling sick to my stomach from the effects of the dope. After a while, Pastor Gerry came over to where I was digging and said, "Anthony, bury your hole now and get back to serving God." And then he walked away. *What? That's it?* I felt confused at first, but I obeyed and buried the hole. It sounded like Pastor Gerry was going to let me stay at the ranch after all.

Just like my mom's kindness had led Maribel to God's grace so long ago, through Pastor Gerry I experienced the Lord's kindness written in Romans 2:4: "The kindness of God leads you to repentance."

God's grace poured over me that day and broke through my stubborn, rebellious heart. I had blown it so much, yet the Lord blessed me with prison discharge papers when my parole was over. Being the recipient of such undeserved favor led me to true repentance. And at that defining moment, I realized God was calling me to serve Him for the rest of my life.

GOD'S RESTORATION

I first came to U-Turn For Christ when I was thirty-one years old. That was over fourteen years ago, and I pray that I can serve in this ministry for the rest of my life. Today I'm the facilities director, overseeing day-to-day operations and special events at the men's and women's ranches. If something's broken, I fix it; if someone needs ministering, I'm there—even if it's two o'clock in the morning. I also advise and consult with the other pastors at the various U-Turn For Christ ranches nationally and worldwide.

If they have a problem with construction, plumbing, electrical, or maintenance, they call me and I advise them. Additionally, I serve as an assistant pastor at nearby Calvary Chapel Romoland. Never in my wildest dreams have I thought God could use me this way, and I give Him all the glory. Every day is a privilege. And I always try to remember to extend God's grace to the men and women at the ranch, knowing that God's kindness can lead to their repentance.

One of the greatest joys the Lord has given to Maribel and me is the opportunity to counsel couples going through marital difficulties. We understand! I remember one couple in particular, Henry and Rachel, whose drug addictions had led to divorce. Henry came to the ranch first, followed by Rachel soon afterward. After God delivered them both from their addictions, it was clear they wanted to remarry. I explained God's design for marriage from Ephesians 5:22-33, asking them to memorize that passage and to keep the Lord at the center of their relationship.

When Maribel and I used to go through rough times, I would call Pastor Gerry and say, "I'm outta here!" Pastor Gerry would always bring me back to 1 Corinthians 13 and remind me to put love into action. I keep this in mind whenever Maribel and I have disagreements now. We don't have a perfect marriage, but when we keep God in the center, He blesses us. I've been privileged to counsel hundreds of troubled marriages through the years and have encouraged couples to be open to God's healing and restoration in their lives.

Today, Maribel's focus is on our home, our marriage, and our girls. She's always there for us. Ashlie is twenty-three now, married, and has her master's degree from Cal Baptist University. Cindy, twenty-one, is newly married and has her BA from Cal Baptist too. Jamie, "my baby," is twenty, lives at home, and is preparing to go back to school soon. Maribel, Ashlie, and Jamie have all gone through the U-Turn For Christ program with me, and that has been instrumental in healing all our lives. I've been blessed to watch my girls grow up in the Lord, and I've seen God restore our relationships as a family. The girls have witnessed firsthand what I've gone through and how much I've been forgiven.

Over the years God has continued to restore my relationship with my mom, my dad, my brother, and other family members. My parents and family used to think, *Little Anthony was a good kid when he was young, but when he got older, he became the worst in the family.* They all used to shut their doors on me, literally, but the Lord has reopened them. Now when they call to talk to me, I share God's Word and tell them what the Lord is doing in my life.

Once or twice a month, I'm honored to travel to Mexico and minister in Tijuana, Rosarito, Ensenada, and Maneadero. I thank the Lord that today I have legal status there, and I look for every opportunity to share Jesus by giving away Bibles, food, and clothing. Taking Bibles into Mexico is a lot different than smuggling drugs or undocumented immigrants, and when I cross the border, now I reach out to the guys who try to clean my car windows and panhandle. They're the ones I used to bring across the border illegally. I've built relationships with many of these guys and have been so blessed to see some of them ask Jesus into their hearts. I've witnessed lives changed and families restored. I've even seen some of them go into the ministry.

As I reflect back, I remember watching Pastor Gerry disciple men in Mexico years ago. He always looked for those on the outside—the wanderers—and he poured himself out to them, just like Jesus did. That's what I try to imitate.

Today, U-Turn For Christ has established a men's ranch in Ensenada, Mexico. Once the men there are off drugs and alcohol, they give back to the community by doing maintenance work at the police stations and reaching out to prisoners. Now that I speak fluent Spanish, I meet with the mayor regularly and seek out volunteer opportunities for the men at the ranch. We've also partnered with an orphanage in Maneadero called The Gabriel House, where severely disabled children live. Every Christmas, Maribel, the girls, and I go to The Gabriel House to hand out gifts to the children. We have no greater joy than to see our daughters bless those who are hurting. We witness tears change to smiles as our girls play with these children and love on them.

After the tsunami hit Thailand in 2004, Pastor Gerry and I took a team from U-Turn For Christ to help with the cleanup. Debris from the storm was strewn everywhere, and as I walked along the beach, I found a little flip-flop that must have belonged to a toddler. I still have that tiny shoe—God has used it to instill a compassion for the refugee children there. We helped set up a camp for the refugees and later a Christian children's home for the orphans left after the tsunami. We also have built a church in Thailand, which still stands today.

In 2005 I worked with a U-Turn For Christ team that provided disaster relief for victims of Hurricane Katrina. I stood in awe at the power of God when I witnessed the destruction there. Strengthened by the love of Christ, we came alongside the hurricane victims in whatever way we could, whether it was feeding the hungry or cutting down trees to clear a roadway. It was the first time I was part of a chainsaw ministry.

I've also traveled to the Philippines to help with U-Turn For Christ ministries in that country. At first I felt uncomfortable in the hot, muggy weather, and I wasn't used to the little kids who clung to me because I'm an American. But after a few trips, I didn't mind any of those things, and God opened up amazing opportunities for outreach, such as teaching Bible studies in prisons and hospitals, give my testimony on the radio, and share at crusades.

In Luke 9:58, Jesus explains to His disciples the high cost of following Him. He says,

> "Foxes have holes and birds of the air have nests, but the Son of Man has nowhere to lay His head."

In other words, we must be willing to give up everything for Him. In these verses, the Lord reminds us that if we're going to come after Him, we need to come wholeheartedly.

God's restoration in my life is nothing short of a miracle. When I recall the old legacy of corruption and crime that I was once so proud of, I'm humbled at how God turned my life around. Not only did He restore my marriage and family, He changed everything. Before I knew the Lord, I was the guy you'd never want to meet. But God showed me grace and covered all my sins. Now I have a new legacy, something of eternal value to pass on to my girls. It's a legacy I don't deserve. If it were not for God's grace, His unmerited favor, I could have never been a part of so many wonderful things. And because of what the Lord has done for me, all I want is to be His servant for as long as I live. Every day my prayer is this: *God, give me the strength to serve You and to die to my flesh.*

I've learned to never lose hope for someone who is struggling with drugs or alcohol. The enemy is real but so is Jesus Christ. Jesus said, "I am the way, the truth, and the life" (John 14:6). If He can change someone like me, He can change anyone who is willing to surrender. For "with God nothing will be impossible" (Luke 1:37).

"This is the life story of Anthony Dowdy. As this book was in the process of being edited, our beloved Anthony went home to be with the Lord on September 10, 2013.

"We mourn the loss of a godly father and diligent servant of Jesus Christ but rejoice in the knowledge that he is in the presence of the Lord. He lived a transformed life to the fullest in the service of our Lord. My prayer is that many will be blessed by his testimony and follow his example. His wife, Maribel, still serves with us at the U-Turn For Christ in Perris, California." -Pastor Gerry Brown

Anthony, Maribel, Cindy, Jamie and Ashlie

Father in heaven, thank you for Pastor Anthony and for the incredible work You have done in his life! You have allowed him to become a strong witness of Your love and grace, because he made a U-turn for Christ in his life and became a bold witness in his Jerusalem

(at home with his family), in Judea and Samaria (in Mexico bringing blessings rather than curses), and in the uttermost parts of the earth (in the Philippines, where the people love him).

Lord Jesus, thank you for how real You are in the way You glorified Yourself using Anthony's life. May his legacy of grace continue to be an example to others. Amen!

ANTHONY DOWDY MEMORIAL FUND:

For more information on how to sponsor others to go to U-Turn For Christ, visit www.Uturnforchrist.com or call (951) 943-7097.

CHAPTER 3

Thus says the Lord, who created you … "Fear not, for I have redeemed you, I have called you by your name; you are Mine."

ISAIAH 43:1

PASTOR MARIO ROCHA
Called To Be His

Sweaty and hot, Mario pushed open the glass door of the Sizzler restaurant where he worked as a waiter. Stopping off at the restroom, he splashed cold water on his face and glanced up in the mirror above the sink. The image staring back took him by surprise—a skinny, sick-looking drug addict with dark circles under his eyes and dripping rings of sweat under his arms. An overwhelming shame washed over him.

Who am I kidding? Mario thought. Anyone can see I'm on dope!

Mario untied his apron and walked out of the restaurant, throwing the apron on the front seat of his car. With tip change still jingling in his pocket from the previous night—along with a half-ounce of weed—he filled up his gas tank and bought a loaf of bread and a jar of peanut butter. Driving home to pack his bags, he decided, I'll leave town again and start over. Things will be different this time—it'll be the good life!

This is Mario's story.

Back home in Topeka, Kansas, I grew up in a tight-knit Mexican-American community, where aunts, uncles, cousins, grandparents, extended family, and many friends all knew each other's business. Living so close to each other, I learned that people talk. And at a young age, I learned they were talking about me.

My grandfather raped his stepdaughter when she was only twelve years old. Nine months after her thirteenth birthday, she gave birth to a son, and that baby boy was me. When my mom's pregnancy became apparent, my grandparents tried to cover it up by claiming she was raped in a dark alley. But the police didn't buy it. My mom's scandalous story circulated quickly, and her classmates in junior high called her terrible names. After I was born, my grandmother switched my mom to a school where no one knew her. I was taught to call my mother by her first name, Patti, and to pretend she was my sister. Yet even as a baby, for some reason I instinctively called her "Mama."

My grandparents taught me to call them "Mom and Dad," even though I knew they were my grandparents. In actuality, my grandfather was both my father and my grandfather. They divorced when I was born, and my grandpa rented an apartment nearby. Still, he spent most of his time at my grandma's house, with me and five of my half siblings: Linda, Stephanie, Steve, Susie, and Cynthia. My mom moved to the other side of town while I was still a toddler. Grandpa drank a lot and even after the divorce, he beat my grandmother. Sadly, he molested his own children too, including me.

One day when my mom was fifteen and I was three, she knocked on my grandma's door with the police. "I'm here for Mario," she announced.

"No—don't take him!" Grandma begged, weeping hysterically as the police pried me from her arms.

While I kicked and screamed, an officer handed me to my mom. Holding me in a tight grip, she hurried down the street where her new husband, Chuck, waited in his car. Grandma tried to run after us, but the police held her back. "Don't take him, please don't take him!" she cried as we sped away. Several weeks later my mom found that caring for a toddler was more difficult than she'd imagined, so she brought me back to my grandma's to stay.

Months later, Grandma took me in her arms and said, "Mario, I need to tell you something. Someday people may tell you that your grandfather is your real dad, but don't believe them. The truth is, when your mom was a young girl, she was raped on her way home from school. And that's how you were born." I was confused by what she said, but deep down, I already knew who my real father was. "And one more thing," she added, "some people will reject you because of what happened to your mom."

Grandma's prediction rang true throughout my childhood. For example, one day after school I went to a friend's house with a few other boys. When my friend's mom saw me there, she quickly took me aside. "I'm sorry, Mario, but you'll need to leave right now," she said. "You see, we're renting this house from my parents next door, and they told me that you aren't allowed to come in because you were born from incest." Humiliated, I grabbed my backpack and ran home.

MASKING THE ANGER

When I was seven, my grandpa died from cirrhosis of the liver, and painful memories of his molestations began to haunt me. I harbored so much hatred and bitterness that I prayed God would let him burn in hell. Soon the anger became my driving force, and I eventually turned to drugs and alcohol to mask it all.

I smoked my first joint at the age of fourteen while on lunch break with my buddies in high school. For the first time in my life, I felt carefree—laughing, giddy, and happy! I went to my next class and slid down in my seat, staring blankly at my math book. I remember a poster tacked onto the classroom wall, with a student sitting at his desk and a caption reading, "Dazed." Ironically, I was just like that kid in the poster, totally zoned out. Suddenly I realized my teacher was asking me a question because I heard her voice calling out, "Mario? Mario…Mario!" I finally looked up and said, "Wha-aat?" I didn't hear the question.

My drug use escalated from there. I gradually stopped going to classes and spent more and more time getting high at school with my friends. By the second semester of my freshman year, I showed up only to get high. Finally the principal and guidance counselor called my grandmother to say I'd been expelled for missing so much school. I never went back.

"Well, don't think you're going to just sit around the house for the rest of the year," Grandma warned me. "You're getting a job!" After lying about my age, I was hired at a nearby pizza place, but it only lasted a couple of months because I skipped work to party. This pattern of working and partying continued for five years, until I had worked at nearly every fast food restaurant in Topeka.

One thing always kept me from going completely wild with drugs and alcohol, and that was my grandma. Standing only five feet tall, she was a little Mexican firecracker. She always cared for me—even spoiled me—and unlike my siblings, I was hardly ever spanked. However, all that changed when Grandma found out I was smoking pot; she became so upset that she actually hit me with a left hook. When I ducked to avoid her, she punched me again with a right uppercut. After she hit me, a neighbor came running through the back door of our house, which had been left wide open. He saw the whole thing and heard all the yelling. "Mrs. Rocha, Mrs. Rocha—stop!" he pleaded.

"Get off our property! And mind your own business!" Grandma yelled between cuss words. He finally left, and Grandma stopped yelling.

Even though Grandma knew I drank and partied, she didn't know the extent of it all because I hid it from her. Sometimes I'd stay out all night and come back the next morning after I was sober. Grandma would chew me out and say, "It's a good thing you're not eighteen because I'd kick you out!"

OVERWHELMING GRIEF

When I was nineteen, Grandma was admitted to the hospital for double-bypass surgery. After seeing my grandpa on his deathbed, I hated hospitals and couldn't bring myself to visit her there. However, I did call the day before Grandma's surgery. "Why haven't you come to see me?" she asked. "You make me feel like you don't love me." I assured Grandma that I did indeed love her and would visit her soon. Because she'd been in the hospital before, I didn't take it too seriously. But the next day when my sister showed up at the house where I was partying, I felt scared.

"Grandma had complications," my sister said, "and you need to come to the hospital right now." When we got there, Grandma had already lost consciousness and was being kept alive on a heart-lung machine. Because of her grave condition, my siblings and I had to decide whether to continue the machine—which would eventually damage her other organs—or let her go. We made the heart-wrenching decision to let Grandma go. Her last words to me replayed over and over in my mind: "You make me feel like you don't love me." And Satan beat me up with those words for many years to come.

Trying to numb my grief, I let loose and got heavier into drugs—cocaine, acid, marijuana, and anything else that didn't require a needle. Whether dealing drugs or ripping people off, all I wanted was to make money and get high. Though I had once believed in God, gone to church every Sunday, and even served as an altar boy, I turned as far away from Him as possible, dabbling in witchcraft and studying satanic books. For five years, my family watched helplessly as they witnessed the horrible mess I made of my life after losing my grandma.

Finally one of my sisters said, "Mario, you need to get out of here. You need to get away from everything and start over." I knew she was right. I wanted to get away too—from the drugs, from the alcohol, and from Topeka, Kansas. But I didn't know where to go.

A FRESH START

Then I remembered an invitation my sister Linda had extended many times over the years: "Mario, if you ever want to get away from the life you're living, my home is open to you." Linda lived in El Centro, California at the time, and I dialed her number.

"Does your offer still stand, Linda?" I asked. "Because if it does, I want to come."

"That's wonderful, Mario. I'll ask Fernando," Linda said. "Call me back tomorrow."

Linda's answer blew my mind. *What do you mean you'll "ask Fernando"? This is your brother calling!* I thought. *You have to ask your husband first?*

At the time, I didn't understand that as a Christian, Linda was following the biblical principle from Ephesians 5:22-23:

> "Wives, submit to your own husbands, as to the Lord. For the husband is head of the wife, as also Christ is head of the church."

Out of respect for Fernando as the head of her family, she was simply checking with him first.

The next day I called Linda back. "You can come!" she said excitedly. I bought a bus ticket, and a few days later Linda and Fernando welcomed me into their home, along with their children, Linda, aged twelve; Fernando, nine; and Uriah, two. "The rules will be the same for you as they are for anyone else," Linda said. "We all go to church. No drugs, alcohol, or bringing women home." I agreed to her rules and was thrilled to land a job right away at a nearby Taco Bell.

One morning soon after my arrival, Linda and I sat in her kitchen, talking together. "Mario," she said. "you know the Lord is the only one who can free you from your addictions." Even though there was so much I didn't understand about God, I knew I needed Him.

"You know what?" I said, "I want that!" So I bowed my head and invited Jesus into my life.

As promised, I attended church with Linda's family, where for the first time, I heard expository Bible teaching, which is studying the Bible from Genesis to Revelation, chapter by chapter, verse by verse. I loved studying the Bible at Calvary Chapel El Centro, and I tried to follow the Lord—a little. After a few months at Linda's, I remember thinking, *Everything is good. I've stopped taking the drugs now, but I can still smoke a little marijuana. It'll be okay as long as I don't get carried away like before.* Of course, Linda didn't know I started smoking pot again.

GIVING IN

One day the manager from a local Sizzler restaurant waited in my drive-through line at Taco Bell, and he overheard my conversations with customers over the loudspeaker. When he pulled up to my window, he said, "Tell me, son, have you ever waited tables?"

"No, sir, I haven't."

"Well, I've been listening to the way you handle your customers, and I think you'd make an excellent waiter." He handed me his business card. "I'd like to train you," he said. "Stop by the Sizzler any time." I did and he hired me.

To work a second job, I had to switch my hours at Taco Bell to graveyard. On my first night shift a co-worker said, "Hey, man, I've seen you carry a Bible around and I hear you're a Christian."

"Yeah, that's right," I said.

"Well, that makes me feel kind of uncomfortable—you know, like you're going to tell on me if I do something wrong."

As a baby Christian, I wanted to appear cool and be accepted. "Hey, you've got nothing to worry about, man," I said. "I'm not like that—I won't try to get you in trouble. You do your thing, I'll do my thing, and we're both good."

"Okay," he said, "but I think I'd feel a lot better if you'd at least do one line with me, just so I know you're not going to hold anything over my head."

After I mentioned that I'd used cocaine in Kansas, he started describing what speed felt like. "It's like cocaine, only more intense," he said. "Just try it!" So I snorted one line. Immediately I was hooked; it did feel like coke, only it lasted a lot longer. From then on, whenever I worked with this guy, I'd do a line. I told myself it was fine, as long as I didn't get carried away.

Now that I was using both speed and marijuana, Linda started questioning me, but I denied everything; however, when I didn't come home for a few days, she called me at work, wondering where I was.

"Look, Mario," she said, "You're a grown man, and I can't tell you how to live your life, but I know what you're doing and you can't do it in my home! I have to think of my children and my husband. So you need to come home now and pack your things."

How can she kick me out like this and call herself a Christian? I thought. Upset—and high—I mumbled, "Whatever," and hung up the phone. I packed up and moved to Calexico, where an assistant manager from Taco Bell let me rent a spare room in his house.

Linda came to visit me a few weeks later, on my twenty-fifth birthday, but I was still mad and wouldn't let her come inside. Besides, there was a joint in the ashtray by my bed. So I talked to her through the screen door.

"Happy birthday, Mario!" she said through the screen. "How are you?"

Somehow the conversation led to an argument and we didn't connect too well that day. At that point, I didn't even care about birthdays.

ON THE RUN

One summer afternoon when I arrived for work at the Sizzler, I stopped at the restroom to cool off and was shocked by the pathetic image staring back in the mirror—I looked skinny with sunken eyes and I was dripping sweat. It was the first time I'd really seen myself for who I was—a full-blown drug addict, and at that very moment I felt embarrassed. I decided to run away again, this time to Santa Ana, where my brother Steve lived. The only trouble with visiting Steve was that he had been in and out of prison so much that I wasn't sure where to find him.

Later that night I pulled into a cheap motel in Santa Ana and rented a room for a week. Sitting on the lumpy mattress, I flipped the remote channels, staring at the black-and-white screen and smoking my last joint. Suddenly, a still, small voice spoke to my heart: "Call your sister, Linda, and tell her you're okay. Stop running away!" In my heart, I answered, *Okay, Lord.* So I dialed Linda's number and as soon as she answered I felt better.

"Linda, I feel like God is telling me to come back to El Centro."

"You don't know how badly I've wanted to jump through this phone and snatch you up," Linda said excitedly. "Praise the Lord! Come back!"

"Well, here's the problem—I'm almost out of money. I just rented a room for a week at this place, and there's a big sign on the window that says, 'No Refunds.'"

"Why don't you talk to the manager?" Linda suggested. "Just be honest and tell her what happened. Meanwhile, I'll put you on the prayer chain at church."

The next morning when I told the manager my story, she looked away and started writing something down. *Wow, she's blowing me off,* I thought. *She's already doing something else!*

"Here's your refund," the manager finally said, handing me a check, "minus the night you stayed here." I couldn't believe it! It had to be God. I called Linda and we both cried together over the phone.

Driving back to El Centro, it was just me and the Lord talking together, and I surrendered everything to Him. *Jesus, I don't know what it's going to take, but I don't want to live like this anymore. I'll go wherever You say and do whatever it takes. But change my life and make me different!*

FINDING TREATMENT, FINDING FORGIVENESS

When I arrived at Linda's, we called around to find a Christian treatment center and found one nearby that took me the next day. Each

MARIO ROCHA: *Called To Be His*

morning began with thirty minutes of silent prayer, kneeling at the side of my bed. During my first prayer time, God showed me a verse I had never seen before, Matthew 6:14:

> "For if you forgive men their trespasses, your heavenly Father will also forgive you."

Whoa! I thought. *Does this mean I have to forgive my dad?*

Every day for the next two weeks, I prayed the same prayer: *God, I don't know how to do this. I've held onto hatred and bitterness for so long that they've been my strength! So if forgiving my dad is what You want, then You'll have to help me do it.*

After praying for two weeks, suddenly forgiveness flooded my heart. What freedom! What relief! It felt like a heavy weight was lifted from my body. In the Lord's great kindness, He gave me a vivid dream of my father that same night. In the dream, my dad was weeping and asking me to forgive him. I said, "Yes, Dad, I forgive you and I love you." Then we wrapped our arms around each other and embraced. I woke up crying and felt so happy for this major turning point.

As I continued on at the treatment center, I noticed some serious doctrinal issues that came up, so Linda and I decided it was best to withdraw and find another program. Many phone calls later, we found U-Turn For Christ, based out of Calvary Chapel Hemet, where Pastor Gerry Brown was an assistant pastor at the time. An elder described the program to us over the phone, and Linda drove me to the church in Hemet to sign the necessary papers, remembering what I had promised the Lord—"whatever it takes." And I meant it.

July 27, 1995, was my first day at U-Turn For Christ, and in my heart I knew I was in the right place. Yet at the same time, I experienced an internal struggle of not wanting to be there, with thoughts like, *Why did they put this place way out in the middle of a desert?*

Back then, U-Turn was a brand new facility—barely nine months old—and it had only one building, a bunkhouse for nine guys. There was no air-conditioning, only a small fan in the far corner of the room. All the windows and doors stayed wide open, and flies buzzed everywhere. But I witnessed God build the ministry little by little, and He allowed me to appreciate these humble beginnings.

LESSONS

Two days after arriving at the ranch, I attended a Bible study that affected me deeply. The speaker said, "You either trust God or you don't. You can't say, 'I trust Him with these things, but I'll handle those.' You either trust Him 100 percent or you don't trust Him at all." Then came the challenge: "Do you trust Him?" I kept asking myself that question, and the next day I snuck off to the back of the property to be alone, wandering through rows of overgrown evergreen trees until I was hidden from view. Then I fell to my knees and started bawling like a baby. *God, why did You bring me here?* I prayed. *What do You want me to learn?* After a while, I sensed His still, small voice saying, "I want you to learn to trust Me, not your circumstances or how nice this place is or isn't. Look at Me. Trust Me." And right there, among the trees, I made a commitment to trust God with every step from that day on. That was eighteen years ago.

The practice of learning the Word of God at U-Turn For Christ changed the way I think, and it eventually gave me the ability to say, "Okay, I'm presented with this tough situation and this trying circumstance—now, what am I going to do?" Not what I'm going to do in light of how I want things to turn out or what I think is best for me, but in light of God's Word. Hebrews 4:12 says,

> "For the word of God is living and powerful, and sharper than any two-edged sword, piercing even to the division of soul and spirit, and of joints and marrow, and is a discerner of the thoughts and intents of the heart."

His Word always gets through to the issues in my heart that I over-look—things I may not see as sin. God gets in there and says, "Hey, you need to look at this!" His Word is life-changing and powerful, and it's what I draw from in every situation.

One of my favorite Scriptures is 2 Samuel 22:4:

> "I will call upon the Lord, who is worthy to be praised, so shall I be saved from my enemies."

God gave me this verse when I first arrived at U-Turn For Christ, struggling with demonic nightmares. At a Bible study one evening, the speaker encouraged us to cry out to Jesus, asking Him to save us from whatever we were going through at that moment. So I cried out and asked God to take away my hellish nightmares.

After I prayed, the pastor began singing this same verse, "I will call upon the Lord," and all the men joined in. The women sang an echo and together it sounded like an angelic chorus. Back in my room, I sang the song over and over before falling asleep. The nightmares ended that night and they never returned.

Over time, I've watched God's loving hand orchestrate my life to the place where He's led me today, as the associate pastor to Pastor Gerry Brown at U-Turn For Christ. When I came here in 1995, I assumed I'd finish Phase I and then leave. But God had another plan. Even during those first months here, I sensed God calling me to be a pastor. But then I read James 3:1:

> "My brethren, let not many of you become teachers, knowing that we shall receive a stricter judgment."

That verse scared me so much that I decided not to tell anyone what God had called me to do.

After eight months at U-Turn, I was recruited to work in the office, answering phones and giving out information. From there, I became the assistant administrator and after that, the administrator. Then in 1999, Pastor Gerry called me into his office and said, "It's time for me to ordain you," confirming what God had already spoken to my heart years before.

Like a deer in the headlights, I was taken totally by surprise and only managed an "okay." I had never told Pastor Gerry what God had shown me, and I knew the Lord was speaking through him.

After this conversation, I remember sitting at my desk, alone in the office. I looked upward and prayed, *Oh God, are You sure You want me to be a pastor?* Then He directed me to Jeremiah 1:5-7, where I found His answer:

> "Before I formed you in the womb, I knew you; before you were born I sanctified you; I ordained you a prophet…. For you shall go to all to whom I send you, and whatever I command you, you shall speak."

This verse was yet another confirmation from God, and a few months later, Pastor Gerry ordained me.

I've watched the Lord use Pastor Gerry in incredible ways and have clearly seen God's calling on his life. In 1998, for example, I received a phone call from my brother-in-law in Topeka, telling me that my sister, Stephanie, had suffered a stroke. Being ten years older, Stephanie had always been like a mother figure to me, and when I heard she wasn't doing well, I knew I had to take the next plane to Topeka to be with her. So I went to Pastor Gerry's office and told him I had to leave right away. "Okay, Mario," Pastor Gerry said, "if you need to be there, then go. But make a phone call first."

"I've done that," I said. "In fact, I've already made several phone calls, but the hospital doesn't give me much information."

Pastor Gerry whispered, "Lord help me," and then he leaned in toward me. "You need to call the hospital and tell them who you are, what you do, and how you're related to Stephanie. Tell them you need more information about your sister because you're about to get on a plane, and you want to make sure it's the right thing to do."

Trusting Gerry's wisdom, I called the hospital and told them I was ready to fly in from California. "Well, as a matter of fact," the nurse said, "Stephanie's actually doing fine now. It was her thyroid. She wasn't taking her medications the way she was supposed to, and her symptoms only looked like a stroke. She's actually going home in fifteen minutes!"

Thank you, Lord! I prayed. This is only one example of how God has directed Pastor Gerry and used him to help me and many others at U-turn For Christ. There's only one condition: you have to trust him.

EVELYN

Over the years, the Lord continued to heal the hurts of my childhood, and this process began when He allowed me to forgive my dad. Though my mom and I have lived apart for many years, I'm thankful that our relationship continues to develop. She still lives in Topeka, and we communicate today by phone and video calls. I'm thankful that my mom and my sisters are all Christians today.

I realize now that the rejection I experienced caused me to push people away and become distant because I didn't want to get hurt again. I was a true loner, and the hardest part about it was that I really wanted to be married! So for many years, I had this ongoing conflict inside.

Ezekiel 36:26 says,

> "I will give you a new heart and put a new spirit within you;
> I will take the heart of stone out of your flesh and give you a
> heart of flesh."

What this means is that God softened my hardened heart and He prepared me for the wife I'd been praying for. I had also prayed for a family—a big family! But first I needed a wife and I wanted to make sure she was the one God chose, not one that I hunted down. Many times people introduced me to different women, hoping I'd find "the one." But it didn't happen.

After thirteen years of waiting and praying, I met her in 2008 at a U-Turn For Christ Pig Roast. Diane Duran, our Phase 2 leader introduced us. "Mario, I want you to meet Evelyn," Diane said. "Evelyn is Pastor Angel's sister." (Pastor Angel used to direct the U-Turn For Christ ranch in Mexico.) The moment I laid eyes on Evelyn, I knew she would be my wife. However, I didn't want my lingering gaze to be misinterpreted, so I looked away. That night, God woke me up at 3 a.m. Typically when God wakes me up, I pray about the first thing that comes to mind. This time I saw Evelyn's lovely face, but I couldn't remember her name. *This is not good timing, Lord!* I prayed. Feeling like I was wrestling with Him, I questioned His leading, *Right now? But I'm not ready and I'm not sure I want this yet.*

"It's time," the Lord said gently.

Okay, I prayed. *I guess it wouldn't be so terrible to say that I met my wife at the U-Turn For Christ Pig Roast.* The moment I prayed this, a peace came over me and I fell back to sleep.

As a single pastor in the ministry, I kept my distance from the ladies at the women's ranch. Too many times we had seen romantic relationships become a distraction, and while the men and women were here, we wanted them to focus only on their relationship with Jesus.

When I met Evelyn at the Pig Roast, at that time she was in the Phase 2 program, and it wasn't until four long months had passed before we spoke again.

During that time, God confirmed in both of us that He wanted us to marry, and when Evelyn was close to graduating from Phase 2, Pastor Gerry gave us special permission to speak to each other at a birthday party we both attended. At the party, we sat across from each other at the table. It was no secret that God had spoken to us, and we both had been waiting for the day when we could finally share this moment with each other. The conversation started when Evelyn slid her Bible across the table to me and said, "Show me the scriptures God has given to you about me."

I smiled, opened her Bible, and read Song of Solomon 4:9:

> "You have captivated my heart, my sister my bride, you have captivated my heart with one glance of your eyes, with one jewel of your necklace." (ESV)

I read a few more verses that the Lord had shown me, and then I slid the Bible back across the table. "Now show me the scriptures God has given to you about me."

Evelyn read a few verses, starting with Psalm 21:2:

> "You have given him his heart's desire and have not withheld the request of his lips."

Knowing God had confirmed that we would be husband and wife, we then talked about what our wedding would be like, how many children we wanted, and even what we'd name them.

Two weeks later, I proposed, and six months after that, on April 11, 2009, we were married with Pastor Gerry officiating. We chose to have our wedding in a secluded area at the ranch, at the foot of three tall wooden crosses, with our families and friends gathered around us to witness our vows. It was truly the happiest day of my life!

The following year in 2010, God blessed us with a son, Samuel, and our daughter, Alexandra, was born in 2011. And because of the Lord's goodness, I'm no longer a loner.

God not only gave me a wife and a family, but also a distinct calling. In my ministry at U-Turn For Christ, the Lord has taught me that I'm a servant of the Most High God. This is my position first and foremost, to serve the men and women He brings to us and help them get to know Him. Those who come here need compassion. They also need firmness and sternness when necessary, but with great care. Jude 22-23 says,

> "And on some have compassion, making a distinction; but others save with fear, pulling them out of the fire, hating even the garment defiled by the flesh."

We need to simply love on them all and say, "I'm no better than you; I'm also a sinner saved by grace. God has done something incredible in my life and He wants to do that in your life too."

BEFORE I KNEW HIM

God called me when I was far away from Him—at my worst, in fact, when I was grappling with addictions and sin. Like Psalm 40:2 says,

> "He also brought me up out of a horrible pit, out of the miry clay, and set my feet upon a rock, and established my steps."

My sister Stephanie tells this story about the first time God called me—years before I even knew Him—and in the middle of my drinking at a party, no less. I marvel at what He has done since then.

She says, "Back in the day, after our parents were gone, I remember my sisters and I were all in the kitchen at home, and Mario had twenty guys downstairs in the basement—getting high, playing loud music, and drinking together. Mario came upstairs, smiling and shaking his head and he looked at me and my sisters. 'I know you guys will probably think I'm crazy,' he said, 'but God is telling me that I'm going to be a priest someday!' We were Catholic, and we all looked at him and laughed in disbelief.

"Yeah, sure, right, Mario!" we said.

"'No, I'm serious! You think I'm drunk or high, or that I don't know what I'm talking about. But God just spoke to me!' He said, 'Mario, one day you will be Mine. You will be a priest.'" We all thought that was the biggest joke ever.

"Well, the laugh was on us because we were the unbelievers. Just look at Mario today. God did exactly what He said He would do— Mario is a pastor and he loves God. Even back then, the Lord was calling Mario, and through all the stuff my brother was doing, God was still with him. The Lord took the dirtiest thing and made it into something beautiful to honor Him. That's the way I look at my brother. When I see Mario, I remember that story of what God showed Mario at the party, and it gives me hope."

Jesus is ready, willing, and very capable of changing a person's life. It all comes down to surrendering to Him. There is no other way, no other cure. For those who may have friends or loved ones struggling with addiction, or any other sin, U-Turn For Christ is a place to find help. Jesus, our loving Savior, is reaching out with love and He wants to set men and women free, once and for all.

> "Be anxious for nothing, but in everything by prayer and supplication, with thanksgiving, let your requests be made known to God; and the peace of God, which surpasses all understanding, will guard your hearts and minds through Christ Jesus." (Philippians 4:6-7)

Keep praying and don't give up! You can be sure that God wants to answer your prayers—I'm a living testimony of that.

· · · · · ⓤ · · · · · ·

Mario, Samuel, Alexandra and Evelyn

Dear Lord, thank you for Pastor Mario and the incredible work that You have done in and through his life.

His example with his wife and children is one for all to follow, and the way he has fallen in love with You and Your Word allows wisdom to pour out of him into the lives of others. He has been my right hand for over eighteen years and a huge blessing, one we don't take for granted.

Please continue to keep him and bless him as he serves You. Amen.

CHAPTER 4

And behold, a leper came and worshiped Him, saying, "Lord, if You are willing, You can make me clean." Then Jesus put out His hand and touched him, saying, "I am willing; be cleansed."

MATTHEW 8:2-3

PASTOR ERIN WINEMILLER
Willing to Surrender

It was a warm evening in June of '93, the week before high school graduation. Erin and his friends cruised through a Santa Ana neighborhood, searching for the party house that matched the address on their flyer. Soon they heard loud music coming from a house down the street, and the address matched. The boys parked and made their way to the backyard, where a standing-room-only crowd had gathered for a night of dancing and drinking.

As they entered the busy and riotous yard, Erin's friend, Alex, grabbed a beer from the cooler.

"Have one, man!" Alex said, tossing the beer to Erin.

Erin caught the cold bottle. "Thanks," he said. Alex knew Erin didn't drink—they'd been hanging out together for a few years now. But with only a week left of school, they both knew that life was on the brink of change. Erin unscrewed the top and took a swig. Then he drank a little more, and a little more, and before the night was over, he had finished all forty ounces and felt pretty buzzed.

The next evening Erin's friends planned to meet at another flyer party, this time in Anaheim, but at the last minute, Erin decided to stay home. He wanted to call a girl instead, and after talking on the phone for hours, he finally collapsed into bed falling into a deep sleep when suddenly he felt someone shake him wide awake. His dad had heard his friends knocking at the front door and let Erin's friends inside.

"Wake up, Erin. It's Alex," one of the boys said, trembling. "He…he was stabbed in the chest at the party tonight."

Erin searched his friend's face. "What happened? Is he okay?"

"He's dead."

This is Erin's story.

As soon as I could walk, my dad started pitching balls to me. Dad was my biggest fan, coaching my teams through the years and sharing my passion for baseball. I played year-round on select leagues, and at Rancho Alamitos High School, I made varsity all four years.

I was a good kid—I stayed out of trouble, never got a tattoo, and got along with my parents. My dad had my highest respect, and I never wanted to disappoint him. One thing bothered me, though, and that was his smoking and drinking.

I promised myself at a young age that I'd never drink or take drugs. Though some of my friends felt differently, it simply wasn't my thing.

Growing up in Garden Grove, California, I had one sister, Jennifer, who was five years younger than me, and we were close. Dad was raised Catholic, and we were taught to believe in God but we didn't know much about Him. The first time I saw the inside of a Catholic church was during my sophomore year, when my girlfriend took me to mass on an Easter Sunday. I tried reading the Bible a few times but gave up because I couldn't understand it.

In 1990, when I was fifteen, one of Dad's co-workers invited my parents to Calvary Chapel Anaheim and they both became Christians. Soon afterwards, my mom and dad asked me to join them at the very first Harvest Crusade held at the Pacific Amphitheater in Costa Mesa. I felt so much peace and joy there, like something I'd never experienced. When Pastor Greg Laurie gave the invitation that evening, I went forward and accepted Jesus as my Lord and Savior. I started going to Calvary Chapel Costa Mesa on Monday nights to hear Pastor Greg teach, and I attended Calvary Chapel Anaheim on Sunday mornings.

Dad stopped drinking when he became a Christian, but he continued to smoke. About six months later, he woke up in the middle of the night and reached for his cigarettes but couldn't find them. So he woke up my mom. "Honey," he said, "where are my cigarettes?"

"I threw them away," she said.

"Why did you do that?"

"Because God told me to."

Dad thought about it a minute and said, "Well, if God told you to get rid of them, He must want me to quit." Then he went back to sleep and he never smoked again.

TRANSITIONS

Stuff started bothering me after I became a Christian. For one thing, my friends and I usually drove around town together on the weekends, doing stupid things and starting mischief. But after going to the Harvest Crusade, whenever we'd pass by a church or see a cross or even a Christian bumper sticker, I'd immediately feel convicted and tell my friends, "I've gotta go now."

They'd ask, "Where you going?" And instead of trying to explain that the Holy Spirit was convicting me about the things we were doing, I'd say, "Oh, it's just time for me to get home." Then they drove me back.

Up until the party with Alex before graduation, I'd managed to keep my promise and avoid alcohol all through high school. I don't know exactly why I decided to drink when Alex offered me a beer. Baseball season had just ended, school was almost over, and I simply made a conscious decision to do it. Looking back, I know now that the enemy was walking around like a roaring lion, seeking someone to devour, just like it says in 1 Peter 5:8.

He caught me off guard, as if he was saying, "C'mon, Erin, just go ahead!" I had tasted beer before, but the guys all knew I wasn't a drinker. Still, when Alex handed me that bottle and we hung out together, it was the first time I ever got drunk.

I couldn't believe it when my friends told me Alex was dead. Alex had been such a great friend to me, and he was a popular, well-liked student. The mood on campus that week before graduation was somber, and adding to our grief, we learned that whoever killed Alex had fled the scene, and no one knew who stabbed him. Needless to say, I took his death very hard. Even my lifelong resolve not to drink or do drugs started to crumble, and I made a new promise to myself: I would continue drinking in Alex's honor. That's when my life began to change.

In the fall, I enrolled at Golden West Junior College, where I played baseball and I also worked part-time in a warehouse. Unfortunately, I couldn't keep my grades up so I quit school after a year and started working full time. A few different jobs followed over the next few years—at the Boys and Girls Club, a car dealership, and a trucking company.

THE PARTY LIFE

I continued drinking and also started smoking marijuana. My friends and I belonged to a tagging crew, which is similar to a gang but not officially. We went to flyer parties together, where tagging crews from all over Orange County converged and we hung out in vacant houses. Typically there would be a DJ, loud music, alcohol, and drugs.

Once in 1994 we were drinking at a friend's house and some of us impulsively decided to drive to Tijuana. One of my friends told me I could sober up enough to drive if I'd take a line of speed, so I did. Then five of us piled into a friend's car, and I got behind the wheel. It didn't take long before we noticed a flashing red light behind us and we got pulled over for reckless driving. The officer walked up to the car door, smelled alcohol, and ordered me to get out for a sobriety test. Surprisingly, I passed, and he let me get back on the road. "It worked!" I said, amazed. After that incident I reasoned I could drink as much as I wanted, and if I ever needed to sober up to drive, I could do a line of speed and be fine.

In June of 1996, my friends and I were riding around in a car in Garden Grove when a man nearby was grazed on the head with a bullet. Someone made up a story of how it all happened, and the next thing I knew, I was arrested and jailed for attempted murder along with several others. A witness singled me out as the driver of the vehicle that fired the shot, but the accusation was false. At the preliminary hearing two months later, witnesses gave differing accounts of the shooting. All charges were dropped, except mine, and I remained in jail. That September my grandfather was in hospice care, dying of cancer, and my parents paid bail so I could see him one last time. He died within a week and I moved in with my grandmother in Garden Grove so she wouldn't be alone. I found a job as a delivery driver for a cabinet-making company while I continued to fight for my innocence in the shooting.

Soon after my release, the phone rang and it was Frankie, a guy I met in jail. "Hey, Erin," he said, "come over and we'll hang out." Frankie lived with his mom in Anaheim, and when I stopped in to see him, he offered me heroin. I had snorted it once before in jail but never thought I'd do it again. After that, Frankie and I started using together every weekend. Meanwhile, a year after my arrest, the charges were suddenly dismissed because all the witness accounts conflicted.

ROSIE

That December I met Frankie's younger sister when she came for a visit over Christmas break. Rosie was a senior in high school and lived with her aunt and uncle in San Francisco. The first time I saw her walking around the corner of Frankie's apartment complex, her beautiful smile captured my heart and I loved her. We only dated for two weeks, and then she returned home to San Francisco. Once back home she called me. "Erin," she said, "I want to come back!" So I sent her a plane ticket, and she moved in with Frankie and her mom to finish her last semester of high school. By this time, Rosie was nineteen and I was twenty-two.

Initially I hid my weekend heroin and drinking from Rosie, my parents, and even my grandma. But as the months passed and I began using more, Rosie knew. In early 1998, we found out that Rosie was pregnant and we told my parents. Later when I confessed my drug and alcohol problem, my dad was distraught—he didn't know I'd ever had a drink, much less used heroin. Dad called Calvary Chapel

Costa Mesa and they referred us to U-Turn For Christ. My parents tried to convince me to go there, but I refused. "I don't want to," I said. "I can do this on my own."

I tried weaning myself off the heroin but I couldn't do it. Then I enrolled in a 21-day detox program with methadone. After finishing the program, I told everyone I had quit using, but I was lying. For the next seven months my drug use spun out of control. Someone gave me cocaine for a toothache, and I started shooting both cocaine and heroin. Rosie said I looked skinny and sucked up, like I had one foot in the grave and one foot in the world. I didn't really care about anyone then, only what I needed to do for the next fix. That September, our first daughter Brittany was born.

RESTORATION BEGINS

On October 21, 1998, my dad's birthday, I woke up knowing it was time to do something. I'm not sure what got into me that morning, but I said to my parents, "All right, let's go to U-Turn For Christ." So they drove me to the ranch.

The first person I met at U-Turn For Christ was Chuck Perry, who did the intake process and checked me into my bunk. I kept wondering when the withdrawals would kick in, so to distract myself, I sat in a chair outside the bunkhouse and started reading a book called *Harvest* by Chuck Smith. As I read through the miraculous stories of guys like Mike MacIntosh and Raul Ries, I began reflecting on my own life and wondering, *How did I get to this point where I have to go to a place like U-Turn?* I had stayed away from drugs and alcohol for so long, but now here I was, twenty-four years old and strung out. *How did it happen?* Then I started bawling and walked back to the office, where Steve Huffine let me cry on his shoulder. He encouraged me and prayed for me. And that was the start of God's restoration process in my life.

Besides getting off drugs, I had other goals in mind when I arrived at the ranch: working out, lifting weights, and getting healthy. But in order to use the weight-lifting equipment, we had to memorize six Bible verses every week. That motivated me, but the first time I worked out, I realized that because of my heavy drug use, I was a lot weaker than I thought.

I fell in love with the Word of God right from the start. The first verse I learned was Proverbs 3:5-6:

> "Trust in the LORD with all your heart, and lean not on your own understanding; in all your ways acknowledge Him, and He will direct your paths."

Memorizing was tough at first—I didn't think I could possibly remember so many verses! But Joe Vasquez, an overseer at the ranch, encouraged me not to give up so easily and to keep trying. As I exercised that muscle in my brain, it got easier. Each week I'd write the scriptures from the memory board on three-by-five cards, and when we'd go out on work crew at the Western Eagle food bank, I'd pull out my cards in between moving pallets. The guys practiced together too as we worked, and we all challenged each other. We shared an excitement for God's Word that inspired us to go beyond our memory verses and memorized entire passages, as well as chapters.

Matthew 4:1-10 tells how Jesus quoted Scripture to combat Satan in the wilderness, and on one occasion at the ranch, I felt like the Lord said to me, "Erin, if you want to overcome sin in your life, you need to know My Word too." David says the same thing in Psalm 119:11:

> "Your Word I have hidden in my heart, that I might not sin against You."

Along with learning Scripture, I also appreciated the Friday night services at the ranch. With worship by Johnny Reno and teaching by Pastor Gerry, Friday nights were full of energy. Rosie and my parents used to come to the services too, and I was so excited when

Rosie accepted the Lord there. Even after I graduated in December we all went back on Fridays for church services. And then later that month on December 23, 1998, Rosie and I were married in the sanctuary at U-Turn For Christ with Pastor Gerry officiating.

A SEED OF DESIRE

So many good things happened at the ranch, yet I still struggled spiritually. A part of me hated the drugs more than anything, yet another part of me thought, *One day I know I'm going to try them again, just once to see what it's like, maybe five or ten years from now.* I prayed over and over, *Lord, I don't want to do this anymore!* But I was lying to myself, and to God, because deep down I held on to a hidden seed of desire to use drugs again. I buried that little seed in the back of my heart, and it didn't take years—it just took me ten days to mess up after leaving the ranch.

I only used once, but that was enough for my family to realize I needed help before things got worse. I stopped going to church at U-Turn with my family on Fridays, and I knew I needed to go back to the ranch, but I didn't want to see Pastor Gerry or any of the guys. One Friday night Pastor Gerry took Rosie aside and said, "If Erin doesn't want to come back, why don't you and Brittany stay here? And if Erin wants to see you, then he'll come."

My sister, Jennifer, found out about Rosie's plan to go to U-Turn and she told me about it. I thought, *No way! I'm the one with the problem. Okay, I'll go back then.* So in January of 1999, I checked in for the second time, ready to repeat Phase 1. I remember it was a Tuesday, and on Thursday I received a letter from Rosie. Her letter didn't say anything about going to the ranch, so I felt confused.

Then I saw Pastor Gerry walking across the campus, and he yelled out, "Hey, Erin, your wife's checking in here tonight." And sure enough, Rosie showed up that evening.

The next day at the Friday service, there was a baby dedication, and I joined Rosie and Brittany on stage to have our daughter dedicated. I hadn't spoken to Rosie since she arrived the day before, so I turned and whispered, "Hey, are you really checking in?"

Rosie glanced over at me. "Don't talk to me," she said.

Rosie moved into the women's ranch and she started Phase 1 a week after me, while my mom helped her with Brittany. I saw Rosie again a couple of weeks later, and we finally talked.

During my second time in Phase 1, I memorized 1 Timothy 5:8, and the words touched me deeply:

> "He who does not provide for his family is worse than an unbeliever."

I remember thinking, *I need to leave and take care of my family!* I tried to use it as an excuse to leave the program, but that didn't work so I stayed. After graduating again, I couldn't wait to buy a bus ticket home so I could go to work and provide for Rosie and Brittany.

BUS STATION DILEMMA

I left the ranch with the best intentions, planning to go straight to my parents' house in Anaheim, where I would stay until Rosie joined me a week later. But when I arrived at the Greyhound Bus Station in Riverside, I looked up at the reader board and discovered there were two different options. I could either buy a ticket to Anaheim, where my parents lived, or I could buy a ticket to Santa Ana, where I used to buy my drugs. Immediately, a battle began raging in my mind: *What do I do? What do I do?*

Okay, I finally told myself, *I'm going to Anaheim.*

After buying my ticket, the burden lifted and I boarded the bus. We were well on our way when I noticed the driver turning off the 91 Freeway and merging onto the 55, headed for Santa Ana. *Where are we going?* I wondered. What I didn't know was that the Greyhound bus stopped first in Santa Ana and then continued on to Anaheim. The battle raged again, *Do I get off or keep going?* When we pulled into the station in Santa Ana, I impulsively jumped off the bus and found a drug dealer. I didn't make it home until the next day.

I repeated Phase 1 a third time. It's all kind of a blur now, but when I returned home after my third graduation, Rosie and I got into a big argument, and I ran off to get high. I ended up at U-Turn for a fourth attempt, and this time Pastor Gerry decided to send me to Maneadero, Mexico, to a similar ranch facility. He offered to let Rosie, Brittany, and our second daughter, Kaitlin, stay in a mobile home behind his house in Perris so he and his wife, Peggy, could look after them.

ONE LAST DRUG DEAL

After a month in Maneadero, I didn't get my way about something and so I walked out and headed downtown to buy drugs. Another guy named Mike left the ranch too, and we ran around together for a week, drinking and doing drugs. Mike had a car that Pastor Gerry had loaned him for the ministry, and we parked it in a friend's driveway and slept in the car at night. When Pastor Gerry heard we'd left the facility, he sent Pastor Anthony and Pastor Mario down to talk some sense into us. One day as Mike and I were on our way to buy drugs, I saw them both in Pastor Mario's car, and they saw us too. I looked over at Mike and said, "Okay, listen. Drop me off up here and let them follow you around the block a few times. Then I'll jump back in the car and we'll ditch 'em."

Mike stopped the car and I ran out to buy drugs under a covered porch area where I couldn't be seen from the road. When I walked back to the street, I didn't see Mike anywhere. *Man, where is he?* I thought. I started walking back to the place where we were staying, did some drugs along the way, and finally decided to take a bus. Just as I stepped onto the bus, I saw Mike's car and jumped off to follow him. Running down the middle of the street, I flagged down the driver of the car, who I thought was Mike. But as I got closer, I could see that Pastor Anthony was actually driving. He slowed down and pulled up beside me. "Look," he said, "you're done. Get in the car and let's go. You can't be doing this."

"No way!" I protested. "I'll walk back to the ranch myself. "

"Listen, Erin," he warned, "Pastor Gerry said this is your last shot. Now get in the car."

Pastor Anthony was my friend, and I didn't want to take Pastor Gerry's kindness for granted. After all, he and Peggy were taking care of my family while I was out here acting like an idiot. So I climbed in the car and we rode back to the ranch in Maneadero. That was the last time I took drugs.

Going through Phase 1 at the ranch in Perris had been easy—even fun—compared to this, but in Maneadero I began to pray, *Lord, it needs to be different this time! I want it to be hard because otherwise, I'll just go right back out there and do it again.* I knew I needed to stop playing games and take responsibility or my life would be a mess forever. Being separated from Rosie and the girls for another three months was definitely the hardest part—I missed them so much. But God answered my prayer and after four months away from home, I finally returned to Perris in 2000, humbled and grateful.

STARTING OVER

Reunited with my family, I slowly built trust with Rosie, as well as with Pastor Gerry and the others in the ministry. I started reading through the book of Matthew, and one afternoon when I was sitting outside the bunkhouse, I read the story about the leper who came to Jesus to be healed:

> "And behold, a leper came and worshiped Him, saying, 'Lord, if You are willing, You can make me clean.' Then Jesus put out His hand and touched him, saying, 'I am willing; be cleansed.'" (Matthew 8:2-3)

The truth of Jesus' words, "I am willing, be cleansed," hit me hard. I recognized that God wanted to do a work in my life and to help me overcome my addiction. It wasn't God's will for me to be out there using drugs and drinking—He wanted to cleanse me from that. It's like He was saying, *Just give it to me, Erin, and I'll take it. But first you need to surrender. Are you willing to surrender so I can heal you?*

The seed of desire had been buried and hidden away in my heart for so long and I had allowed such ugly fruit to grow from it. The Lord showed me that He wanted me to live victoriously; He was willing to cleanse me. My part was to surrender. So with my whole heart I prayed, *God, You know what? I don't know how to get rid of this sin. Somehow, in a sick way, I enjoy using drugs, but I really don't want to do it anymore. I give up! I surrender!* I gave it all to Him and He was faithful to take the desire away. It was gone!

When I finally got off drugs, I had no idea the Lord would start working in every other area of my life too. I didn't know He wanted to change my vocabulary, my dress, and everything else that wasn't bringing Him glory. With the Lord in my life, I stopped cussing and dressing like a hoodlum. Through all the changes, He helped me understand more clearly what Jesus did on the cross for me. He brought me to the place where all I wanted to do was please Him—no one else.

Eventually Pastor Gerry asked me to pray about staying on at the ranch to work as an assistant overseer. God had used Pastor Gerry tremendously in my life—he was like a dad and treated me like a son. He and Peggy went out of their way for our family and were always there for us. So Rosie and I prayed and decided to stay. In 2004 I was ordained as a pastor, and in addition to working at the ranch, I began serving as an assistant pastor at Calvary Chapel Romoland.

AN EXAMPLE TO FOLLOW

Over the years I went on several mission trips with Pastor Gerry, but the most memorable one was our trip to the Philippines in February of 2006. When we arrived on the east side of Samar in Borongan, I called Rosie to check in on her and the kids, and she sounded relieved to hear my voice. "Are you all right?" she asked anxiously.

"Of course," I said. "What do you mean?"

"There was a big landslide in the Philippines today."

"Really?" We hadn't heard about it, so Pastor Gerry and I walked to an Internet café and checked the news. The landslide had occurred in a small village on the neighboring island of Leyte, about eight to ten hours away. Immediately we packed up vans and traveled to the village, where we stayed four days and prayed with Philippine nationals who had lost loved ones. We also assisted the U.S. military who were rescuing children and teachers buried in a school.

Out on the mission field, Pastor Gerry was always working. Sometimes I wondered, *When does he sleep?* He just goes on and on and on—this is normal for him. We didn't depart at the end of the day and go home; instead, I kept serving right alongside with him. Pastor Gerry's work ethic is amazing. The way he puts the Lord first in everything rubs off on all who minister with him. On a mission trip, it's all about Jesus, and when we return back home, you can find him serving first thing on Monday morning in the U-Turn office—and it's still all about Jesus.

THE PRIVILEGE OF MINISTRY

At every U-Turn For Christ leadership meeting, the first thing we do is worship and then we get right into God's Word learning new lessons every day. We need His direction because at the ranch, people come to us in crisis. We can never get to the place where we think, *It's just the same old song, the same story. I've dealt with this before so I don't need to take it to the Lord.* We can never tell someone, "Brother, your problem is easy. Now let me tell you what to do." Each person is different, and each one needs individual attention.

It's God's ministry and I know I have to represent Him in the way He wants me to. That means giving everything, 100 percent, and not to show off myself but to glorify Him. When I'm ministering to someone, I pray for wisdom and the Holy Spirit brings scriptures to my mind to use in counseling. Sometimes He gives me something to share and then says, "That's what you need to be doing too!" I love the way God works His Word into all of us.

The ministry here is unique because it's not centered on "the ministry" but on what Jesus Christ can do in a life that's totally surrendered to Him. U-Turn For Christ teaches people how to be respectful, how to work, lead a productive life, and glorify the Lord in everything they do. We help people get back to the basics and to sit at the feet of Jesus for a few months, simply serving Him.

What He's done in Rosie and me has rippled out to different family members, one life at a time. Several have gone through the program at the ranch, including my sister Jennifer, Rosie's brother Frankie, her sister Tania, and one of my nephews. By His grace, each one is serving the Lord. We try to minister and encourage them by living as an example rather than Bible-thumping. Our desire is to be a light and draw them all to the Savior.

Today, God has completely restored my life. Rosie is my best friend and she definitely is the best thing that has ever happened to me. She's never given up on me and she has loved me through the good and bad. She's seen my life up close, and in her own words, she watched me change from "a scrawny-looking guy" into one who is healthy and active. But more importantly, Rosie has seen my heart change. Before I came back to the Lord, she said that my focus was entirely on myself. But if you asked her today, she would tell you my life is about "loving the girls, being the best husband I can be, and leading our family in a way that glorifies the Lord."

We now have three daughters: Brittany, sixteen; Kaitlyn, fourteen; and Alicia, seven. Raising our children in the ministry has been such a blessing. God gives me wisdom to train them in the ways of the Lord, and my greatest joy is to be their dad. My all-time favorite thing to do is to spend time with my girls, playing with them or watching their soccer games. Both Brittany and Kaitlyn are involved with the youth group at our church, and Brittany embarked on her first mission trip to the Philippines in 2013. And today all the girls attend a Christian school.

I currently serve as the administrator at U-Turn For Christ, overseeing the daily operations of the office and setting up mission trips. I also continue serving as an assistant pastor at Calvary Chapel Romoland. Every day I witness miracles firsthand, watching lives transform from the time they arrive until they finish the program. I'll never forget how the Lord delivered me and how far He's brought me since I first came to U-Turn in 1998. God is so good, and I'm completely humbled by His willingness to cleanse me, to change me, and to use me. He is willing when we surrender it all to Him.

Brittany, Erin, Alicia, Rosie and Kaitlyn.

Lord, the miracles You perform amaze us all, yet the work You have done in Erin shows the power of Your love. Erin's story reminds me that You are longsuffering so that we will come to repentance, as it says in 2 Peter 3:9. Thank you for not giving up on us.

And thank you for allowing Erin to be used so effectively in the ministry, reaching out to others and blessing us with his abilities to manage and administrate.

Most of all, thank you for the gift of watching his family reunite. Because Erin has chosen to follow You, Rosie now has a real husband, and the girls know how much their daddy loves them.

Bless Erin's life, Lord! Amen.

CHAPTER 5

"For I know the thoughts that I think toward you," says the Lord, "thoughts of peace and not of evil, to give you a future and a hope."

JEREMIAH 29:11

CARMEN MEZA
A Future and a Hope

Drifting in and out of consciousness, Carmen winced with pain, unable to move. In her mind, the frightening scenes of that morning still haunted her: Jose's uncontrollable rage, his angry punches, and finally, the moment he threw her in the closet and slammed the door. Now lying motionless in that small, dark space, Carmen finally blacked out. Hours later, she woke up and realized that someone had moved her to the cold bathroom floor.

"Help!" she cried out, but no one answered. In agony, Carmen crawled out of the bathroom, moving slowly through every room of the house in search of a phone. But there was no phone. And there was no one to help.

This is Carmen's story.

By the time I came to the ranch at U-Turn For Christ, I was so angry that if someone in authority said, "Do this," I wouldn't do it. And if someone said, "Don't do this," I *would* do it. No one knew this better than my cousin, Lance. After all, he's the one who convinced me to go to U-Turn in the first place. So when Lance found out I was leaving the program after only a month, he showed up right away.

"I won't try to stop you, Carmen," Lance said matter-of-factly when he found me fuming and ready to walk out. "Besides, your bags are probably already packed. So go get your stuff, make your phone calls, and start walking."

As my cousin spoke, I cussed him out in my mind. Even though my graduation from Phase 1 was only weeks away, I'd had enough! Only thirty days earlier Lance and his wife, Yvonne, had brought me to the ranch, trusting God to free me from drugs and to heal my broken heart.

"Remember," Lance continued, "the same door that opened when you came here will close when you leave. And after that, in a week or in a month or a year from now, you'll call me, because you always do, and I'll come and get you no matter where you are. I'll bring you right back here because I love you and because God has a calling on your life. And then you'll start all over again. So go ahead and leave, Carmen."

Exasperated, I yelled, "I'm not leaving!" Then I ran back to my room in tears. Later that night as I stepped into the shower stall and turned on the spray of warm water, I fell to my knees and prayed desperately, *If You're really the God that people say You are, then come into my heart and change me. Help me and give me strength not to walk out through the gate!* God graciously answered my prayer, and a month later I graduated from Phase 1.

GROWING UP

As a fifteen-year-old unwed teenager, my mother gave birth to me in the border town of Calexico, California. I never knew my biological father because he left before I was born. My mom eventually married another man, had my brother Mike and my sister Maria, and then fled that abusive relationship. I was five when she moved us to Hemet, California, where we lived next door to my grandma, my mom's mother. My mom remarried right away and then she started drinking. When my new step dad moved in, he began molesting me.

No one knew he was molesting me, and at five years old, I was too scared to talk about it. My step dad was a big man, 170 pounds, and he'd slip into my room at night while everyone else slept, climb into my bed, and then get up and leave when he was done with me. I tried to cope by blocking it all out, but by the time I turned thirteen, I knew that what he was doing was wrong. So one night I mustered up the courage to confront him. When he walked into my room, I warned, "Stop! If you touch me again, I'll call CPS—and the police!"

He left quickly, and I noticed he tried to be nicer to me after that. But because he had abused me for so long, I hardened my heart and resolved to never love any man, never get married, and never have children. I didn't want my kids to endure the same thing.

Although my step dad was manipulative, my mom was warm and loving. Mom smothered me with hugs and told me she loved me; however, she was also quiet, isolated, and frequently depressed. I knew she would do anything for me, but because she didn't speak much, we had difficulty communicating.

Sometimes she'd go on drinking binges for days at a time, and twice she was admitted to a psych hospital for overdosing on sleeping pills and trying to kill herself. Whenever Mom wasn't able to look after us, it was my responsibility to care for my younger siblings and to cook.

Eventually Mom quit drinking when I was a teenager, and she gave birth to a fourth child at that time, my youngest sister, Socorro.

With Grandma still living next door, my brother and sisters and I spent a lot of time over there, especially after school. Several of my aunts and cousins lived with her, and on holidays we all gathered at her house for family parties. I dreaded those parties because my uncles would drink, take drugs, and get into arguments. Some of my relatives died from their addictions, and it frightened me so terribly that I promised myself I'd never drink or take drugs. In high school, though, my friends talked me into trying marijuana and meth, but I didn't continue using them.

LIFE WITH JOSÉ

As a teenager I experienced bouts of depression, suicidal thoughts, guilt, and shame. I tried to ignore these feelings by staying busy. At age fifteen I took my first job, a paper route, and I delivered papers every day after school for two years. A couple of years later I worked at a restaurant called Pioneer Chicken, where I met my future husband, José. When José walked into the restaurant for the first time, I noticed him right away—he was charming and good-looking. He must have thought I was cute too because he asked for my phone number, and soon we were talking on the phone for hours at a time.

We dated for a year and had a great relationship, or so I thought. José promised to take care of me and to give me the world. We married in 1987, when I was eighteen and he was twenty-three, but just two months later he started abusing me, first verbally and then physically. The trouble began at night whenever José wanted to be intimate. We had talked about my step dad's abuse, and José had been sympathetic at first. But later he began saying things like, "You must have provoked your step dad" or "I know you really liked it," just to torment me. That soon led to his accusation that I was seeing

CARMEN MEZA: *A Future and a Hope*

someone else, which was never true, so I would pull away and he would get mad. But despite the problems we had, our first daughter, Monique, was born in 1990, followed by José Jr. in 1991, and Andrea in 1993.

During this time, José worked for the waste management company and I worked as a certified nursing assistant, first in a convalescent hospital and later in a cardiologist's office. Once when I was in my early twenties, José came home from work late one night and threw me up against a wall, injuring my back. Without revealing how I got my injury I asked my doctor for advice about my back pain. He said I had herniated disks and prescribed a narcotic for pain. It didn't take long before I became addicted to the pills.

Struggling with suicidal thoughts, I started seeing a psychiatrist, who prescribed antidepressants. Because I worked in a doctor's office, I had easy access to drugs, and I used whatever I could get my hands on—Vicodin, Soma, Oxycontin, Norco, and Percocet.

In the late '90s, a patient named Gerry Brown came to see the cardiologist's office for a follow-up after a heart attack. I escorted him back to a room and hooked him up for a treadmill test. Then I received a phone call. It was my mom and she was upset about my brother, who was on heroin. Gerry overheard our conversation and after his test was over, he handed me a business card for U-Turn For Christ. "If your brother ever wants help or decides to go to rehab, call me," he said. I thanked Gerry and gave his card to my mom.

Even though I believed my brother needed help, I continued taking pain pills for over eight years. Then at age twenty-nine I stopped cold turkey. While coming off the drugs, I went into a severe depression that lasted about two weeks. I stayed in bed with the covers pulled up over my head, sleeping a lot, and I didn't take my kids to school. My oldest daughter, Monique, who was thirteen at the time, took care of her younger brother and sister while José worked long hours.

After I had spent two weeks in bed, José came home from work, walked me into the bathroom, and shut the door. "We have to do something to get you out of bed," he said as he pulled out a bag of crystal meth. "This will help you stay awake." He made sure I took the first line, and after that, I was hooked. Then he handed me some pot. "When you need to go to sleep, use this." Having meth and pot around was never a problem because José's friends at work kept him supplied. Now I had two new addictions.

José continued to abuse me. Sometimes after he beat me up, the kids and I went to a friend's house or a hotel room to get away. But during our separations, José always managed to track me down and persuade me to come home.

DIVORCE

Several months later my in-laws came to visit. While they were there, my mother-in-law agreed to watch the kids so that my mom, José, and I could go to the casino on a Friday night. But José decided not to go at the last minute, so Mom and I went alone and stayed out all night. When we returned the next morning, José beat me up, worse than ever before. He hit me hard and long, and when I didn't get up, he threw me into a closet, where I blacked out. At some point he came back to check on me and move me into the bathroom. Then, before leaving the house, José and my in-laws removed all the phones to make sure I couldn't call anyone for help.

By Monday morning, I'd recovered enough to go to work. Without thinking about it, I pulled my hair back in a ponytail, and got dressed for work. I tried to make sure my bruises were covered up, but a co-worker noticed a large black-and-blue mark on the back of my neck. Alarmed, she took me aside and whispered, "Carmen, what happened?" This nurse was familiar with my situation at home, and before I could answer, she said, "You need to file a report now! And if you don't, I will." I felt afraid, but I went to the police station anyway. They told me to call 911 when José got home that evening, so I did. Then a police officer came to the house, arrested José, and took him off to jail. After his arrest, the kids and I went to live with my mom. The day I moved in with Mom was September 11, 2001, the same day the Twin Towers fell in New York.

Deep down, I didn't want my marriage to end, and I became more and more miserable. After José was released, I received a court summons and learned that he had filed for divorce after thirteen years of marriage. There was nothing left to do, so I pawned all my jewelry and hired a lawyer.

When I appeared in court, apparently Jose had told someone that I was on drugs. So after I tested positive, the judge took my kids away. Then José informed the court of my step dad's abuse, and the judge forbid my children from being placed with anyone in my family. José couldn't take the kids because of his drinking history, so finally my attorney turned to me and asked, "Where do you want your kids to go, Carmen?" The only person I could think of was my childhood friend, Nora, and her husband, Jaime, who were both stable and drug-free. During the court recess, I called Nora to ask if she'd consider it. She said yes.

After my children left, I no longer cared about anything. I quit my job and started using heavily going from party to party. Sometimes I'd stop at my mom's to take a shower and then go back out on the streets. At first I visited my kids regularly, but eventually I stopped seeing them. I used heroin, speed, crack—whatever my friends had. I wasn't eating much and became very skinny. Over a year's time I dropped 100 pounds and eventually weighed only 97 pounds.

One day I ran into Nora and the kids on the street. When my children saw me, they started crying. "Please, Mom, come home with us," they begged. "Please come back!" I wanted to do the right thing, so I went home with them to Nora's house. But in the middle of the night, the drugs started calling me. All I could think about was getting high, so I left.

WALTER

Desperate to get high, I rang the doorbell at a friend's house, but no one answered. As I turned to leave, I saw a kind-looking gentleman sitting in a chair on the front porch. He smiled and said, "Hi, I'm Walter," so I sat down and talked to him. Walter was small, thin, bald, and had deep blue eyes. He told me he was renting a room from my friend, and then he said he was blind, which intrigued me. Right away I sensed that he wasn't a threat. He shared that he was diabetic, which got my attention because it meant he had needles. He also said he sold pot to make money. After we talked, Walter and I started hanging out together, and later I moved in with him. I was hired as his caregiver through the county's support services, and we stayed together for three years, from 2003 to 2006.

Walter wanted to marry me, but all I wanted to do was get high. In spite of our living arrangement and smoking pot together, Walter told me he was a believer, and on Sundays he'd drag me to church at Calvary Chapel in Temecula. I had grown up Catholic and didn't know anything about having a personal relationship with Jesus or the importance of reading the Bible. Walter would say, "Carmen, go to God and everything else will follow." I went forward at an altar call in 2005, but looking back, I realize that I didn't really understand what it meant.

Walter and I went to rehab and AA meetings together. We would stop using drugs for a little while and then relapse. We argued a lot because I wasn't committed to rehab. Once we got into a terrible fight and I pushed Walter so hard that he broke his thumb. He got so upset that he told me to get out. He called my mom to tell her what happened and asked her to come and get me. My mom called my cousin, Yvonne, who picked me up and took me back home with her to Murrieta.

"I've missed you, Carmen," Yvonne said kindly on our drive back to her house. "Everyone in the family has missed you." Yvonne and I had grown up together, but because of my drug use, I had distanced myself from my family over the past few years. As we talked, Yvonne noticed how unhealthy and sad I looked, and she could see I desperately needed help.

"We're selling our home, Carmen," my cousin continued. "We're moving to Hawaii to start a U-Turn For Christ there." Yvonne met her husband, Lance—now my cousin too—when she went through rehab at the ranch several years earlier. Now Lance was a leader in the ministry.

"Maybe you can help us get our house ready to put on the market," she offered. "I'll pay you. You could even come with us to Hawaii and help us take care of the girls. Trinity is four years old now and Tara is one."

I figured I had nothing to lose, and in my mind I was already buying pot with the money I earned. I pictured myself playing with the kids all day and then partying on the beach at night. Without Walter, José, or my kids, I was free! "Yeah, okay," I agreed.

After settling in at Yvonne and Lance's house, Lance came home and greeted me. "I hear you've decided to go with us to Hawaii," he said.

"Yeah, I'm going!"

"Okay," he said. "There's just one thing you'll need to do before we go."

"What's that?"

"Go to the women's ranch at U-Turn For Christ."

"You're crazy!" I said. "I'm not going to any women's ranch. There's nothing wrong with me! Besides, I could never live with a bunch of women."

Lance repeated his conditions, calmly but firmly. "If you want to come with us to Hawaii, you'll have to go to the ranch first. We're not leaving for three months, and the first program, Phase 1, only lasts two months. So you'll be back in plenty of time for Hawaii."

I stayed with Yvonne and Lance for the rest of the week, helping them clean their house, and all the while I missed my old life. I tried calling Walter, but he wouldn't answer. Finally, he returned my call, but Lance picked up the phone first. "Back off, Walter," I heard Lance say, "and leave her alone. Listen, she's agreed to go to rehab—isn't that what you want?"

Walter got excited when he heard I was headed for U-Turn. "That's great!" he said. "Can I go too?" So Lance arranged it and Walter arrived at the ranch a few days before me.

THE FIRST MONTH

The day before I left for the ranch, I went for a long walk in Lance and Yvonne's neighborhood. Even though I didn't have a real relationship with the Lord, I still prayed sometimes. *Okay, God,* I said, *I know I don't really know You, but please help me because I don't want to go to this place!* The next morning I picked up my last prescriptions of Vicodin and Soma from a pharmacy and downed my last dose. That evening, Yvonne and Lance drove me to the ranch.

Soon after I arrived, I plotted how to pull Walter out of the program and spend time with him. But it wasn't as easy as I thought because he was in the men's section and I was in the women's. The only time I saw Walter was at church on Sunday mornings and in a discipleship group on Wednesday nights. Even then, I could only watch him from a distance, and there was no way to get his attention because he couldn't see me! I felt frustrated. After a month of this, I decided, *With or without Walter, I'm outta here!* Word got to my overseer that I was planning to leave, and that's when Lance came and told me to walk out. Only my pride and rebellion kept me at the ranch, at least initially.

During my last month in Phase 1, I spent a lot of time crying and seeking God. I didn't see stars or miracles, but as the time drew near for my graduation, I realized I wasn't ready to leave the ranch after all. One day Pastor Gerry arranged a meeting with Walter and me. Seated together in his office, Pastor Gerry turned to me and said, "Carmen, Walter loves you and wants to marry you. What do you have to say?"

I swallowed hard and thought awhile before answering. "I love Walter too, but I know I've manipulated him in the past and I don't want to do that again. He deserves better. And I'm not ready yet—I want to become the woman God wants me to be, whether it's for Walter or not." So we left it at that. Walter graduated from Phase 1 and traveled to the Philippines for ministry. Not long after that, I heard the sad news that he had passed away, apparently from his diabetes.

It felt like everything was against me. But as I began to really listen to God's Word, a scripture I heard in a Bible study spoke to me:

> "'For I know the thoughts that I think toward you,' says the Lord, 'thoughts of peace and not of evil, to give you a future and a hope.'" (Jeremiah 29:11)

Weeks later, a speaker named Rosalie came to the ranch and she shared the same verse with me personally. I pondered the words over and over because at the time I had no hope and no future. The Lord definitely gave me that verse, but I didn't understand what it meant. I couldn't see. But all that was about to change.

SOUTH CAROLINA

A week before my graduation from Phase 1, my overseer, Marilyn, told me she was leaving soon for South Carolina, where she was going to help open a new U-Turn For Christ ranch there. "Would you consider going with me, Carmen?" she asked.

But I'm going to Hawaii, I thought. *Or…maybe I should go to South Carolina instead.* Confused, I finally answered, "I don't know."

"Why don't you pray about it?" Marilyn suggested.

"Wait, where's South Carolina?" I asked. I didn't even know where it was or what it would be like.

I did pray and God gave me peace about accompanying Marilyn. "What's six more months?" I said. Little did I know that as Marilyn and I began preparing the women's dorm, God would use that time to also begin healing my broken heart. One day as we hung pictures on the walls, arranged furniture and decorated each room, the Lord brought Proverbs 14:1 to mind:

> "The wise woman builds her house, but the foolish pulls it down with her hands."

God showed me that I was once that foolish woman, tearing down my own house by allowing drugs to take over my life. But now, by His grace, the Lord was helping me become a wise woman by pouring His Word into me.

When the dorm rooms were finished, the Lord started bringing women to the new ranch, and I remember crying out to Him, knowing I'd be leaving South Carolina soon. *Lord, give me a hunger for Your Word. Help me pay attention. Give me wisdom and discernment. Guide me, Lord.* At this point I was done with Phase 2, and I received a surprise phone call from Pastor Gerry's wife, Peggy. "Carmen, we've been praying," she said, "and God keeps putting you on our hearts to come and run the women's ranch here."

I couldn't believe it. *Thank You, Lord!* "Okay," I said, wondering what God would do next.

A NEW CALLING

Unexpectedly, in my new role as overseer of the women's ranch, I began to see myself in those who came to the program—women who had been molested or abused, and women who had lost their children because of drugs. I marveled at the compassion and understanding God gave me for each one as I realized that I had experienced many of the same things. And I began to see why He had allowed those terrible things to happen, not because it had been His will, but because He wanted to turn it all around so that I could help others.

The apostle Paul describes this in 2 Corinthians 1:3-4:

> "Blessed be the God and Father of our Lord Jesus Christ, the Father of mercies and God of all comfort, who comforts us in all our tribulation, that we may be able to comfort those who are in any trouble, with the comfort with which we ourselves are comforted by God."

God graciously allowed me to comfort hurting women with the same comfort He had lavished on me.

A typical day at the women's ranch began at 5:30 a.m., when we woke up and met together to read a chapter of Proverbs. Then we had breakfast, did chores, and left the ranch to serve at different job sites. One group of women went to a local food bank called Western Eagle to pack boxes of food for needy families, while another group went to the Murrieta Bible college to do housekeeping. Others cleaned the church in Romoland or served at a local thrift store or a coffee shop.

Wherever we went, we made God the center of our day. We practiced our memory verses while making beds and cleaning rooms, and we shared answers to prayer while packing food. After serving all morning, we took a break for lunch and read a psalm together, then we continued working through the afternoon and returned to the ranch at 4 p.m. Next, we had a break, ate dinner, recited our daily memory verse aloud, and then gathered for a Bible study in the evening. This would lead into Bible reading and prayer, counsel from the leaders, and finally bedtime at 9:30 p.m. Our days were busy and full of blessings!

MIRACLES

I see miracles at the ranch every day. When a young girl named Kelsey (name changed) came here a few years ago, she went through alcohol withdrawals and was tormented by hallucinations and voices inside her head. Convinced she had a phone implanted in her ear, Kelsey thought she could control the phone with an imaginary button located on her clothing. She thought the voices belonged to family members—her mom, dad, brothers, sister, and uncles—all telling her to leave the ranch and meet them down the hill at the end of the road.

"Don't answer the voices," we told Kelsey. We gave her different scriptures to repeat out loud, such as James 4:7:

"Submit to God. Resist the devil and he will flee from you."

The pastors laid hands on her and we all continued praying. One day Kelsey and I were cooking in the kitchen together and I asked her to stir something in a pot on the stove. She said, "But the voices are telling me to leave right now."

"Don't answer them," I said, "just call on the name of Jesus. Keep calling out to Jesus!"

Kelsey began praying out loud, *Set me free, Jesus. Take these voices away. Please help me, Jesus.* Moments later, Kelsey snapped out of it and the voices and hallucinations stopped. I get chills thinking about it! When her family came to church that night, Kelsey was a different person. The Lord completely restored her, and she became a wonderful example to the other girls, a living testimony of God's grace. Kelsey has been clean and sober for over five years now and is married with a beautiful baby girl. She still has a strong relationship with Jesus Christ, and she boldly proclaims how He set her free from her addictions.

Sometimes women who come to the ranch miss their children so much that they decide to go home and take care of them. We try to counsel them to stay at the ranch instead so they can come to understand that when they're stuck in an addiction, they're not equipped to raise children properly. While these women are here, they have an opportunity to learn the biblical principles and build a new foundation for their lives in Jesus. As they grow in their relationship with Him, they discover that His Word has something to say about whatever situation they're in, including parenting.

Isaiah 55:11 says,

> "My Word…shall not return to Me void."

We see this verse played out daily at the ranch as women memorize Scripture and learn how to live it out. For example, the women are encouraged to write notes to their children and tell them what God is doing in their lives. In this way, they learn how to become that wise woman of Proverbs 31, and they will eventually go back to build their house on the foundation of the Lord. A house with this kind of biblical foundation can withstand the storms of life. We teach women to have strong and loving relationships with their children, husbands, and other family members.

THE HEART'S DESIRE

David tells us in Psalm 37:4,

> "Delight yourself also in the LORD, and He will give you the desires of your heart."

Since coming to the ranch, the greatest desire of my own heart has been to reconcile with my children—Monique, Andrea, and José Jr. During Phase 2 in South Carolina, I began writing to my children, but they didn't respond. So I tried calling them, but they didn't answer. One time when I called, Nora answered the phone and said, "Your children don't want to talk to you, Carmen."

I felt so sad, but I also knew it was my own doing. Then I read the story of Abraham in the book of Genesis and how God called him to lay his son Isaac on the altar. I also read about Joseph, who was separated from his family for years and then finally reunited with them. The Lord used those stories to inspire me with the hope of seeing my own children again someday—not in my time but His. And so I believed He would bring them back. When I gave my kids over to God and put them on the altar, it freed me to pursue a deeper relationship with Jesus for myself, even though my children made it clear that they wanted nothing to do with me.

By 2010 I had been in the ministry for four years, praying continually, *Lord, please restore my kids to me.* My entire church joined me in prayer for them too. During a Wednesday night message, I remember Pastor Gerry once shared, "Many of you sitting in this sanctuary are separated from your children because of your own sin. Know this—the Lord wants to restore them to you. But let's say that God brings your kids back to you right now and He even sets them in your lap. Are you really ready for them?" After hearing that sermon, my prayer changed to this: *Prepare me for them, Lord. Prepare me.* And He began doing that.

One day Pastor Gerry's wife, Peggy, suggested, "Carmen, why don't you take your kids a box of food and put it by their front door? Whether they want it or not will be up to them. But when they see your consistency, maybe they'll have a change of heart." So every few weeks I called Nora to tell her I was coming over, and I left two boxes of food at her door. I left things I knew my kids would enjoy, like Oreos, peanut butter cookies, Captain Crunch, Trix, Fruit Loops, and pasta. The first time I came, I knocked on the door but no one answered so I just left the boxes. The next time, one of my kids answered the door and said, "Thanks, Mom," but with a bad attitude. Another time one of the kids said, "Hi, Mom," and gave me a hug. Little by little, they saw that I wasn't high on drugs or talking nonsense or cursing like I'd done in the past. Because of the Lord, they saw that I was a different person. And as they saw this different mom, their hearts began to soften. The Lord was restoring our relationship, but now my kids were experiencing their own problems.

When José Jr. turned eighteen, Nora called me one day to tell me he had started drinking, smoking pot, and using drugs. "You need to come and pick up Junior," she said. "I don't know what to do with him." Pastor Gerry and Peggy counseled me to bring my son to the ranch. The pastors here took him into their care and discipled him. Junior accepted the Lord at a Harvest Crusade and after that, he accompanied Pastor Gerry on mission trips to the Philippines and to Mexico.

A few months after Nora's call about José Jr., she called again to say that Andrea, then seventeen, was using drugs. Nora didn't know what to do with her either, so Andrea came to the ranch too. "Let the other leaders deal with her," Pastor Gerry advised, "and you back away." While Andrea was on drugs, she got pregnant but was afraid to tell me. She tried to make herself miscarry by punching her stomach, but after hearing testimonies from the other women at the ranch, she finally got the courage to tell me she was pregnant.

"Okay, Andrea," I said, "since abortion is out of the question, now you're going to become a mommy. That's what an adult Christian woman does—she takes care of her baby." My beautiful grandson, Josiah, was born April 20, 2012—a healthy, happy baby—and I have the joy of watching him grow and play while he and Andrea live nearby with my mom.

FAMILY UPDATE

Andrea is now twenty years old. She has gone back to school and works hard at being a good mom to Josiah. Junior is twenty-one, working, and helps out at the ranch every other weekend. Monique is twenty-three, working, and I look forward to what God has planned for our relationship. I have given my ex-husband José over to the Lord, and I pray with all my heart for his salvation. I've learned to forgive him and love him with Christ's love.

My mom still lives in Hemet with my step dad and with Andrea and Josiah. Mom and I have a good relationship and she is at peace, knowing I'm doing well. My brother Mike went to U-Turn For Christ after prison, and he served in ministry there for five years. Today he is the overseer at the U-Turn For Christ men's ranch in Needles, California.

My cousins, Yvonne and Lance, still live in Hawaii with their girls after moving there in 2006. Since I came to U-Turn, Yvonne says she's seen a new confidence in me, and an assurance of who I am in Christ. She's watched me forgive those who have hurt me, and she's witnessed the joy God brought as my children and I were reunited.

Yvonne says, "Carmen has nothing to hide anymore. She'll tell you what you need to hear, and she's not afraid to say, 'Hey, you need Jesus! And you need to ask Him to change you!' I admire her for that."

HOPE FOR TODAY AND TOMORROW

Today I serve as assistant overseer of the women's ranch, and I also work in the U-Turn For Christ office. It's such a privilege for me to minister to the women, love on them, and take them to Jesus and His Word every day. Whenever I feel like I'm not good enough, or like I can't do something, God brings me back to my life verse, Jeremiah 29:11. I cling to these words and hold on to their promise of hope, remembering how far God has brought me since I came to the ranch in 2006 and heard that Scripture for the first time. Back then, my only hope and future was finding the next high on drugs. But today because of Jesus, my glorious hope and future are found in Him!

Andrea, Carmen and José Jr.

Lord, Carmen's life was one of hurt and pain until You lavished her with Your love and compassion.

Thank you for the radical God-fearing woman she has become through You. Please continue to show her how valuable she is to You.

And please use her to bless others in the same miraculous way that You have touched her life. In Jesus' name, Amen.

CHAPTER 6

I carried you before you were born. I will be your God throughout your lifetime—until your hair is white with age. I made you and will care for you. I will carry you along and save you.

ISAIAH 46:3-4 (NLT)

PASTOR JOHNNY RENO
Abandoned to His Arms

On a balmy night in July of 1958, the Flying Tiger aircraft descended into the Portland International Airport after a 16-hour flight from Seoul, Korea. Eighty Korean orphans, from infants to teenagers, traveled aboard, ready to meet their American adoptive parents for the first time. Gathered outside, the crowd of new parents stood together, anxious to catch a glimpse of their soon-to-be children, who had all been adopted through the Holt's Adoption Program, founded in 1956 by Harry and Bertha Holt.

One father in the crowd, Gilbert Reno, had been waiting at the airport since early morning for his adopted four-and-a-half year old son. Gilbert watched excitedly as the Flying Tiger taxied off the

109

runway and came to a full stop at the terminal. This would be the second Korean adoption for Gilbert and his wife, Anita, with an infant daughter joining their family only months before. Gilbert fixed his eyes on the plane's side door until it finally slid open, and he watched as the babies were brought out first, carried in large wicker baskets by their adult caretakers. The older children disembarked next, and near the end of the line, Harry Holt himself descended the passenger stairs, holding another large basket.

Mr. Holt recognized Gilbert in the crowd, and smiling broadly, he walked toward him and held out the basket. Gilbert nervously peered inside and caught his breath. Dressed in only a diaper and a tiny T-shirt lay a very thin, sickly child, listless and still.

This is Johnny's story.

That little sick boy in the basket was me—John David Reno. I have no memories of Korea nor of my arrival in the United States. Dad says that when he first saw me, I had a weak, quiet cry. Boils covered my body, and I had a staph infection on the back of my head and my hands. I couldn't walk or even stand up, and I showed no emotion, making no effort at physical contact.

Mr. Holt lifted me carefully from the basket and placed me in my father's arms. Then Dad and I flew home together to Hemet, California, where I met my mom and three siblings: six years, three years, and five months. Just a year earlier, Mom and Dad had lost an infant son, Robert, who lived only twenty-four hours. Devastated, they tried to conceive again without success. So they explored adoption and learned about the Holt's Adoption Program, which started placing Korean children in families after the Korean War, when many babies were fathered and left orphaned by American GIs.

My parents put their name on a waiting list with the agency and soon adopted their first orphan, four-week-old Susan. When they picked her up and saw the plane full of Korean children, they vowed to adopt another one soon, and immediately put their name back on the list, this time requesting a boy. A few months later Mom received a call from a Mrs. Bray at the agency. "We have a little boy ready for you," she said.

"Wonderful!" Mom exclaimed.

Mrs. Bray continued, "I must tell you, Mrs. Reno, that the child is extremely sick and malnourished." She went on to explain that I'd been abandoned during the severe famine after the war and was taken to an orphanage in Puson, South Korea, where there was a high mortality rate. Harry Holt's daughter Molly, a registered nurse, had visited the orphanage and when she saw me, she knew I'd die if I didn't get help. So she took me back with her to the Holt's orphanage in Ilsan, and that's when the agency contacted my parents.

While waiting for my adoption to be finalized, Mom was surprised to find out she was pregnant, and her doctor urged her to forego my adoption. "You already have two older children," the doctor said, "along with the baby and another one on the way." But Mom dismissed the doctor's concern.

"We're committed," she replied. "We've seen John David's picture and we're already in love with him!" This, of course, meant my parents had three new children in one year, and according to Mom, it was quite the year!

A FAMILY OF MY OWN

Despite knowing about my fragile health before I arrived, both my parents were thrown a little when they saw me. Mom says I was "a tiny mite" with huge dark eyes, a distended tummy, stick arms and legs, and a shaved head to prevent lice.

Without birth records, my history from Korea was unknown. My parents were told that I had been abandoned and the orphanage found me. No one knew how old I was, and doctors at the Korean orphanage estimated my age from my tooth and bone structure to be about three. They even gave me a birthday: May 9, 1955. When I arrived in the States, I weighed a scant eighteen pounds, the average weight of a nine-month-old. That first year at home, I came down with one illness after another—mumps, measles, chicken pox, and whooping cough. Mom says she could hardly set me down and that I soaked up her hugs and clung to her like a little koala bear.

According to Mom, I didn't speak for an entire year and I often stared at the ceiling. But with good nutrition and lots of love, I blossomed and thrived. I ate like a vacuum cleaner and picked up every crumb that fell. After a year of nurturing, I walked into the kitchen one morning and pulled on Mom's dress. "Food, food!" I cried, and those were my first words.

The emotional scarring of my early neglect took longer to heal, however, and I was told that for months I woke up screaming with night terrors. Then gradually they stopped.

Our family continued to grow, with a new brother born in 1959 and two more Korean sisters adopted in 1963, bringing the count in our family to eight children. When I started school, I became a popular student, an extrovert with lots of friends, but I was also teased a lot because I looked different.

My parents provided a wonderful home life, and I felt like I had the best mom and dad in the whole world. My father took us on vacations and we went fishing and hunting together. We did chores together, planted gardens, and took care of farm animals—horses, chickens, goats, and a cow. When I was eight years old, I helped milk the cow and goats morning and night. I delighted in caring for the animals, and I think it made my dad happy that out of all the kids, I was the only one who really loved doing it. I woke up every morning before sunrise to feed them.

FROM SKEPTIC TO BORN AGAIN

Dad ran a successful real estate business while Mom stayed home with the kids. Once when Dad sold a house to the pastor of the First Baptist Church of Hemet, the pastor asked my father a life-changing question: "Gilbert, if you died today, do you know if you'd go to heaven?" Dad got upset. After all, he took his family to church every Sunday, did good deeds for others, and was president of the Kiwanis Club. Besides, Dad had never heard about being born again. Then in 1964, when I was nine, Dad was sitting in his chair one night watching Billy Graham on TV. With a beer in his hand and tears in his eyes, he prayed to ask Jesus into his heart. Soon Mom became a Christian too, and my parents' decision changed the course of our lives.

We started attending the First Baptist Church of Hemet, where the pastor gave an altar call after every service. I didn't want to go to hell, so I went forward each time, and I'm sure people thought, *Boy, this guy needs a lot of saving!* All I knew was that I was always in trouble for not obeying my parents. Whatever they said not to do, I'd go do it and get a spanking. Then one day the pastor took me aside and said, "Johnny, I've noticed that you come forward for altar calls a lot, sometimes twice a week. And I want you to understand that when God gives you the gift of salvation, He doesn't take it away every time you do something wrong. So you don't have to keep going forward, okay?" Finally, I got it.

Dad became a pastor when I turned twelve and gave up his real estate business for full-time ministry. He moved our family to Spokane, Washington, where he worked as an American Sunday School Union missionary, planting churches in Northeast Washington and Idaho. Suddenly I was a preacher's kid, and it seemed like I was in church 24/7. For me, it was a lot of pressure! I wanted long hair, and my dad liked it short; I liked tight jeans and he liked baggy pants. I started living up to the wild and rebellious image of a PK.

After a year of piano lessons, Mom let me buy my first guitar at K-Mart for fifteen dollars. I earned all the money myself from mowing lawns. I taught myself how to play and was pretty serious about the guitar, practicing for hours at a time. When I replaced the catgut strings with steel strings, sometimes I'd play until my fingers bled.

TEENAGE TRAVAIL

On my thirteenth birthday, my parents informed me that I was actually older than I thought I was. Because I was so small as a young child, they had taken a year off my age. What a bad birthday surprise that was! Something changed inside of me that year; my life felt chaotic and I started having issues with being adopted. I felt abandoned and grew more aware of how different I was from other kids. Not only did I have dark skin, black hair, and slanted eyes, I didn't even know where I came from or how old I was! I felt like a freak, like I was from the moon. I remember looking in the mirror, hitting my face, and wishing I could die. I was convinced I'd be dead by the age of sixteen.

Then I began having migraines that made me go blind and pass out. Sometimes the pounding pain lasted for days. My parents took me to many doctors, who determined the headaches were stress-induced. I felt crazy, like I was being oppressed by an evil spirit. I remember once banging my head against the wall and cutting myself. Finally I decided I didn't want to live by the rules anymore and started sneaking out the basement window to run away from home, sometimes every other week. I wanted to stay out all night, smoke cigarettes, and drink. The first time I got drunk was from a neighbor's supply of vodka, which belonged to my friend's dad.

As I became more and more incorrigible, I was made a ward of the court and sent to a Christian ranch for troubled boys in Naches, Washington. When I arrived, the other boys, who were mostly foster kids, asked, "What are you here for?"

"Running away from home," I said. Then they all laughed because they were locked up for more serious offenses, like car theft and attempted murder. They bragged about their crimes and thought it was pretty funny that all I'd done was run away. I remember thinking, *I can't wait to turn sixteen because then I'll join the army!* After staying a year at the boys ranch, however, I changed my mind and returned home.

My parents had two more biological children while we lived in Spokane, giving us a grand total of ten kids—five biological and five adopted from Korea. Surprisingly, even with ten children and Dad in full-time ministry, our family life remained pretty normal. Mom was patient and kind with all of us and she left the discipline to Dad. After I'd been back home from the ranch a few months, I once again decided that I didn't want to follow the rules, so I moved out and lived with my girlfriend and with friends. I found a part-time job and worked throughout high school. Eventually I became the night manager of a boat company, and without my parents' restrictions, I started using drugs, smoking, drinking, and having sex.

BACK TO CALI

By 1976, at the age of twenty-one, I left Spokane and moved to Southern California. There I lived with one of my sisters and found a construction job in Hemet. I met a nice family in town, the Gibbels, who used to know my parents, and they invited me to their home Bible study to help with the music. I agreed; after all, they were very kind to me. Every week right before Bible study I'd get stoned and then show up to lead music. After I'd attended for about a month, one night the Bible teacher announced, "If anyone wants the Lord's help for anything, stand up now and we'll pray for you." I stood right up, stoned and higher than a kite. Then I thought, *What are you doing, Johnny? Sit down!* But instead, I began crying like a baby. I prayed, *Lord, if You're really real, I need You to save me!* People started praying for me, and I left that night delivered from pot. Later

I found out that these people had been meeting thirty minutes before the study started each week, just to pray for me. They knew I was high, but they kept right on praying.

After that night I felt different. Suddenly I wanted to read the Bible and go to church whenever the doors opened. I wanted all my friends to come to Jesus too, so I kept hanging out with the old crowd, telling them they needed the Lord. They said, "Johnny, you're no fun anymore! You're a crazy Jesus freak and we don't like that."

I tried to be a good witness, but after a while I started feeling weak and soon I was backsliding. When I'd come down off drugs, I'd wish so hard that I could stop and be free. Backsliding and coming back to the Lord became my pattern over the next few years, and deep down I knew it was a selfish way to live. Some of my old friends told me later that they came to the Lord through my changed life and witnessing to them. I'm thankful that in spite of my failings, God's Word did not return void just like Isaiah 55:11 says,

> "So shall My word be that goes forth from My mouth; it shall not return to Me void, but it shall accomplish what I please, and it shall prosper in the thing for which I sent it."

About this time, I met a woman and led her to the Lord. I found out later that she had been raised as a Jehovah's Witness. Soon we both fell away and moved in together. She had one son, Kory, whom I considered my own, and when she became pregnant with our son Joshua, we decided to get married. Yet we lived in a divided house—while I tried to follow the Lord, she was drawn back to her JW faith. We'd been married only a few months when I arrived home from work one night and found all the lights turned off and the house empty. I remember switching the lights back on, taking a shower, and crying out to the Lord. I felt like I was losing it. *Lord*, I prayed, with tears streaming down my face, *You have to help me or I'm not going to make it.*

In that still, small voice He answered, "She's not coming back." Later I found out that my wife's mother and friends had moved her out and that she had returned to the JWs. She wanted a divorce and I was devastated. I started attending Calvary Chapel Hemet, and on my first Sunday morning there, the Lord spoke to me during communion and said, "This is where I want you to learn My Word."

Newly divorced, I felt the Lord giving me the desire to go to Bible college. However, I didn't have money for tuition, and I couldn't stop working because I had to pay child support. One afternoon while I was out driving, I prayed, *God, if You really want me to go to Bible College, please send someone to buy my car.* I drove a couple more blocks, and then saw a mailman go by in his mail truck, waving me down. I pulled over and rolled down my window. He stopped and called out, "Hey, I just wanted to say that if you ever decide to sell your Corvette, I'd love to buy it."

I couldn't believe it! "As a matter of fact, I am selling it!" I said. I quoted a price and then followed the guy to his house, where he gave me cash to hold the car, and later he paid the rest. I was so happy! Soon I enrolled at Calvary Chapel Bible College in Twin Peaks and had enough money to cover expenses for the next two years.

SERVING THE LORD

I was on fire for the Lord and had big hopes that He would use my life. Along with my studies in Bible college, Pastor Chuck Smith of Calvary Chapel Costa Mesa allowed me to oversee the construction of a new library on campus. After completing my first year, I was invited by Calvary Chapel South Phoenix to help start a house ministry for those in town who were homeless or addicted.

We made sack lunches once a week and brought them to a park where the winos hung out. I played guitar and we shared the gospel. Hundreds came to the Lord that year, and we even saw some delivered from demons. For those on the street who were serious about living out their faith, we brought them home, took care of them, and discipled them.

Sometimes people in the park got angry as we shared the gospel and they threw stuff at us. Once while I was preaching, a man broke his wine bottle on the ground and yelled, "I'm going to kill you!" Then he started chasing me down the street, but he was so drunk that I outran him, even with a guitar and Bible in hand. By the time I left South Phoenix a year later, we had eighty people in the house ministry.

I returned to Hemet and started my own concrete and masonry contracting company. God blessed my new business abundantly. I went back to Calvary Chapel Hemet, and married a wonderful woman there. We hosted the youth group in our home and that's where I met Pastor Gerry Brown, who served as an assistant pastor at the church. He brought his daughter to the youth group, and recalling our meeting, he says, "I remember Johnny as joyful and excited about using his gift of music for the Lord."

Unfortunately, I got beaten down spiritually and my wife and I started backsliding. We used drugs together about one weekend a year, which soon became a pattern for us.

At thirty-nine years old, I had everything I'd ever wanted—a successful business, a custom-built home, lots of money, and the Lord's favor. About this time, my wife began taking diet pills and she gave me a few to try. That was the beginning of the end for me. Things got so dark and evil that my wife couldn't take it anymore and she divorced me in 1995. I don't blame her—I would have left me too! After she was gone, I started using crack cocaine and crystal meth, and my life became a living hell on earth. I'd tried crack cocaine before but didn't get high on it. However, when I used it this time, it bit me like a snake and I went downhill fast. Alone and depressed,

I slept through both Christmas and New Year's Day. Then I shut down my construction business and filed for bankruptcy. I couldn't work anymore because of my drug use.

WRONG WAY

Sometime during January of 1995, I took my handgun, some cash, and my drugs, and I headed to a party in San Diego with the plan to take a bunch of drugs and then shoot myself. Thankfully God intervened. On my way there late at night, I stopped at a head shop, bought a box of crack pipes, and then drove to Washington Blvd. A guy was standing on the corner and I pulled over. "Hey, where's the party with all the chicks?" I asked.

"I'll show you," he said, and the next thing I knew, he hopped right in and told me to turn the car around. Wouldn't you know it, a flashing red light appeared behind us and the police pulled me over for making an illegal U-turn.

The officers took one look inside the car and handcuffed my passenger; it turned out he was an unregistered sex offender. Then they found the gun, the glass pipes, the crack cocaine, speed, and marijuana. I was pretty stoned, so they handcuffed me too and drove us both to the downtown San Diego police station. There, they weighed the cocaine in front of me. At the time, the law stated that carrying over half an ounce of a hard drug was illegal. I had three-quarters of an ounce, so I went straight to jail. But the next night my lawyer paid my bail and I was released. Then I called someone to pick me up from jail and bring more drugs. I felt like a pitiful mess.

My lawyer advised me to take a plea bargain, to plead guilty to transporting illegal drugs with the intent to sell. But I hadn't done it; I was much too selfish to give my drugs away or sell them! Still, I took his advice because my alternative was six months behind bars. I realize now that I was too wasted to make a good decision.

I'd never been in trouble like that before, yet there I was, going through divorce court, bankruptcy court, and facing a drug charge all at the same time.

After pleading guilty, I asked my attorney exactly what it all meant. "Johnny," he explained, "you've just pled guilty to something worse than murder in the eyes of the DEA (Drug Enforcement Administration). Now they'll always be in and out of your million-dollar house, your cars, and your life. If you don't stop using drugs, you'll go straight to prison for five years. But if you get clean and stay sober for five years, you can pay me to go back to court and have your record expunged."

I tried my best to sober up on my own. I went to AA Twelve-step programs, checked myself into substance abuse hospitals, and I even went back to church, but nothing worked. Meanwhile, bad things started happening to me, like guns shoved in my side, bricks thrown through my windshield, and my leather car seats slashed. I even found my dog dead and hanging on my front gate. I was robbed, harassed, poisoned, and lied about.

Some people told me these things never happened and it was only my paranoia. They said I was crazy to think the DEA would waste their time on me. "You're a nobody!" they insisted, and I always agreed. Yet I knew I needed to keep forgiving and blessing those who wanted to harm me. The Lord taught me to trust in Him, no matter what. And He taught me to pray for those who mistreat me.

I continued going to church, even though I wasn't able to get off drugs completely. I knew I had wrecked my life and didn't know what was going to happen. Then I ran into Pastor Gerry again and shared what was going on. He handed me his U-Turn For Christ business card and said, "Johnny, if you need help, give me a call. I'd love to help you." Pastor Gerry remembers our encounter too.

JOHNNY RENO: *Abandoned to His Arms*

He says, "When I saw Johnny that day, he'd changed dramatically. He looked skinny and frail from all the drug abuse and lack of nutrition. His demeanor was subdued and down. He seemed absent and empty, as if he had a deep longing inside."

After one more drug spree a couple of months later, I took out Pastor Gerry's card and dialed his number. "I'm in trouble," I said. "Can you come and meet with me?"

"Of course, Johnny," Pastor Gerry assured me, "I'll meet you anywhere. I want to help you," he continued, "but more importantly, the Lord wants to help you." It was the middle of the night, and I didn't want to leave my house or even go outside. But finally I agreed to meet him halfway at a local Circle K market.

Later, I confided to Pastor Gerry that I was convinced everyone was after me. He explained that this feeling was common for people who use speed, because the drug deprives them of sleep. And without sleep, of course, the brain doesn't function right. Everything becomes confusing regarding what's real and what isn't.

Pastor Gerry didn't judge me, and it was only because of his kindness and love that I even went to the U-Turn For Christ ranch. He understood my paranoia, my drug use, and my legal issues, and eventually he helped me with all of them.

GOD GOT A HOLD OF ME

After taking drugs for eight solid months, my life was out of control. I knew I was headed for an early grave, just like I had imagined as a kid. Besides ruining my physical and mental health, I was also concerned about my spiritual health. Sadly, I had also done a lot of damage to the people I loved the most, and I felt so lost that I believed the Lord would never take me back again. But when

I arrived at the ranch, God got a hold of me and He saved my life. On my first night there, He miraculously delivered me from crack cocaine, without going through withdrawals! God loves us so much. Hosea 14:4 tells us,

> "I will heal their backsliding, I will love them freely, for My anger has turned away from him."

That's what God did for me, yet the process was a battle. The first week, I wanted to be somewhere else—anywhere else but the ranch. I felt afraid and worry consumed me. I remember walking into the chapel sanctuary and praying, *God, You have to speak to me!* I sat down in a chair with my Bible and it fell open to Mark 6:50. Those red letters jumped out at me:

> "Be of good cheer! It is I; do not be afraid."

At first I thought, *Man, that's not what I want to hear right now.* But then I realized it was exactly what I needed to hear, and God began filling me with a total peace. I surrendered to Him, knowing I was safe and right where He wanted me.

One of my favorite memories in those early days at the ranch was working as a cook with two other guys who were both new Christians. While cooking together, we discovered we all had similar troubling circumstances, with failed marriages, lost jobs, and people we had hurt. In between meals we sat down with our Bibles to seek the Lord, lifting up our lives to Him moment by moment.

We read the Word together out loud, repeated God's promises, and prayed for each other. After a while, instead of only looking at my own problems, I started caring about theirs too. Often one of us said, "Let's pray about that and ask God for a miracle." We all saw Him work in our families and do miracles in our lives.

Pastor Gerry reminded me that because I had known the Lord earlier in my life, I recognized that my sin of choice had taken me away from sweet fellowship with Him. That's why I had so much anxiety at first. But the blessing of this ministry is that we witness a peace come over individuals here, and that happened with me. Though I was still paranoid, there was also a sense of confidence that God would be with me and be there for me every step of the way.

A HEART TO WORSHIP

Shortly after the Lord delivered me from crack cocaine, Pastor Gerry asked, "Hey, Johnny, you play guitar. How about if you help out with worship?" Soon my longtime hobby of guitar playing became so much more. The Lord blessed my life with a deep desire to thank Him for His grace and mercy, and to sing about all He had done for me. What a privilege it's been to help lead worship at both U-Turn For Christ and at Calvary Chapel Romoland. Over the years, I witnessed men and women go through the same things I struggled with and I've been so blessed to see their lives restored by Jesus.

As a worship leader, I experienced the truth of Psalm 40:3:

> "He has put a new song in my mouth—praise to our God;
> many will see it and fear, and will trust in the Lord."

Worshiping the Lord, praising Him, and then listening to the teaching of His Word always changes us.

Often at the ranch I've heard Pastor Gerry ask, "What does God say about this area in your life?" Or as Romans 4:3 says, "What saith the Scripture?"(KJV) For me, the Bible came alive at U-Turn. When I struggled in an area, I searched the Scriptures to find out what God said about it. Then I believed it and applied it to my life.

James 1:22 instructs us to "be doers of the Word and not hearers only" because otherwise, we're just lying to ourselves. Without the truth of God's Word, we have nothing solid to base our lives on. Thousands of men and women at U-Turn For Christ have been set free from their addictions, and they're still free because they've stayed in the Word. King David said,

> "They cried out to the LORD in their trouble, and He saved them out of all their distresses. He sent His Word and healed them." (Psalm 107:13, 20)

That's what happens here at U-Turn For Christ.

My life verse changes now and then, but I always come back to the same one, Proverbs 3:5-6:

> "Trust in Lord with all your heart, and lean not on your own understanding. In all your ways acknowledge Him and He shall direct your paths."

Sometimes the Lord says to me, "Johnny, will you trust Me in this?" or "Johnny, you don't have to understand everything. Just put Me first in whatever's going on right now and then you'll know I'm directing your life."

A PARTNER IN MINISTRY

As a worship leader at U-Turn, I determined not to look at the girls—that is, until a tall blonde named Kirby walked into the sanctuary one day. When I saw her, I remember praying, *Oh, Lord, what am I doing?* I confided in Pastor Gerry and he said I could talk to her when she finished Phase 1. So after she graduated, I asked her out. The first few times I asked, she said no, so I figured, *Oh well!* But eventually we talked as friends and got to know each other better. Soon, in Pastor Gerry's words, "She fell in love with Jesus and then she fell in love with Johnny."

After I had been single for seven years at U-Turn, Kirby and I were married on April 30, 2002. She has become my biggest blessing here on earth, and whenever I think of God's grace in my life, I think of Kirby.

We serve in ministry together at the ranch, with Jesus as the center. Kirby co-writes songs, helps organize the music, prays for me, and encourages me as I lead worship at the ranch and at Calvary Chapel Romoland. She also teaches Bible studies and loves on the women here. I tell everyone that Kirby is the best part of me. She is endearing, quiet, kind, joyful, and patient. Best of all, she loves Jesus deeply, and then she loves me, even with all my flaws.

Marriage is tough sometimes, especially in the ministry. Yet our marriage gives me one more reason to confess our Lord Jesus Christ because He means everything to us. Kirby and I have six wonderful young adult children and seven grandchildren (so far) between us. We love each one so much and pray for them all daily.

A THANKFUL HEART

Today my dad continues to serve the Lord in Spokane, conducting Bible studies for older adults once a week. He prays for people, evangelizes, and witnesses wherever he goes. We've grown close in our Christian fellowship over the years, and he even flew to California to attend my ordination as a pastor in 2004. I'm close to my mother as well, and I'd like to thank both my parents for adopting me and loving me as their own. I'm so grateful that they brought me up in a Christian home, and I love them very much.

The Lord has used Pastor Gerry greatly in my life, not only as my pastor but also as my friend. I want to thank him and his family for all the love and care they have extended to me.

Regarding my ministry at U-Turn, Pastor Gerry says, "The anointing God has on Johnny's life is incredible. He is an exceptional one-on-one evangelist, perhaps the best I've ever met, and the Lord uses him powerfully to help those struggling with drug and alcohol abuse. In this ministry there are many who deal with paranoia, and in the midst of Johnny's struggles, the Lord uses him to counsel others. They learn from Johnny's example, and as he continues to bow at the feet of Jesus, he leads others to bow before Him as well.

"Ephesians 6:12 reminds us that 'we do not wrestle against flesh and blood' but God gives us what we need to pull down the strongholds of our mind. At times, Johnny's mind is where his battle is, and I believe the Lord has allowed him to be tested in this way so he can depend on Him all the time. Johnny has learned to keep his focus on the Lord and to keep worshiping Him."

As Pastor Gerry said, I still deal with paranoia today, and whether my fears are perceived as true or untrue, they are real to me. Only those who have gone through it can really understand. My friends here at U-Turn For Christ are the ones who have stuck by me no matter what, and most of all, I know that God sees all and He knows everything about me.

FOR THOSE WHO STILL WAIT

When men and women come to the ranch and meet the Lord, they learn how to walk with Him daily, how to be a blessing, and how to give instead of just take. Then they go back to their families, churches, and communities, and they use the truths they've learned here to serve the Lord.

Jesus said,

> "If anyone desires to come after Me, let him deny himself and take up his cross daily and follow Me." (Luke 9:23)

At U-Turn, people learn how to give their lives away and help others. If you have kids who are rebellious or without Christ, or family members addicted to drugs or alcohol, please don't ever give up on them. Pray and believe God's promise that "with God all things are possible" (Matthew 19:26). We know our loved ones must choose the Lord for themselves, but just as someone prayed for me, God wants us to stand in the gap for the lost and the hurting. He cares about our family members. He understands our weaknesses and wants us to "come boldly to the throne of grace that we may obtain mercy and find grace to help in time of need" (Hebrews 4:16). Jesus is "not willing that any should perish but that all should come to repentance" (2 Peter 3:9).

God has no favorites. He loves your family as much as any family. He wants to save your children, brothers and sisters, moms and dads, grandpas and grandmas, your friends, and all people everywhere. Maybe God has you reading this for such a time as this, to be a light to those around you. Or maybe you're reading this and you are the one who needs to be set free from drugs, alcohol, or any other sin you wish you could stop. Know this—there is no salvation without Jesus (John 14:6). You need Him to save you.

The Bible says, "Now is the day of salvation" (2 Corinthians 6:2). Today, you need Jesus! Just give yourself over to Him, and allow Him to save you.

I hate drugs and what they did to me. I never want to forget where I was before I had the Lord in my life. I never want to forget how hopeless, helpless, and lost I felt. God knows what it will take to heal his sinning kids, and He allows hard places and bad storms to make us stop. Yet even in those storms, Jesus comes to us. I still sin, but my sin of drugs is over. First Peter 4:1 says,

"He who suffers in the flesh is done with sin." (AMP)

I praise Him for that! Even though I was raised in a Christian home and used to feel like I lived at church, I had to come to the place of knowing the Lord personally. My Christian environment couldn't save me. I still experience repercussions and consequences of my involvement with drugs, but God is with me through it all, and He makes it all worth it. And from the time I made that illegal U-Turn and got arrested, God led me to another U-Turn, a life-saving place called U-Turn For Christ. Now He's given me the rest of my life to serve Him, and with whatever time I have left, that's what I want to do.

AN INVITATION

The Father gave His very best, Jesus, and this is where we all need to start. If you've never received the Lord Jesus into your heart, or if you're away from Him now, please pray this prayer, which is based on John 3:16, knowing that God wants to save you and your loved ones:

> "For God so loved (insert your name or a loved one's name) that He gave Jesus, His only begotten son for (name), that if (name) believes in Him, (name) should not perish but will have eternal life. In Jesus' name. Amen."

God loves you and will never turn you away. But it's your choice. You have to come to Him and repent, to turn away from your sin. I pray that you will cry out to the Lord Jesus today and receive His help. And if the Lord wills, perhaps you'll direct others to U-Turn For Christ, where together we can see them get on the right path, one that the Lord always planned for their lives.

> "Then you will call upon Me and go and pray to Me, and I will listen to you. And you will seek Me and find Me, when you search for Me with all your heart." (Jeremiah 29:12-13)

Then we'll all rejoice with you. To God be the glory!

Johnny and Kirby

Dear Lord, it has been a joy to watch the way You have used Pastor Johnny all over the world for Your glory!

Please continue to bless the gift of music and evangelism that You have given him as he presses on to bring You glory with every breath.

I pray that You will give us many more mission trips together. In Jesus' name we pray, Amen!

CHAPTER 7

In this is love, not that we loved God,
but that He loved us and sent His Son.

1 JOHN 4:10

PASTOR ALEXANDER YOUNG
Unconditionally Loved

Reaching into his suitcase, Alex pulled out a green acrylic cross and a framed picture of baby Jesus, both treasured gifts from his mother. He carefully arranged the cross and picture on his hotel nightstand, and then he sat on the bed and dialed his mom's number. "Hi Mama! I've got my altar all set up right here by the bed," Alex said, hoping to reassure her. "Don't worry, okay? I'm doing good, really. Everything's in place now so I can pray. I'm protected."

Alex's mother knew her son was living in darkness. "Come back to Jesus, Alex," she pleaded. "Please, son. Come back."

"I will, Mama," Alex said. "I promise I will…someday."

This is Alexander's story.

As the sick child in the family, my parents coddled me. I contracted spinal meningitis and rheumatic fever at the age of fourteen months, leaving my immune system compromised. After a month-long hospitalization, I continued to struggle with fatigue, shortness of breath, fevers, and every airborne illness that came my way. I spent a lot of time at home with my mother, and even my Marine Corps sergeant dad went easy on me when I was young, reserving his discipline for my less fortunate siblings. Our busy Samoan household consisted of my parents, four sisters, two brothers, nine cousins, and me—all living under one roof in Gardena, California. I was the middle child, the special one.

A former drill instructor, Dad enforced strict rules to keep his family in line, and we all knew he meant business. We learned about God at an early age, and we were all required to attend Mass every Sunday at the local Catholic church. School ranked high on Dad's list too, and he would often say, "Study hard, get a scholarship, and no girlfriends until college!" He denounced laziness and insisted we always do our best. Unlike Dad's tough military presence, my mom showed great compassion and tenderness to her family. Whenever she spoke, I would listen because I likened her voice to the voice of Jesus, and she always pointed me to God. It was her beautiful face I saw when I was sick, and rested in her soft embrace when I hurt.

When I started school at the age of five, I went home sick a lot and fell behind. So from ages five to seven I was placed in special education classes. But by fifth grade, I became an honor student and the teachers said I could skip the sixth grade. "You're *too* smart!" my mom teased. Seventh grade proved to be my most productive year, and proud of my academic achievement, my mother had high hopes for me. She dreamed I'd become a doctor or a lawyer someday, and more than anything, I wanted to please her. But I had a dream of becoming a famous athlete. My talented older brother, Donovan, was my inspiration, and I wanted to do everything he did: football, basketball, wrestling, track, and powerlifting. When I was only ten, Donovan trained me on the weight bench, and I worked hard to build up my strength and endurance.

DREAMS AND DISTRACTIONS

Unfortunately though in junior high I joined the party scene and began drinking with older friends. On my fifteenth birthday I received fifteen joints from a relative, and after sharing a few with the homies, I sold the rest and made my first drug deal. Also at age fifteen, I met my future wife, Valerie, and we fell madly in lust. My dad warned me, "Be home by 10 p.m. or you'll be locked out!" But I wanted to spend every moment with Valerie, so I'd just stay out late waiting until the wee hours of the morning to sneak into my room, suffering the consequences of getting caught! With so many of us coming and going through the house, it was hard for Dad to keep up with who was coming in from work and who was breaking curfew! But thank God a new day awaited and Dad would be up early and off to work.

I continued pursuing my athletic passions in high school, and although fame eluded me, I was popular and well-liked by my peers. For two years, I played offensive guard on our school football team and I competed in weightlifting as well. With above average upper body strength, I set a school record for the bench press, lifting 435 pounds.

While outwardly I grew stronger, inwardly I developed a covetous mentality—an insatiable appetite for new things. As a kid, I didn't mind wearing hand-me-downs, but when I became a teenager, dressing fashionably was an absolute must! I knew we had no money for luxuries so I didn't even bother asking my dad for the things I craved. If I saw something I liked, I simply took it. For example, when I wanted new training shoes for football, I went straight to a department store, tried on the shoes I liked, and then walked out the front door. It's a good thing the shoes were Nike cross trainers because I broke them in quickly, running a half mile down the street to avoid mall security. In my heart I knew stealing was wrong, but at the time I saw no alternative.

One Saturday night during my junior year, I went out drinking and smoking pot with my friends and I arrived home late. Unexpectedly, Dad met me at the front door. "Are you drunk, Alexander?" he asked sternly.

"No, sir!" I said. I knew that coming home drunk was disrespectful to my parents. Dad and I got into a heated argument but I refused to back down and simply tell him the truth of where I'd been.

Finally Dad said, "It's my way or the highway, Boy!" I chose the highway, and Dad kicked me out of the house. That night, and for many nights to come, my girlfriend Valerie's bedroom window became my front door, without her parents' knowledge. Yet because I was such a mama's boy, I would go home during the day to see my mom while Dad was at work, and I'd pick up a change of clothes while I was there.

My mother's constant example of Jesus' love humbled me. She didn't hesitate to correct me, but she always forgave me, in the same way 1 Peter 4:8 tells it:

> "Above all, love each other deeply, because love covers over a multitude of sins." (NIV)

Weeks later, when Dad's anger subsided, I apologized for my rebellious attitude and made peace with him.

THE NAVY YEARS

The following year in 1980 I graduated from high school, joined the U.S. Navy, married Valerie, and became a father—all in twelve months! Our son, Royce Alexander, was born August 9, and suddenly I had a family to support. The Navy sent me to Tennessee, where I trained to be an aviation electrician's mate, and then they shipped me out on the USS Enterprise. I traveled to ports around the world and maintained electrical equipment on naval aircraft. While on the ship, I continued weightlifting and competing, earning second place in the Sixth Fleet Powerlifting Tournament. When we'd pull into ports, I'd drink heavily and sample drugs. While in Mombasa, Africa, some friends and I purchased a huge amount of weed, and we smuggled it back onto the ship to sell to our shipmates. We made a lot of money from that purchase, and drug dealing started looking pretty attractive.

My fourth year in the Navy was the most challenging. My marriage fell apart, my work performance declined, and my mental and spiritual state suffered. To cope with it all, I drank more, got into fights, and cheated on my wife. Needless to say, I was in a lot of trouble. I was also charged with Article 87 Missing Movement on the USS Enterprise. In other words, I wasn't on the ship when it left port. For that offense, I was thrown into the brig for thirty days. Later, while based at NAS Miramar in San Diego, I physically challenged the Military Police, as well as my superiors, and I was placed on base restriction. Facing court-martial for assault and battery, I learned that my sentence would be five to ten years in confinement with hard labor. When I met with the judge to advocate about my case, he left me with these parting words: "The only way you can beat this is if you die tomorrow."

In my mind, I saw no options so I took the judge's advice and proceeded to plot my suicide. Working under a supervised release, I pretended to take my supplements one morning at work but I swallowed a handful of sleeping pills instead. Thirty minutes later my supervisor found me passed out on the floor and called an ambulance to rush me to the hospital. After they pumped my stomach and flushed out the pills, I was transferred to the psychiatric ward, and doctors determined I had a mental breakdown. A month later they concluded I was too unstable to continue active military service, and by God's grace, they cancelled my prison sentence. Since I had performed so well during my first three years in the Navy, I was awarded an honorable discharge.

THE JET SET

When I left the military, Valerie and I tried to work out our problems but we weren't able to reconcile, so we filed for divorce in 1984. Single again at twenty-one years old, I returned to Gardena to piece my life back together. I felt like a little boy stuck in a man's body. My lean, muscular physique had always helped me step up to any challenge in the past, but this time my appearance wasn't enough. I decided that more schooling would help me, so I enrolled in an accelerated electronics course at DeVry University. Three months into it, I challenged the course and was forced to quit because I didn't pass the exam. Alcohol still had a powerful hold on me and it clearly affected my ability to concentrate and study.

After DeVry, I supported myself by becoming a drug dealer. At first I didn't actually take the drugs; I only sold them. But then I started partying with an old girlfriend and got addicted to cocaine. Soon my need for the drug became greater than my supply, and when I could no longer make a profit, I began hustling and pushing drugs heavily. I hooked up with friends who were in drug cartels in Guadalajara, where I witnessed frightening drug deals gone bad. It was all a wake-up call from God, and by the late eighties, I realized I had to get off cocaine to stay alive.

I began powerlifting again, and through intense weight training and dieting, I gradually replaced my drug high with an adrenaline high.

With more upper body bulk and strength, I landed a job as a personal bodyguard for singer-songwriter Stevie B, and for two years I toured with his band and lived in the limelight. Most of his staff partied on tour, but I chose to abstain so I could maintain my focus and strength. I escorted Stevie B to concerts, handled security, and accompanied him to autograph sessions. Despite my jet-set lifestyle, I never forgot my Catholic upbringing, and I took my altar with me wherever I went. When I checked into a hotel, I set out the gifts from my mother—the small green cross and the picture of baby Jesus—and then I'd add a photo of my son, Royce. The altar was my place to pray, and it helped me feel close to God.

Working as a bodyguard seemed like the perfect fit for me. I even had plans to expand my business. Then in 1990, my plans were cut short when I was injured in a motorcycle accident while on tour. Hobbling around on an injured leg, I was forced to quit my job. By this time I had moved to Hawaii and was dealing drugs again. Every day I'd call my mom to tell her I was all right, even if I wasn't. I knew she worried about me, and her loving reminders to follow Jesus gave me peace of mind. Even though I didn't do what she said, I'd listen respectfully and say, "I got it, Mama!" I worried about my mother— she had diabetes and suffered from its debilitating effects for years. As often as I could, I sent her money, jewelry, and gifts.

I sent money and gifts to Royce as well. Valerie and I shared custody of our son, and though I wasn't there for him like I wanted to be, my mom and sisters helped take care of him, and he grew especially close to my mom. I tried to buy Royce's love with material things to make up for my absence, but by the time he reached his teens, I realized that I'd been a deadbeat dad.

STRUNG OUT AND SEEKING

I lived in Hawaii for eight years—dealing, trafficking, and transporting large amounts of cocaine and meth. During my last few years on the island, I was so addicted to meth that I wandered the streets like a homeless person. I also took up gambling. My family worried about me, and some of my siblings flew to Hawaii, begging me to come home and clean up my life. At one time I even convinced my brothers and cousins to partner with me and expand my drug dealing! Yet my mom was the only one who still captured my attention. "Alex, give your life back to Jesus," she would say. But even though she had my attention, she didn't have my obedience. Proverbs 22:6 promises,

> "Train up a child in the way he should go and when he is old he will not depart from it."

It doesn't say children won't stray. And I strayed a lot.

In 1997 my family finally convinced me to leave Hawaii and return to Gardena. Once I was back at home, my younger sister, Fa'a Tui, who worked at Calvary Chapel South Bay, told me about a Christian ranch called U-Turn For Christ where I could get help for my addictions. However, I wasn't interested in rehab and told her, "I already gave my life to the Lord, and now you want me to go there? No, thanks!" Over the next few years, Fa'a Tui kept talking to me about the ranch and I kept saying no, I wasn't interested.

Surrounded by my family, I stayed clean for six months, but then the old party crowd found me. Physically and mentally I was at my worst, beat up by poor choices. My older sister Ekelani said my clothes were always dirty, that I reeked of cigarette smoke, and I looked like a lost, broken person. I hung out with the druggies in town, and sometimes my family didn't see me for a week.

Mom often sent one of my siblings out looking for me to bring me home for a shower and a change of clothes. No matter how many times I disappointed my mother, she never gave up on me. She always believed and hoped that I would come back to the Lord. With all her heart, she believed what 1 Corinthians 13:4-8 declares:

"Love suffers long and is kind…does not behave rudely, is not provoked, thinks no evil…bears all things…hopes all things, endures all things. Love never fails."

That's how my mom loved me.

On May 2, 2000, the unthinkable happened. My beautiful mother had a heart attack and passed away in her sleep. God granted her parting wish—to be ushered into His presence at home, sleeping in her own bed next to her husband, with her children and grandchildren nearby. Although I was strung out on drugs, my mother's death devastated me. I went to the mortuary to view her body and felt so sorrowful for causing her to worry about me all of her life. I wished I had come back to the Lord when she had asked me to, and that she could have seen my transformation with her own eyes. It saddened me to think about all those years my mom prayed for me, and that she never saw her prayers answered.

My siblings and I were all supposed to speak at my her funeral, but I was so high that all I could say was, "Jesus loves you and I love my mother!" At the service I assured my family that I would turn my life around, but I was still so far away from restoration. I knew it would be a hard journey, and I was hesitant to take that first step.

SAYING YES

Six months after my mother's death, I had a dream about her. In my dream, she was scolding me, telling me I was very sick and that I needed to call my brother Donovan to take me to the hospital. Then she added, "And why haven't you come back to Jesus like you promised?" When I woke up, I called Donovan and we went to the ER, where I was diagnosed with heart failure, high blood pressure, sleep apnea, bronchial asthma, and pulmonary edema. I'd gained a lot of weight, going from 265 to 405 pounds in only a few years, and my lower legs were swollen and discolored. That day in the hospital, my drug use came to a screeching halt. My brothers and sisters arranged an intervention right there in my room, pleading with me to get help. This time I said yes, and after my hospital discharge, I resolved to prepare myself to enter U-Turn For Christ.

I took a crash course in God's Word over the next several months, devoting myself to Bible study and prayer. Whenever the doors opened at Calvary Chapel South Bay, I showed up—for the men's study, midweek services, and Sunday mornings and evenings. I also began an intense physical training schedule. I exercised at the YMCA, did brisk walking, ate a strict diet, and took vitamin supplements. Within a year, my weight dropped back to 265 pounds.

FOOLS' DAY

I purposely chose to begin U-Turn for Christ on April 1, 2002. When my dad and Donovan dropped me off at the ranch, I thought, *Now I'm going to give back to God what the world took away. So April Fool's to you, Satan!* I was hungry and desperate for God, and soon I met other guys there who were in that same desperate mode. The Lord wasted no time getting my attention, and during our first Friday night worship service, we raised the roof in song. The Lord lifted my spirit and I felt comforted and loved. Even on that first night, I sensed God's call to serve in the ministry at some future time. There was no audible voice, but He simply spoke to my heart, and I knew this would be the final U-turn of my life.

A few weeks later on a warm spring evening, I sat outside the bunkhouse memorizing a list of Scriptures for Phase 1. It was about 10:30 p.m. and most of the other guys were already inside. A soft breeze blew as I camped out in front of the "memory board," which was a large white board with twenty-four memory verses written out in black lettering. We were required to memorize all the verses in two months, so my goal was to learn three per day. As I repeated the verses out loud, the words started coming alive in my mind, instructing me about what it means to truly surrender to God and serve Him. I felt excited—and convicted!

One verse especially captured my attention, 1 John 1:9. It says,

> "If we confess our sins, He is faithful and just to forgive us our sins and to cleanse us from all unrighteousness."

While meditating on these words, memories of my mother came flooding back and I began to weep. I missed my mama so much! I cried out in prayer: *Lord, I know You've brought me here, and I'm not going to let go of Your robe until You bless me with a revelation of Your will for my life.* Then another verse on the board jumped out at me, Jeremiah 29:11: "'For I know the thoughts that I think toward you,' says the Lord, 'thoughts of peace and not of evil, to give you a future and a hope.'" Assured that the Lord held my future, I surrendered everything to Him in that moment.

Over the next couple of days I was assigned to a work crew that traveled to Calvary Chapel Bible College in Murrieta for the day. Our job was to break up asphalt from an old tennis court and then load the pieces onto a truck. But something unexpected happened one day while we were out there, and all I remember is one minute I was loading asphalt and the next minute I was waking up in the ER, with a voice saying, "Alex, Alex—can you hear me?"

"Where am I?" I asked.

"You're in the emergency room at Temecula Hospital," a nurse said. "You fainted."

After a few more fainting spells, the doctors concluded that I needed a pacemaker to regulate my heartbeat. Hearing the news, I cried out, *Lord, when I gave You my life, I didn't expect this!* While waiting for my procedure date, I was reassigned to a new job in the mechanics shop at the ranch, where the staff kept a close eye on me. In June of that year, doctors inserted a pacemaker, and Pastor Gerry graciously excused me out of the remainder of the program so I could recover.

OLD FRIENDS REUNITE

I moved back home and got plugged in at Calvary Chapel South Bay. Several months later, my pastor, Steve Mays, offered me a job on the church staff, working in security. One of my responsibilities was to lock up the church each night after everyone went home. One night I had an overwhelming desire to visit an old drug buddy, Danny. As I pulled up to his house, a feeling of bondage fell over me, but I ignored it and knocked on the door anyway. Danny welcomed me inside, and three visits later, I was hooked on meth again. Thankfully, God intervened quickly, and I was arrested for identity theft soon after that.

Proverbs 4:14-16 offers a clear warning for those who are tempted to make foolish choices like mine:

> "Do not enter the path of the wicked, and do not walk in the way of evil. Avoid it, do not travel on it; turn away from it and pass on. For they do not sleep unless they have done evil; and their sleep is taken away unless they make someone fall."

I confessed my sin to my pastors and apologized for bringing shame on the church and on myself. After serving sixty days in jail, Pastor Steve had compassion on me and assured me that my sin had been covered under the blood of Jesus. He arranged intense counseling for me, three times a week with another pastor. The battle to return to drugs was fierce, and my restless spirit taunted me. I caved in one more time and then resigned from the church. Pastor Steve helped me get back into U-Turn For Christ for a tune-up in 2004. As Pastor Steve said goodbye, he exhorted me to "forsake all this world has to offer and follow Christ."

I had been at the ranch about a month when Pastor Gerry called me into his office. "God has laid it on my heart to raise you up for leadership, Alex." Then he offered me the position of head overseer at the men's ranch. Because of all I had brought upon myself in the past year, I was filled with the fear of the Lord at his offer. Yet I humbly accepted, and this time I determined to serve God well. Over the next two years, Pastor Gerry faithfully mentored me. Every morning we took a five-mile walk together, praying and fellowshiping while I soaked in all the wisdom I could. Pastor Gerry poured his vision into me—to take in those who are lost and beat up, and watch the Lord transform them into His servants. A strong leader, Pastor Gerry reminded me so much of my dad and he always steered me into doing what was right. Sometimes his corrections hurt my pride, but eventually I was able to pray, *Thank you, God, for molding me!*

NONE OF THESE THINGS MOVE ME

When I prepared to come to U-Turn in 2002, I listened to a powerful Bible teaching by Don McClure based on Acts 20:24:

> "But none of these things move me; nor do I count my life dear to myself, so that I may finish my race with joy, and the ministry which I received from the Lord Jesus, to testify to the gospel of the grace of God."

This verse helped me through many difficulties in the ministry, including a second pacemaker procedure in 2006. At that time, I was hospitalized for an infection in my heart, and the doctors replaced my faulty pacemaker with a new one. After a month in the hospital and numerous complications, I prayed, *Lord, I know my life is in Your hands, but these doctors are making a mess of things!*

The Lord answered gently, "Is this going to move you, Alex?"

I see now that it was all preparation for challenges yet to come. Acts 20:24 continues to teach me to not be moved but let the Lord take control when my circumstances become overwhelming.

As head overseer at U-Turn, God taught me many lessons. One morning at a leadership meeting, Pastor Anthony rebuked me for something I didn't do. Later that day I started arguing with him about it, and as our voices escalated, Pastor Mario walked over to see what was going on. In a soft, calm voice, he said, "I need to see you both in my office right now."

Closing the door behind us, Pastor Mario asked, "Now what's going on?"

Pastor Anthony told his side first, and by the time he finished, I was in an uproar. "How can I respect him?" I said, glaring at Anthony.

Pastor Mario challenged me. "Who are you?"

"I'm just a servant, trying to do my job," I answered.

"And what's another name for a servant?"

"A bond slave."

"And what rights does a bond slave have?"

"None." And before I could say anything else, I broke down crying. Suddenly it didn't matter who was right or who was wrong. I apologized, thanking Pastor Anthony and Pastor Mario for standing their ground and dealing with a knucklehead like me. God used this conflict to teach me that I can't serve if I'm not surrendered. Jeremiah 12:5 says, "If you have run with the footmen and they have wearied you, then how can you contend with horses?" This passage really spoke to me, and showed me I had to get along with the leaders in God's camp if I wanted to lead others.

The Lord also showed me that the men in the U-Turn program follow what they see in their leaders, and they mirror my example, good or bad. If I complain about what I'm going through, pretty soon I'll hear them complain too. It's a repetitive cycle, and if I don't go to God with my own sin, others will follow me in it.

KAUAI

After ministering at the Perris ranch for two years, and then serving two years as head overseer and administrator in Kauai, I was asked in 2008 to serve as the U-Turn director in Kauai. The Lord gave me such a heart for this community. Every day people come to us asking for help for a lost son or a daughter, or for themselves. The enemy tries hard to take these dear ones back, but he's losing because through Christ, we are victorious! We reach out to widows, orphans, and the homeless, giving whatever we have in the name of Jesus. We have our challenges in Kauai, but we believe God's promise:

> "In all these things, we are more than conquerors through Him who loved us." (Romans 8:37)

I raise awareness about the destruction of addictions through mission trips, conferences, the Rotary Club, and other community organizations. The Lord took me out of my comfort zone and opened doors to speak and promote the ministry to many community leaders and pastors. He's given me a vision to eventually open up facilities on all the islands of Hawaii and throughout the South Pacific.

I also have a heart for the country of Samoa. After the 2009 tsunami, I took a team to Leone, where my mother was born and raised, and we fed the people there. As I witnessed the devastation, I remember praying, *Lord, I believe You're showing me all this for a reason.* Since that trip, my prayer has been to return to Samoa and open a U-Turn For Christ ranch there. Wherever I go, the desire of my heart is to "deliver those who are drawn toward death, and hold back those stumbling to the slaughter" (Proverbs 24:11).

FAMILY RESTORATION

When my sister, Ekelani, visited me in Kauai recently she was so happy to hear praise reports like, "Pastor Alex is such a blessing to us" and "Pastor Alex helped my son who almost committed suicide." She knows I want to raise men up in God's Word and restore them so they can go back to their families and friends and be lights for Jesus. Ekelani says, "I've always loved my brother but we share a deeper love now because we're both walking with the Lord. Alex lives his life completely for God and my family is proud of him."

My Marine sergeant dad is now in his seventies and still lives in the same house in Gardena where we grew up. These days, I take every opportunity to tell him, "Thank you for being the father God called you to be!" Dad did everything in his power to help his children love the Lord, and I will always be grateful to him.

My son Royce is in his thirties, happily married with two children, and he lives on the East Coast working as a web designer. I thank the Lord for my son! We have a good relationship—better than it's ever been. When I truly surrendered to the Lord, He opened my eyes to the importance of my relationship with Royce and God has restored that.

In 2004, I earnestly began praying for the Lord to bring me a wife. I thought it would only take a year, but eight long years later, God answered my prayer. He brought Jen to me and we were married on October 10, 2012. God is so good, and He is faithful! Our marriage has been a true blessing from Him.

Proverbs 18:22 promises,

> "He who finds a wife finds a good thing, and obtains favor from the Lord."

I believe in this promise. Jen is such a good, God-loving woman, and keeping my commitment to her has been a wonderful journey.

I know she is God's precious daughter, and every day I have the joy and privilege of loving her. It is my complete duty and honor to do so. The saying is really true, "Happy wife, happy life!"

I thank God for all my family. I realize now what I put them through, and that helps me relate to others who struggle with drugs and alcohol, because I understand! Whenever reconciliation happens within a family, it's a beautiful thing to see. All who embrace it are blessed.

MAMA'S BOY

My mother's prayers ushered me into the kingdom of God, and I've dedicated my life to Him in honor of her. When my mom went to heaven and I couldn't call her anymore, I called on Jesus instead. That's when He showed me I'd been looking for Him all along! He's given me the same grace I first saw in my mother. And just like her love for me was unconditional, His love is also unconditional—and I've finally connected the two. Someday when I'm in heaven, I'll see my mother's pretty face again, and with tears of joy I'll say, "Thank you, Mama, for all you did for me."

I tell every guy I meet, "You're a mama's boy! You may not admit it or confess it, but when you experience the love of Jesus, you come to know the depth of love that every mama's boy knows." His love is perfect, and neither "height nor depth, nor any other created thing" can ever separate us from that love (Romans 8:39). My mother not only introduced me to Jesus, she also loved me the way He does. And that's why I'll always be a mama's boy, showing her honor by sharing the unconditional love of Jesus with others.

Jen and Alex

Oh God, You have chosen to use Pastor Alex in such special ways. He is a big man with an even bigger heart, and the gentle spirit that You've given him is proof of Your power to change a man.

Though Alex once used his size and strength to intimidate, he now glorifies You and uses his body to motivate and inspire others to serve You.

Bless Alex, I pray, as he continues to give his all for You. In Jesus' name, Amen!

U-TURN FOR CHRIST KAUAI
Pastor Alex and Jen Young
Physical address: 4523 Ioane Road, Anahola HI 96703
Mailing address: PO Box 1781, Kapaa HI 96746
Office: (808) 820-8014
Mobile: (808) 651-2081
email: uturnforchristkauai@gmail.com
website: www.uturnforchristkauai.com

CHAPTER 8

And Joshua said to the people, "Sanctify yourselves, for tomorrow the Lord will do wonders among you."

JOSHUA 3:5

PASTOR DUNCAN MUYA

Wonders Among You

Alone in Pastor Gerry's office, Duncan stood before a large world map taped to one wall. As he studied the colorful pins dotting the map, he pondered the location of each U-Turn For Christ ministry around the world. Duncan knew the Lord had a calling on his life, but he still wasn't sure what it was. Where do I fit in, Lord? he prayed. Is it New York? California? Where do I fit?

Just then, a vivid image appeared in Duncan's mind—an image of another map, but this one was of Kenya, the country of his birth. The map in his mind was dotted with pins too, and each one represented a U-Turn For Christ location yet to come.

Excitedly, Duncan cried, "Lord, are You serious? You're going to take me to Kenya and give me a map in my office, with little pins for my country?"

This is Duncan's story.

I had plenty of attention growing up. I loved being the last born of four children, and all that attention was a good thing. Raised in Nairobi, Kenya, East Africa, with one older brother and two sisters in the middle, I became an outgoing and fun child. Yet I wasn't a foolish boy. Dad recognized my potential early, seeing that I was very bright, and he had great hopes for my future. He says I was a jovial, outspoken kid. When visitors came over to our house, I would entertain them, offering them something to drink and making them feel right at home.

Dad worked as an architect and provided well for our family. We never experienced poverty. I even had a bicycle, something most Kenyan children did not own. Dad took us places and was always there for us. He loved our family very much, but he drank a lot. Often I'd hear him say, "My drinking isn't hurting anyone!" And as far as I could tell, it didn't hurt me.

At the age of thirteen, I left home for Kianyaga High School, a boarding school on the outskirts of Nairobi. My fun-loving nature followed me into ninth grade. There, I got into fights, but all in the name of fun. I was a good actor so I joined the drama club and I also played on the school basketball team. When I found out there was a big market for marijuana and cigarettes at my school, I became the school trafficker. I'd sneak out to the nearest town to buy cigarettes and marijuana, smuggle them back to my dorm, and then sell them to other students at twice the cost, even though I didn't need the money.

When I was sixteen, my mum called me one day at school and exclaimed, "Your dad is born again!" I didn't believe her. But when I came home the following weekend, I could tell Dad had changed. It was a good thing, really, but at the time I didn't think so. All I knew, my father was different and I didn't like it. He used to be fun but after he stopped drinking he became very serious. Suddenly he was praying, hosting Bible studies in our home, and telling us to read our Bible. We had to go to church earlier and stay later than everyone else. He'd never asked us to do those things before and I resented it.

SEEDS OF REBELLION

For as long as I could remember, my mum had been a devout Christian, but I was not. To me, God was a killjoy and Christianity was for old people who said things like, "Don't do this or you'll go to hell." Dad's requirements were a drag to a young boy like me, and they left me feeling confused.

Recalling this time of change, Dad says, "Before I accepted Christ, my wife Lucy was a member of the visitation ministry at church, and she called on the sick and bereaved. Sometimes when I'd accompany her on a visit, the host would mistakenly refer to me as "Pastor Muya." I would vehemently deny being a pastor. Yet deep inside I knew something was missing in my life.

"Then one Saturday night when I was drinking alcohol with others in the village, I saw a man get hit over the head with a bottle. As I watched him fall to the concrete with a thud, I woke up from my drunken stupor. It dawned on me that if I had been this man who died, I would have gone to hell. The following Monday at work a fellow employee asked if I wanted to accept Jesus, and I did not hesitate."

Church attendance was a mandatory cultural practice in Kenya until we turned eighteen. Even before Dad became a Christian, we always went to church, end of story, but I never took it seriously. After Dad was saved, my rebellious side came out even more, and I began smoking marijuana and drinking regularly. Whenever the boarding school captain caught me selling, I'd get into fights with him about it. As a form of discipline, I had to remove tree stumps from the school property, and I was also suspended three times.

Dad remembers, "Many times the school's head teacher called to tell me that Duncan was spending time with the wrong company and smoking bhang (marijuana). Like any parent, I defended my son outright. But later I knew better. Duncan's behavior and attitude changed so much in high school. While under the influence of drugs, he would stay out late and leave his well-furnished bedroom to seek refuge in dingy neighborhoods."

At seventeen, I was expelled from boarding school and I finally admitted that I'd been smoking marijuana and drinking. Dad became zealous to get me back on track. Recognizing my increasing rebellion, my parents knew I needed a fresh start, and they worked hard to save enough money for us to move to America, the land of opportunity.

During my visa interview at the U.S. embassy in Nairobi, I was threatened with being left behind if drugs were found in my system. So I stopped smoking marijuana temporarily until the drug test was over. I arrived in the U.S. at the age of eighteen and moved with my family to Murrieta, California, in 2001. The most difficult part of living in the States was that I didn't know how to relate to white people, Mexicans, or the array of other cultural groups in this country. But over time, as I got to know different people and cultures, relationships got easier. And because foreigners often congregate together in the U.S., we lived in a close community with Kenyans and Somalis.

I lost an entire year of school in Kenya, so I enrolled at Murrieta Valley High School for my senior year. There I acquired a new group of partying buddies who introduced me to crystal meth and crack cocaine. I soon tried them both, without even knowing what they were. Following high school graduation, I spent the summer working at a gas station in Temecula, and in the fall, things took a turn for the worse. Feeling young and carefree, I quit community college after only one semester so I could party more and have a good time.

THROWING MY LIFE AWAY

My drug use escalated over the next two years, and all my dreams of becoming an architect like my dad or a pilot like my brother slipped away. I began working for a car dealership and when they changed ownership, the new owners decided to give everyone a drug test. I knew I'd fail the test so I quit my job and sold meth instead. Soon I was a full-time druggie. I felt bold on meth and thought it was the best thing that had ever happened to me. Even though I appeared outgoing on the outside, deep down I actually felt shy. My reserved nature led me to try and prove myself by doing crazy things with others. On meth, I was bold with the opposite sex—something I had never felt before. And on meth, I robbed a gas station and ran with the best of them. I earned respect from the other guys and felt accepted. But in my right mind, I could never rob anyone.

My relationship with my parents worsened, and Dad and I argued a lot. He recalls, "It's difficult to describe the agony that my wife and I went through when Duncan was on drugs and alcohol. He seemed unsettled and stressed, and he behaved strangely. He brought awkwardly dressed, peculiar characters to the house—all the bad kinds of people that parents do not want in their homes. Things became very strained, and we finally asked Duncan to leave in 2003."

I found an apartment in Temecula and moved out. Still trying to prove myself, I hung out with guys who committed crimes and did crazy things. Because I had worked at a gas station, I knew how to open cash registers and get the money out. My friends and I moved in groups, so I was never alone in a robbery. One time I had a run-in with a rival group of Asians who mistook me for a gangbanger—which I wasn't—and they beat me senseless. They stabbed me on my arms and neck, and they left me with bruises all over my body. When Dad found out that I was in the hospital, he came to visit me. I had so much respect and reverence for my father because in the

Kenyan culture, the father always has the final say. I knew I had disappointed him, and his visit was shameful for me.

Not long after, two other gas stations caught me on camera, and the police started looking for me. Drug dealers came after me too because I owed them money. I owed my landlord as well, and when I wasn't able to pay my rent, I got kicked out of my apartment. I started living in my 1989 Pontiac, parking at motels or parks and sleeping in the backseat of my car.

One time a detective called me and asked, "Why are you running with these people? Are you hungry? Are you broke?" I remember thinking, *No. I don't have to live this way.* His words definitely got my attention. I thought, *Is something bigger going on here? Is something leading me to change my life?*

I couldn't be on the streets much longer because I knew the drug dealers would catch up with me. I couldn't go home and face my parents because I knew the police were asking them where I was. Sometimes I would watch to see when my parents went out, and I would show up at home and my sisters would let me inside for a quick shower and something to eat.

Dad says, "We went for weeks without knowing where Duncan was. One day we received a package in the mail containing Duncan's license, his college card, and his workplace I.D. The sender told us he had collected them from the middle of a street somewhere in Temecula. It's difficult to describe the heartache we felt at the time. We had no clue where our child was, or even if he was alive."

Feeling bombarded on all sides, I realized I had nowhere to go. So one October evening in 2004, I called home and asked my parents for help. They waited up for me until I knocked on their door at 1 a.m.

Dad remembers, "When we opened the door, Duncan's appearance was beyond description. He stood there in tatters, looking skinny and unkempt, and holding a filthy backpack."

Once inside the house, I confessed, "I have a drug problem." My mum, being a Kenyan lady, had no idea what to do. My confession of drugs and crime was quite a shock to her. The next morning my parents called Calvary Chapel Costa Mesa, and they were told about a drug rehab program in Perris called U-Turn For Christ. "Maybe they can help you," they said.

The next afternoon Dad and Mum drove me to the ranch. I thought it looked like a camp for hard heads, a place where families take their loved ones when there are no options left. I felt completely lost. At twenty-two years old, I'm not sure that I wanted to completely change my life as much as I just wanted a break from the street.

FIRSTS

I considered myself a wanna-be gangster, and in the room opposite mine at U-Turn For Christ I noticed three guys who looked exactly like I wanted to look. They were tall, big, buff, and intimidating. One of them was Pastor Alex Young, the head overseer. I loved Alex's size, his discipline, and his love for God. He was bold and articulate, and I respected him because he didn't have to curse to get respect.

One day I smuggled in some cigarettes and felt guilty about it so I gave them to Alex. He told me to go dig a hole and it made me mad. I raised my voice and started cursing. With wisdom, Alex calmly looked me straight in the eye and lovingly counseled me. He treated me like a young brother in the Lord. After that day, Alex took me under his wing, becoming like a big brother to me, and this little brother wanted to go everywhere he went.

Following that incident, at my first Friday night service, the worship leader led a song called "Who Am I?" by John Mark Hall of Casting Crowns. Hearing the words broke me into a million pieces:

Who am I, that the Lord of all the earth
Would care to know my name
Would care to feel my hurt?
Who am I, that the bright and morning star
Would choose to light the way
For my ever-wandering heart?

Not because of who I am
But because of what You've done
Not because of what I've done
But because of who You are.

I am a flower quickly fading
Here today and gone tomorrow
A wave tossed in the ocean
A vapor in the wind
Still You hear me when I'm calling
Lord, You catch me when I'm falling
And You told me who I am
I am Yours, I am Yours.

Who am I, that the eyes that see my sin
Would look on me with love
And watch me rise again?
Who am I, that the voice that calmed the sea
Would call out through the rain
And calm the storm in me?
Not because of who I am
But because of what You've done
Not because of what I've done
But because of who You are.

I am Yours, I am Yours
Whom shall I fear?
Whom shall I fear?
'Cause I am Yours.
I am Yours. (Lyrics © Sony/ATV Music Publishing LLC)

After the song I shed tears like never before. The experience felt like a wake-up call from God, and that night I gave my life to Him.

One month into my time at the ranch, I had to face the music of the police and appear in court. The judge sentenced me to three years probation for my criminal offenses. A month later I finished Phase 1 and was invited to stay on at the ranch for training in ministry. When my parents came to celebrate my Phase 1 graduation, Dad says, "Duncan's bright smiling face and appearance were restored, and by the time he graduated, he was the son we had known in his early days, before drugs. He could concentrate, have meaningful conversations, and make plans. He was like a new creation."

Even though I never considered myself a leader, God raised me up to serve as an overseer. At twenty-two years old, I sometimes felt intimidated by the other guys, especially the gangster types. But the Lord encouraged me from Joshua 1:6 to "be strong and courageous" and after a while, I began enjoying my role as overseer. I loved the thrill of being around the other men and I liked instructing them. God had given me a gift for leadership.

NO SUNDAY MORNING CHRISTIAN

At another Friday night service, I remember praying, *Lord, what do You want me to do with the rest of my life? I don't want to do anything boring. I don't want to have a nine-to-five job and be a Sunday morning Christian. I want to do something exciting for You!*

Some of the ideas that crossed my mind included joining the military, the Peace Corps, the Red Cross, or the Coast Guard. Because I was still very young, all these options seemed viable.

Then the Lord brought Ephesians 3:20 to mind:

> "Now to Him who is able to do exceedingly abundantly above all that we ask or think, according to the power that works in us."

I sensed the Lord saying, "Duncan, I will show you much greater things. If your heart is willing to follow Me, I will do things beyond your imagination." Humbled by these thoughts, I prayed, *Okay, Lord. You have me. You have me. I am all Yours.* After that night, Ephesians 3:20 became my life verse.

I knew I wanted to serve the Lord—all my chips were in. But God's sanctification had to occur first in my life before He could do something wonderful with it. I had to be dedicated with my whole heart to serve Him. Joshua 3:5 says it this way:

> "Sanctify yourselves, for tomorrow the Lord will do wonders among you."

I also had a strong desire to go to college. So after eight months at the ranch, I left when an opportunity opened up to attend Joshua Springs Bible College in Yucca Valley, California.

Growing up, I was exposed to God's Word but I never read the whole Bible. At Bible college I had the privilege of studying all sixty-six books, and I really got into it. As I learned to read and study the Scriptures more intently, I found that it answered all of life's questions and satisfied my thirst. I trained to be a minister and graduated two years later. Pastor Gerry ordained me in 2007 and invited me back to the ranch for an internship in ministry. There I waited on God for the next step.

During my internship, I went on a mission trip to Mexico with Pastor Gerry. While we were there, Pastor Gerry sensed my anxiety about the future and said, "Stay in the Word, Duncan, just stay in the Word." His advice helped me simplify ministry, and I came to understand that as long as I remained plugged into God's Word and continued in prayer, the Lord's direction would come, and every decision would be guided by Him. Pastor Gerry's counsel taught me that if I don't have God's love and His Word in me, nothing I do will be worth keeping.

After the Mexico trip, I remember standing in Pastor Gerry's office, staring at the map on the wall and praying for guidance. I still get goose bumps remembering the moment when God showed me I would start a U-Turn For Christ in Kenya. That was my God moment. Six months later, in January of 2008, I stepped onto Kenyan soil and thought, *This is it, Lord, this is it!*

And then God whispered to my heart, "Duncan, everything is set for you to do this ministry, and everything you do will be anointed." That's how it all began for me as the pastor and director of U-Turn For Christ Kenya.

BRINGING U-TURN TO KENYA

God did things in reverse order when He called me to Kenya—He spoke to my parents about it before He spoke to me. The house we grew up in, which stands on four acres in Nairobi, was locked up and empty for many years, and my dad felt uncomfortable leaving it there desolate. The Lord told him the house was to be used for something, so Dad contacted different churches in Nairobi to see if any of them wanted to rent it. But no one responded. So when my parents learned that I was going to open a new U-Turn For Christ facility in Nairobi, Dad said, "Why don't you use our house until you find your own property? Use the land and do what you want with it." Later, my parents generously donated their large four-bedroom home to the ministry.

Dad says, "My wife and I could not hide our excitement and joy over having our lost son brought back to us. Our greatest wish was to help another child rehabilitate from drugs and alcohol so that other parents could have the same joy. That's why we decided to avail our home in Kenya for the ministry."

Kenya is a beautiful country. The equator cuts our county in the middle and geographically our ministry is located about fifteen miles north of Nairobi. U-Turn For Christ Kenya is out in the country, on a farm, and our neighbors are the cows and plantations. With six to eight months of rain per year, it's very green here, and we're all farmers at U-Turn For Christ Kenya. We grow our own food and eat from the land—grains, maize, kale, and carrots. We also raise ducks, goats, and chickens, and we have two milking cows. Besides farming, our men also serve in the community. We do groundskeeping and heavy labor for Dream Children's Home, a local orphanage, as well as groundskeeping for other neighboring ministries.

Alcohol is the drug of choice in Kenya, and traditional brews are the most popular. With half the population below the poverty level surviving on less than two dollars a day, many people make these brews themselves, like moonshine in the U.S. Traditional brews emphasize the word "spirits" because they're made for witch doctors to use when calling in spirits. People with money drink store-bought beer, but those without money drink these cheaper, potent brews, called *chang'a*, which literally means "kill me quick." Because of different levels of fermentation and potency, those who consume chang'a can potentially go blind. Or, if a brew sits too long, inhaling the fumes can make a person feel lightheaded. In addition to alcohol, marijuana is also abused in our country.

BASICS OF MINISTRY

Our schedule at U-Turn For Christ Kenya revolves around God's Word and serving the Lord. The men are so hungry for the Word that we even offer Bible studies during free time. I challenge the men to memorize Scripture and they love it. In my office, I hang up a few U-Turn For Christ T-shirts on my door, and whoever learns the most verses each week earns a free T-shirt. The shirts aren't for sale, and we only have a few at a time so they are a prized commodity. The challenge offers the men an incentive to gain what is most important. It trains them to keep their thoughts on Christ rather than on sin and depravity. As it says in 1 Corinthians 2:16, "But we have the mind of Christ."

Another aspect of learning God's Word is that I don't believe serious Bible reading can be done while a person is lying in bed. So at U-Turn For Christ Kenya, I don't allow the men to read their Bibles in bed. I make sure they are upright and away from their bunks to get as much of God's Word into them as possible. I've also made it a policy that the only languages the men are allowed to speak here are English and Swahili. With forty-two different dialects spoken in our country, this makes communication easier.

In general, Kenyans are intellectuals, and the Twelve-step program is the most widely accepted form of drug and alcohol treatment here. So U-Turn For Christ is not a concept that is well-received in our country. Yet it's mind-blowing to see what God has done through this ministry. Aside from slots on a government website and some magazines, our best advertisement has been word of mouth, and hundreds of men have completed our program with good results.

BEYOND MY IMAGINATION

God answered my prayer—ten times over—for something exciting to do. There's never a dull moment in my job at U-Turn For Christ Kenya. The men keep me on my toes both physically and spiritually. We pray together, work together, and have a good time. I have four staff members, including another pastor, Villias Urio. With the addition of a new bunkhouse in 2010, our capacity has reached thirty, and we typically have fifteen to eighteen men in the program. We now have a new U-Turn office on our property, and today my wife and I use the original house as our residence.

Let me tell you about my beautiful wife. Back in 2009 I met Susan Njeri Kabira under unusual circumstances. I saw her walking down the street in Ngong (a town southwest of Nairobi) when a drunk man started hustling her. I intervened and the man left. Later, Susan and I met again at a hair salon and discovered that we went to the same stylist. We began talking at the salon, and I found out she was a believer. Our friendship grew and eventually we became serious. On January 1, 2011, we were married and we are learning about marriage together, with an empty canvas between us to paint a picture of our new life together. Marriage has made me a better leader and taught me to think of others more than myself. Today Susan works full-time for one of the leading providers of Internet and television in the country, and she also teaches Sunday school.

ALL OVER THE MAP

Though I felt lost as a young man, God made my destiny clear in my later years. Bible college instilled in me a great thirst to be educated, and after returning to Kenya, I earned my bachelor's degree in theology through the African International University. I graduated in 2011 and Lord willing, I hope to pursue a master's degree in leadership.

My parents have relocated to Kenya and are now retired. They love the Lord and do whatever they can to help this ministry. Dad is now an ordained pastor and sits on the board of trustees for U-Turn For Christ. Mum makes sure she's here on visiting days, faithfully encouraging the women whose sons or husbands are struggling. She's convinced that God has called her to do this. My parents both love this ministry. Dad says, "We have seen the Lord use Duncan's life to bring many lost souls to the Lord Jesus Christ. All over Kenya, we hear from U-Turn graduates who have returned to school, to jobs, and to their families. Our relationship with Duncan and Susan is great and we support and encourage them in this work. God has done wonders!"

In 2014 we planted a new church, Calvary Chapel Ngong Hills, where I serve as pastor. The church is less than a mile away from

U-Turn so we can walk there. About twenty people from the surrounding community attend, and our men from U-Turn help with ushering, cleaning, and maintaining security at the church. In the March 2014 online newsletter from Calvary Chapel Ngong Hills, we describe the purpose of our fellowship: "Church should be a place where a sinner feels welcome. Calvary Chapel will break the barriers and stigma of drug addicts in Kenya and let people see what men and women saved by grace can do."

There's a great need for U-Turn For Christ facilities throughout the continent of Africa, and we're praying for that. Someday I hope to hang a map in my office with pins all over Kenya and Africa at large. Here in Nairobi, we pray to have a women's ranch some day in a separate location.

My vision for the future is that U-Turn For Christ will eventually become a self-sustaining institution in this country. In other words, men will not only come here to be rehabilitated and find Jesus, but they will also receive vocational training in mechanics, carpentry, welding, or other vocational job skills. This type of ministry has the potential for locations in every part of Kenya.

THE ULTIMATE PAYCHECK

I used to think that being on meth was the best thing that ever happened to me because it helped me feel bold and accepted. But after finding myself in trouble with the law, running from the police, getting beat up, owing people money, and feeling scared all the time, I realized that being on meth was a complete deception. The enemy did a number on me, and the truth is that U-Turn For Christ was the best thing that ever happened to me because that's where I found Jesus. It's wonderful! Now He gives me boldness to lead others and do the work He's called me to do. He equips me through the power of the Holy Spirit in my life.

> "I have been crucified with Christ; it is no longer I who live, but Christ lives in me; and the life which I now live in the flesh I live by faith in the Son of God, who loved me and gave Himself for me." (Galatians 2:20)

I love discipling the men at U-Turn For Christ Kenya because when I was a young believer, so many men poured into my life. Pastor Gerry discipled and trained me, and many others had a great influence on me, like Pastor Alex, Pastor Anthony, Pastor Erin, and Pastor Mario. I've learned that the most important part of discipleship is to be disciplined in my own private devotions. I make sure I'm in God's Word and let it fill me first. If someone asks me a question about the Bible, I want be on my toes so I am able to answer correctly. It's my challenge to do this.

There's an unexpected, wonderful reward in my ministry at U-Turn For Christ Kenya, and it is this: the men call me after they graduate. They call and say, "Pastor, I found a job!" or "Pastor, come to my wedding!" or "Pastor, will you officiate at my wedding?" Truly, that is my paycheck, and I witness wonders in all these things.

To all who read my story, you were made for God's glory. It doesn't matter what you look like or what you think you look like, God wants to use you in a great way. But you must sanctify your life first, so that the Lord can do wonderful things with your life tomorrow. He wants to love on you and anoint you for His work and His kingdom. Perhaps someday He may even guide you to Kenya.

Duncan and Susan

Lord, Pastor Duncan is another miracle story in the never-ending line of people who come to you and admit, "I'm wrong and You are right. Help me!" From there You take the broken, and by Your amazing grace You do things with their lives that no one could have imagined.

Many years ago Duncan learned the valuable lessen of staying in Your Word. May he never forget that lesson and may he pass it on to all those You have put under his care.

As You show Duncan Your goodness, please continue using him to introduce many more of his fellow countrymen to You. We pray that you will bless him and his family. In Jesus' name, Amen.

U-TURN FOR CHRIST NAIROBI, KENYA

Pastor Duncan Kabira Muya & Susan Njeri Kabira
Office No: 0716886548
To call from the U.S.: 011-254-0716886548
email: dm@uturnforchristkenya.com
website: uturnforchristkenya.com

God is faithful, who will not allow you to be tempted beyond what you are able, but with the temptation will also make the way of escape, that you may be able to bear it.

1 Corinthians 10:13

PASTOR JIMMY ESTHER
Strong Enough to Serve

The outdoor amphitheater and park-like setting made for an idyllic venue as the U-Turn For Christ mission team set up for an outreach in Calbayog City, the Philippines. Jimmy eyed the burlap bags of rice and the bins of equipment still in the pickup. A former champion wrestler, Jimmy felt most useful when he was moving, lifting, or hauling things.

"What do you want me to do next, Pastor Gerry?" he asked. "Move the rice?"

Pastor Gerry shook his head. "No, I want you to grab a hairbrush and some barrettes out of this bin, and then go stand over there by the amphitheater entrance."

Jimmy wondered if he had heard right. "What?" he asked. Feeling confused, he thought, I came all the way to the Philippines to brush hair?

As Pastor Gerry walked away, Jimmy was left with nothing else to do but obey orders. So he rummaged through the bin until he found a bag full of hair accessories and a new hairbrush. Then, with brush in hand and pockets full of elastic bands and barrettes, Jimmy positioned himself near the entrance and waited nervously. Soon villagers began entering the amphitheater. One eight-year-old girl walked up to Jimmy and he swallowed hard. "Would you like me to brush your hair?" he asked.

Smiling shyly, she said, "Yes." Then she added, "In a ponytail." Jimmy brushed her long black hair and then awkwardly wrapped an elastic band around it a few times. Within the hour, a line of girls formed, from preschoolers to teens, waiting for a turn. And for the next few nights of outreaches, the girls kept coming while Jimmy brushed hair, arranged ponytails, and fastened colorful barrettes in their hair.

This is Jimmy's story.

Brushing a girl's hair? I wasn't very good at it. And I'm sure there were some lopsided ponytails in the crowd. But the girls were patient, showing me how they wanted their hair done and then guiding me along. Probably the biggest surprise of all was that I had fun!

Pastor Gerry definitely took me out of my element. That's one thing I love about him, the way he encourages us to try things we've never done before. He's always telling us to "be ready in season and out" (2 Timothy 4:2 ESV), so I knew I had to try the hair thing. God does that with us too, putting us in situations where we have to trust Him completely. He may not place us where we want to be, but it's always where we need to be. And no matter what, whenever we choose to obey Him, we're blessed.

A COUNTRY BOY

All my life I've been a worker, a heavy lifter, a doer. I don't preach and I don't teach—I just work. I've always been athletic and my work ethic probably took root in the fifth grade, when our family moved from the city to the small farm town of Hickman, California. My dad transferred to Hickman with his job as an accountant, and we lived on a fifteen-acre almond farm, which Dad kept as a hobby. My younger brother, Christopher, and I helped Dad with the farm, and along with my older sister Sherry we all grew close, working and playing together out in the middle of nowhere. I had my first paying job at age twelve, helping a horse and cattle rancher down the road with his fields and animals. And all during this time, Mom took us to a Catholic church every Sunday, so I always believed in God.

I had my first drink in the third grade. After Dad came home from work, he always had a beer, and one time when he stepped outside I grabbed his can and started swigging on it. That habit quickly stopped when Dad put a cigar butt in his beer can and I ended up with a mouthful of ashes. At age thirteen I started drinking and smoking weed every weekend, out in the fields with the nearby farmers' kids.

Without much to do in the country, my friends and I rode dirt bikes in the surrounding orchards. In between the rows of almond and walnut trees, there was a flat surface where farmers drove their tractors. That's where we rode our bikes, turning corners and creating huge ruts between the rows. Farmers didn't like it because when the sweepers came through at harvest time, they couldn't pick up the almonds and walnuts that fell into the ruts. So workers had to go back later and dig out the crop by hand. Though we never got caught for all the trouble we caused, we were often chased out by farmers, neighbors, and even the sheriff.

DOUBLE STANDARD

As a freshman at Hughson High, I used LSD and meth, and I drank more than ever. Still, I stayed active in sports, participating every season in football, baseball, track, or wrestling. I was even part of the wrestling team that won our district championship. During my senior year the wrestling coach invited me to Hume Lake Christian Camp, and for the first time I heard that Jesus loves me, He died for me, and has a better life for me. God's Word pierced my heart and I gave my life to Christ that week.

After camp I had a different perspective about God and I wanted to follow Him. I quit drugs and drinking but unfortunately I didn't have anyone to show me how to live day by day as a Christian. I continued hanging out with the same friends and eventually went back to using drugs. I didn't go back to drinking though.

My wrestling coach was also a pastor at our local community church, and I attended there off and on during high school. I served at the church too, helping out with sound and mentoring high school kids. But when I wasn't at church, I smoked weed and did drugs, and needless to say, I wrestled with the Lord about my lifestyle. After a while I started doing meth again, and my church attendance stopped. I'd miss church for months at a time, depending on my meth use, and then suddenly show up again. Because I lived in a small town, people talked and they treated me differently when I came back. But I didn't care what they thought.

After high school I was hired full time at a milk creamery and worked there four years. One summer my sister Sherry and I took a road trip to Wyoming to visit our grandpa. Still on meth, I got pulled over for speeding in Nevada. The officer searched our car, found marijuana, and arrested me on drug charges. Since it was my first offense, they were lenient and sent me to a thirty-day rehab and charged me a fine. In rehab, I learned more about doing dope than I had known before, and it didn't help my recovery at all! As soon as I was released, I started smoking weed again.

A year later I failed a drug test at work and lost my job at the creamery. Then I left town to party for six months, and for all that time, I saw little signs of the Lord trying to get my attention, speaking to me through people, billboards, and the radio. Finally, I was done partying, and with my sister about to be married, I got in touch with my mom and made it to the wedding. That weekend I reached out to the pastor at my church for help. He told me that the church was running a Twelve-Step Christian ministry called Unity House and he invited me to go.

On my first visit to Unity House, I walked through the front door and said, "I'm here!" I liked the people there, and I stayed involved in the ministry for a few years. During that time, I went back to school to study environmental technology, and later I worked for a geologist, monitoring ground water.

Meanwhile, Dad bought more almond orchards in nearby Chowchilla and Livingston, and when I turned twenty-two, he hired me to take care of his properties. I did all the physical labor—irrigating, mowing grass, fertilizing, and trimming the trees. I moved into my own house across the river from my parents and stayed clean and sober for a year. Then while working in the orchards one day, I ran into some guys I used to party with in high school, and before long, I was back to taking meth and smoking weed.

FIRED

When my brother Chris came home on break from college, he went to work with me in the fields. He saw me partying out there and told Mom, "You know, Jimmy's really not working it."

Mom remembers, "While Chris was off at college, Jimmy worked the orchards, but when Chris came home, he did the job for two. Jimmy used to tell his little brother not to do drugs, so when Chris saw his older brother like this, it hurt him a lot. I always knew when Jimmy was on drugs because he'd get very mellow. Normally, he was happy-go-lucky, active, and had lots of energy. But on drugs, nothing fazed him. It went on like this for eight years—he'd stay off of drugs for a couple of years and then go back to it. This time, I think he was waiting for us to rescue him."

When Dad found out I was on dope again, everything came crashing down. First, he fired me. Then my friend Chance Mason invited me to come over for a visit. I rang his doorbell and as he opened the door, I saw my pastor, my roommate, and my parents all sitting in the living room waiting for me. Instantly, I knew what was happening. After voicing their concerns and their love for me, I looked over at Chance and said, "Well, it's about time." The truth was out.

At that point, I was so deep into the drug scene that I didn't know how to stop. My pride held me back from asking for help, yet it didn't take much convincing. The Lord had already been drawing me, and that push was exactly what I needed to get back to serving God. "This time I'm not dealing with psychologists," I told everyone. "I know God has something for me in this life, and I want a program that's 100-percent Christian."

News traveled fast in Hickman and people found out I was looking for a Christian rehab. A friend referred us to U-Turn For Christ, and when I heard the name, I knew it was where God wanted me. My parents offered to pay the fee, and a week later they drove me all the way to the ranch in Perris. My mom recalls that day in 2000 when I entered the ranch at age twenty-seven.

"When we dropped Jimmy off at the ranch, his dad said, 'You can't come home.' Do you know what it's like to say that to your child?"

ONE GOAL

I liked the ranch immediately. I liked the big open space away from the city, with only a few structures on the property. I also liked the animals, especially the goats and the pigs. I think it all appealed to my redneck side.

I had one goal when I came to the ranch and that was to get back in a relationship with God. U-Turn For Christ helped me do that. Mom says, "Jimmy needed a new start and he found it at U-Turn. He was thrilled to go."

After finishing Phase 1, I stayed on to serve in landscaping with Art Gonzalez. Every day we worked out in the hot sun, pushing lawn mowers, pulling weeds, and having great fellowship together. Art smiled a lot and he always lifted me up. Often I'd hear him exclaim, "Praise the Lord!"

Once when Art and I went out on a job, the weeds in a particular area were especially tough to dig out. Art heard me sighing deeply and after a while he looked over and said, "Jimmy, I want you to pray this prayer: Lord make my hands like little shovels so I can pull these weeds out faster." I laughed out loud at his suggestion, but then I realized he was serious.

"Do it!" he said.

So I prayed the prayer, and to my surprise, everything flowed after that. It almost seemed like the dirt wasn't there and those stubborn weeds started popping out. That experience stuck with me, and later on I tried it with the young guys I worked with. They laughed too, but a couple of them actually prayed and were blessed when the Lord answered their little, insignificant prayer: *Lord, please help me with this, make the dirt softer, and make my hands like little shovels.*

USING WHAT YOU'VE GOT

I had it in my heart to go into ministry someday, and after completing Phase 2 and getting a job, I shared my desire with Pastor Mario. "Pray about it," he advised, "and see what the Lord has for you." Six months later, in 2002, Pastor Mario and Pastor Gerry asked me to serve in Mexico as overseer for a youth ranch on the Baja Peninsula, working with junior high and high school kids.

Down in Mexico, every Sunday morning we'd minister at the Oaxacan camps, where Mexican farm laborers lived. Sunday was their only day off, so we'd go out to share the gospel, help with physical needs, and cook lunch for them. Once when Pastor Gerry came to Mexico for an outreach, he joined us at the camps. The night before, we packed up all the barbecues so we'd be ready to leave the next morning, but without my knowledge, one of our cooks removed the grills from the barbecues and forgot to replace them. The next day when we unpacked our cooking gear in Oaxaca, we discovered there were no grills and it stressed me out. *How are we supposed to make lunch?* I thought. We were too far away to drive back and get the grills. I looked over at Pastor Gerry and was surprised to see a big grin on his face. "You know what, man?" he said. "Let's pray that the Lord shows us how to use what we've got."

"Yeah, but we've got nothin' right now" I said, feeling frustrated.

Pastor Gerry held up some throw-away tins that had been used for starting a fire. "Well," he said, "we've got some tins…" and then he proceeded to set the tins inside the barbecue, place hot dogs over them, and cook our lunch. Seeing Pastor Gerry's example taught me that even when I plan and try to execute everything perfectly, sometimes things just don't work out. And when that happens, God provides a way, and the ability to improvise. I can still thank Him and be joyous for whatever He gives. James 1:2-3 says,

> "Count it all joy when you fall into various trials, knowing
> that the testing of your faith produces patience."

That scripture assures me that God allows us to be tested. In every
trial He waits to speak and help us, and as we lean on Him, He helps
us endure.

AN ATTITUDE

As the months passed, I started getting a big head. My attitude
changed, and I decided I didn't need to go to Bible studies or morning Proverbs anymore. I also stopped doing my own devotions and
reading the Word. About that time a guy was sent from Perris to
our ranch to be disciplined, and late one night I caught him outside,
sneaking onto our property with meth and weed. We both sat down
to talk about it and soon we were doing the drugs together.

Dealers were easy to find in Mexico so for the next two to three
months, I continued using. My attitude got worse and others noticed.
Word about me traveled to California so I was given a drug test and
failed. It didn't take long before Pastor Mario and Pastor Anthony
came down to see what was going on. Pastor Mario took one look at
me and said, "Jimmy, you're looking a little skinny in the face."

But Pastor Anthony confronted me head on. He gave me another
drug test, which I failed, and then he said, "You need to leave."

After serving a year in Mexico at the youth ranch, I got in my truck
and headed for Perris. I knew I wouldn't be allowed to return to the
ranch, yet I was drawn back to Perris because I'd made a commitment to the Lord. And even though I had messed it up, the Lord
placed it on my heart to fulfill that commitment. I slept in my truck
on the streets in Perris, and I spent my days sitting in my truck or
walking around with a lot of time to think. The leadership knew I
was out there in my truck somewhere, but they didn't contact me.

I began reading my Bible again, trying to hear from the Lord. One night as I sat in my truck feeling like an idiot, God spoke to my heart. "You need to come back to Me, Jimmy, and surrender everything," He said. "And you need to do it now." The Lord's presence seemed so real that I felt like He was hugging me, right there in my truck. I gave myself to Him again that night, and He turned my life around.

LOVED AND FORGIVEN

The next morning I called the ranch. In fact, I called every day after that, talking to Pastor Mario, Pastor Anthony, Pastor Erin, and others. But there was no invitation to come back. After a week of calling, the pastor I spoke with said, "Pastor Gerry asked me to give you a message."

"Really?" I asked, surprised.

"Meet him in his office tomorrow morning at eight."

After living in my truck for a month, I waited in Pastor Gerry's office the next morning, feeling broken. There I was, the guy who had been given the opportunity to run a U-Turn facility in Mexico, the head person. But I'd gone off and used dope and then stayed there as if nothing had happened.

Pastor Gerry walked in and I stood up to look him in the eye. "I want to apologize, Pastor Gerry, for slandering the reputation of U-Turn For Christ in Mexico," I said. "Will you forgive me?"

Now, I'm pretty good at reading faces—and the only thing I could see on Pastor Gerry's face was unconditional love. What I'd done was like a slap in the face. But once I asked for forgiveness, he never held it against me or conveyed disgust toward me. I can't imagine a more compassionate response than his.

"Jimmy, I want you to read Matthew 18," he said thoughtfully, "and call me tomorrow. I'll pray about what to do and let you know."

"Whoever causes one of these little ones who believe in Me to sin, it would be better for him if a millstone were hung around his neck, and he were drowned in the depth of the sea. Woe to the world because of offenses! For offenses must come, but woe to that man by whom the offense comes! If your hand or foot causes you to sin, cut it off and cast it from you. It is better for you to enter into life lame or maimed, rather than having two hands or two feet, to be cast into the everlasting fire. And if your eye causes you to sin, pluck it out and cast it from you. It is better for you to enter into life with one eye, rather than having two eyes, to be cast into hell fire." (Matthew 18:6-9)

After reading these verses, I started to see my sin from God's perspective. As leader of the youth ranch in Mexico, I realized I had caused one of God's little ones to sin, and the graphic analogy Jesus shares in this passage showed me the horrible effects of that sin. I also saw my need to cut off all drugs and alcohol from my life, once and for all. I couldn't just pick them up and use again if I felt like it. In the same way that Jesus described cutting off a hand or foot that causes a person to sin—for me, cutting off drugs and alcohol had to be a complete amputation.

I thank the Lord for Pastor Gerry's willingness to show me the severity of my sin and pray with me. God opened up my eyes to see how far I had strayed and what to do so I'd never repeat it.

The next day when I called the ranch, Pastor Gerry invited me to come back. As I moved my things to a top bunk that afternoon, I'm told that someone walked up to me and said, "I don't like what you did, and if it was up to me, you wouldn't be here." Apparently, I didn't hear it, but nothing could have taken away the gratefulness I felt to be back. I roomed with the guys in Phase 1, and I served every day on a work crew, without privileges. Eleven months later

Pastor Mario wanted to talk to me. "Why do you think the Lord has kept you here so long, Jimmy?" he asked.

"He's teaching me patience."

"Yes," Mario agreed, "but I also think He has a calling on your life. There's a position open here for head overseer, and Pastor Gerry and I both believe it's for you." Humbled by his offer, I accepted, and for the next five years I served in Perris, assembling work crews, scheduling teachers, and helping to discipline and counsel the men.

Pastor Gerry continued reaching out to me and even brought me into his family. I became close to his sons, Danny and Josh, and I often hung out with them or spent the night at their house. Pastor Gerry's graciousness was a gift I could have never imagined.

DOING TIME IN TEXAS

In 2004 Pastor Gerry sent me to Texas, where I served as overseer of a new U-Turn For Christ in San Angelo. Soon after I arrived, Hurricane Katrina hit Louisiana and we moved our fifteen guys to a facility in Baton Rouge, Louisiana. There we joined in the disaster relief effort and worked at a food bank for hurricane victims. When we returned to Texas several months later, our San Angelo facility had been changed into a youth ranch, and a more challenging group of guys arrived. I remember telling people, "We don't get the choir boys here—we get the ones that the parents can't handle."

One of the boys in our program decided to report that a U-Turn assistant had "kicked him in the butt." When the police showed up, other kids began making up stories, saying they'd been hit, beaten, or shoved. Both assistants were arrested, and although I wasn't implicated in any of the stories, I was arrested and held responsible as the head overseer. The youth ranch closed down, and all the boys were sent back to their homes. Only the adults in first and second phase stayed on, and no more applicants were received into the program.

Sitting in jail, I wondered if I'd end up going to prison for something I didn't do. *This is too rough, Lord,* I prayed. *I can't do this!* I felt so alone, having no contact with the outside world. But every night the Lord comforted me with His Word and reminded me He was with me through verses like Matthew 28:20.

> "Teaching them to observe all things that I have commanded you; and lo, I am with you always, even to the end of the age."

I often repeated 1 Corinthians 10:13, and it became my favorite verse:

> "No temptation has overtaken you except such as is common to man; but God is faithful, who will not allow you to be tempted beyond what you are able, but with the temptation will also make the way of escape, that you may be able to bear it."

God's Word gave me a joy I couldn't comprehend as well as the tools to rely on Him, not only in jail but also later on.

After bail was posted twenty-two days later, I found work outside the ministry. Meanwhile, the U-Turn facility closed down while police conducted an investigation. They concluded that the kids from our youth ranch had lied, and all charges were dropped. A year after the arrests, our U-Turn doors reopened and we participated in a few outreaches with other churches in San Angelo.

I'm humbled as I reflect back on the opportunities the Lord has allowed me to be a part of, such as the trip to the Philippines, where I brushed hair. On that trip, I did other things too, like set up for the worship band, make balloon animals, and pass out candy to the kids. Even in these small ways, my desire was to draw and influence others to come to Christ.

During our mission trip to Thailand, I got to mix cement and help build a church. The Lord knows how much I love to work with my hands, and I thank Him for each chance He gave me to serve. When I think of how He redeemed my life from serving the enemy, it makes me want to do more for Him.

A LIGHT IN PAYSON

In 2010, after I spent five years in Texas, Pastor Gerry asked me to serve as the overseer at a new U-Turn For Christ in Payson, Arizona, where Harold Fleeger was director. Payson is a small mountain town with about 15,000 people, and it reminds me of where I grew up. The U-Turn facility there is situated right in the middle of town, giving us the opportunity to be a bright light in the community.

A few months after moving to Payson, I was ordained by Pastor Gerry at Calvary Chapel Romoland. Mom and Dad both came to my ordination and were blessed to witness that day. "It was thrilling for Jimmy's dad and me to watch our son become a pastor," Mom says. "We were so proud of him."

For me, becoming a pastor meant that I knew I had to step up and be a real man of God. Even though I'd already been leading others, after I was ordained, I wanted to lead and serve the Lord even more.

Since 2013 I've served as the director and pastor of U-Turn for Christ in Payson. We average about eight men in our facility at a time, but we've had up to twenty. The churches in town help us by sending out elders to teach Bible studies with our men, and we enjoy a great relationship with these fellow believers. A couple of churches have even supported us financially.

Some residents of Payson have a hard time affording help with cleaning, yard work, and moving. So our work crew from U-Turn goes out regularly to serve the community, without asking for anything in return. We want our neighbors in Payson to know we're there to help, and we tell them, "God loves you, and we're doing this for Him because He's called us to do it." We also serve at nearby Tonto Rim Christian Camp three times a week, doing everything from maintenance to cleaning cabins to digging trenches.

Sometimes people pull into our U-Turn facility and say, "What's this place about?" I tell them U-Turn is a Christian discipleship ministry. We help men turn away from sin in their lives and get them on track with Jesus Christ as their personal Lord and Savior. Then I invite them to church! Some have taken me up on my invitation and now attend Calvary Chapel in Payson.

LESSONS TO LEARN

I'm a person who feels good about doing things quickly and efficiently. I like to give 100 percent, the way the Lord wants us to. Colossians 3:23 reminds us,

> "And whatever you do, do it heartily, as to the Lord and not to men, knowing that from the Lord you will receive the reward of the inheritance; for you serve the Lord Christ."

When I work with guys who are coming off the streets and coming off drugs and alcohol, I realize they've been serving themselves and doing things half way. I can't just open up the Bible and yell or flip out at them. The most important thing I can do is be patient and humble and show them love, just like others have done for me.

Every day God teaches me patience and I get tested a lot! Out on the farm where I grew up, I was used to taking direction, and when I was told to do a job, I did it then and I did it right. But some of these guys aren't used to doing things that way. And I've learned that I can't give them a job and then walk away. I have to stay on them and remind myself that they probably don't know how to do the things I take for granted—simple things like rake a yard or stack wood. So I teach them how, with patience and humility from the Lord, because that's what God asks me to do.

"Likewise you younger people, submit yourselves to your elders. Yes, all of you be submissive to one another, and be clothed with humility, for God resists the proud, but gives grace to the humble. Therefore humble yourselves under the mighty hand of God, that He may exalt you in due time, casting all your care upon Him, for He cares for you." (1 Peter 5:5-7)

HEART OF THANKS

I'm thankful for the Christians in my life who never gave up on me. Friends who were always there for me when I fell and backslid. God used these people to influence me and bring me back to Him. They didn't judge me, and they always received me with open arms.

When I used drugs, I stole a lot from my dad and it crushed our relationship. We couldn't spend more than two days together without arguing about something stupid. But God restored us, and now we spend as much time together as possible. Mom says, "Jimmy's closer to his dad now than he's ever been." My relationship with all of my family is wonderful, and I thank God for that.

I'm grateful to Pastor Gerry for the forgiveness and restoration he extended to me, and for giving me another chance to serve the Lord. Pastor Gerry has shared that his vision is to see a U-Turn For Christ in every state of the U.S. My own vision is to continue serving the Lord wholeheartedly, and ultimately to see every man and woman follow Him and serve Him.

Helping the guys who come to U-Turn is such a privilege. They arrive so torn and broken by the world, and I get to come alongside and teach them to become godly men and serve others. It's a humbling place to be, and I'm continually reminded of where I came from and how far God has brought me.

When my mom came to Payson once for a visit, I heard her say, "Jimmy's probably happier than he's ever been." She's right. I love what I do. My greatest joy is to see a guy come out of the life I once lived, the knucklehead drug life, and watch him become a man who jumps at the chance to help others, regardless of race or religion. Or to witness a father who once said, "I don't ever want to talk to my son again," and then see that father and son restored. Or to meet someone new in the program who is completely selfish and then watch him transform into a man who thinks of others more than himself.

If you have loved ones who struggle with drugs or alcohol, I encourage you to never give up on them. Pray for them and keep loving them, just as Christ loves us. Pray they will repent and be reconciled to God, because that is His desire for each one of us.

> "Now then, we are ambassadors for Christ, as though God were pleading through us: we implore you on Christ's behalf, be reconciled to God." (2 Corinthians 5:20)

Jimmy with his dog, Zoey

Lord, we thank You for Jimmy and ask Your blessing on him. Thank you for how You're using him to oversee the ministry of U-Turn For Christ in Payson, Arizona. May he share Your hope and direction with the men who come into that facility. We ask that You will completely cover him and the ministry.

Fill Jimmy with Your Spirit and allow him to continue to represent You well, as he looks to You and gives You all the glory and honor. In Jesus' name, Amen.

U-TURN FOR CHRIST PAYSON, ARIZONA
Pastor Jimmy Esther
509 W. Frontier Street, Payson, AZ 85541
(928) 468-6336
email: uturnforchristaz@gmail.com
website: www.uturnforchristaz.com

CHAPTER 10

Though one may be overpowered by another, two can withstand him. And a threefold cord is not quickly broken.

ECCLESIASTES 4:12

PASTOR THOMAS & CRYSTAL MENDEZ
God in the Center

Grateful for a day off, Crystal sat outside the women's ranch house, soaking in the morning sunshine. With pen and notebook in hand, she stared at a blank page and prayed, "Lord, where do I start? I've never planned a wedding before!"

A slim figure suddenly cast a shadow across the blank page, and Crystal looked up to see her future mother-in-law, Sue, standing next to her. "All set, Crys?" Sue asked excitedly. With her hair styled and a new outfit on, Sue looked ready for a girls' day out.

"Oh my gosh, I almost forgot you were coming, Mom! So, where are we going again?"

Sue grinned. "I'm taking you to David's Bridal! After all, with you and Thomas getting married in three weeks, we have some serious shopping to do."

This is Thomas and Crystal's story.

Thomas: I never had a girlfriend before. In fact, at twenty-one years of age, I'd never felt anything for a girl except to use her. But then one day at a dope house, I met the most beautiful woman I'd ever known. When I saw Crystal for the first time, she was only eighteen years old. Something about her made me think, *I'd get right to just see her get right!* Sitting next to her on the couch, I was hardly aware of the crowd of dopers all around us—shooting up, snorting, smoking, and getting high. About twenty minutes after meeting her, I leaned over to her and whispered, "I'm going to marry you." She just laughed.

How did we end up at a dope house together? I'll start at the beginning. I grew up in Anaheim, California, with my older brother Ralphy and my little brother Bobby. Mom met Dad right after he got out of prison, when she was eighteen. Both of them were heroin addicts and they never married. Dad used to beat her up, but I don't really remember that because he left when I was three.

My brothers and I spent a lot of time alone because Mom liked to party. She had different boyfriends at the house, and when I was nine, one boyfriend offered me a joint and I fell in love with the high. Best of all, it helped me to deal with the loneliness I felt. Dad came by now and then to say hi, but he never had a steady place to live until I was a young teenager. That's when he got a new girlfriend with her own apartment. Sometimes I'd stay with him, especially when Mom and I weren't getting along. But then he'd get locked up again and I'd have to go back home. This went on for several years.

GRANDMA'S INFLUENCE

Even with all the chaos in my life, I knew the Lord. For as long as I could remember, my grandma picked up my brothers and me every week to take us to Sunday School at White Avenue Baptist Church in Pomona where she lived. Grandma loved her church so much that she drove to Anaheim and back again to take us with her, almost an hour's drive each way. In 1993, when I was eleven, Grandma took us all to the Harvest Crusade at the Anaheim Stadium. At the end of the service, Crystal Lewis sang, "Come Just as You Are," and I felt the Lord calling me to accept Him. I turned to my mom and said, "I want to go down on the field!"

"Then go down," Mom said. Ralphy came with me and he accepted the Lord too. Soon after that, I was baptized in front of the congregation at White Avenue Baptist Church.

As I got older, it was harder for me to follow the Lord, yet I still felt His conviction in my heart. Soon my mom and brothers and I stopped going to church, and I began smoking weed heavily. I stole beer from Mom and drank it when she wasn't around. Eventually I had a stepsister, Ayanna, who was born after my mom had an affair with the mailman. I also had a stepbrother, Gabriel, from my dad and a different mom, but Gabriel didn't live with us.

Growing up, I hung out with Ralphy and we were very close. With gang activity in our neighborhood and two meth cooks on our street, we saw a lot of destruction. I remember watching neighbors on meth who picked at their faces, and others who ripped their skin off because they thought worms were crawling out of their muscles. After witnessing these things, I told myself, *I'll never do that! I'll never take those drugs!* But by the time I was fifteen, Ralphy and I were friends with those same gang members, and we got used to the robberies, car thefts, drugs, parties, stabbings, and shootings. At eighteen, I had my own apartment and Ralphy and Dad lived with me.

One night some friends and I drove out to Whittier Blvd. in L.A. We pulled into a supermarket parking lot and started talking to a couple of pretty girls standing there. I talked to one girl who was being followed by her husband, and when he saw me standing next to my new Honda Accord with Anaheim Angels stickers on it, he got mad. Gangs from L.A. and Orange County didn't get along, and he didn't like my stickers so he pulled his car up beside me. Because I was drunk and was the one with the biggest mouth, I said, "Come on, get out of your car." I had a twelve-inch screwdriver right behind me on the seat of the car, and I was ready to reach for it at any moment. I kept egging the guy on, but I think he got scared when he saw I had four other guys with me. Suddenly he pointed a gun, and I felt something hit me.

I pulled up my shirt and saw a drizzle of blood flowing down my chest. "Hey, I'm shot!" I yelled. The guy sped off and my buddies and I got back in my car. I handed a friend the keys, and he flew down Whittier Blvd. We didn't know where we were, so my friend flagged down an ambulance and we followed it to the hospital. On the way, it got hard for me to breathe and I thought, *I'm going to die.*

At the ER, I was transferred onto a gurney, and I heard a doctor say, "There's another one." They lined me up next to six other guys who had been shot that night. The one next to me was shot five times in the chest. I waited a long time, coughing up blood and getting Demerol for the pain. Four hours later they wheeled me in for an x-ray to look for the bullet. Even with a small camera inserted inside my body, they couldn't see anything. So they took me to surgery and discovered that the bullet had entered an inch away from my heart, punctured a lung, and grazed my colon. They moved around some organs, still looking for the bullet, but it was never found. So they sewed me back up with forty-two staples and said, "We'll just let the fat build up around the bullet. You'll be all right."

DREAM JOB

This all happened on a Friday night, and by Sunday afternoon I was discharged, just in time to start a new job on Monday with WFS Financial, a Fortune 500 company. I landed the well-paying job after three rigorous interviews and was hired to do payment processing. Even though I couldn't stand up completely straight, on Monday morning I buttoned up my new dress shirt and walked very carefully so I wouldn't snag any staples. *I don't want to tell anyone what happened and ruin all this,* I thought. No one ever knew.

Three months later I was back on Whittier Blvd. with my friends and watched another guy get shot. Then it hit me, *What the heck am I doing here?* But for the next two years, I partied every weekend and holiday with friends, clubbing all night, drinking all day, and seeing how many women we could hook up with. The higher we got on speed and pot, the more beer we drank.

Pretty soon my partying progressed beyond the weekend, and I started doing lines of speed in the restroom at work. I'd leave on my lunch hour to smoke a ball of speed at home, then rush back on the 5 freeway from Anaheim to Irvine. My lunch breaks got longer, and I started missing entire days of work because I was coming down off speed and wanted to sleep. My manager really liked me because I was a good worker when I was there so he gave me chance after chance. But finally after two years I was fired. My drug use became an everyday thing and I lived for the next high. I tried to collect unemployment but my supervisor went to court and sued me for misconduct, so I had to pay all the money back.

MEETING CRYSTAL

Because I partied so much, I lost my apartment and moved in with a cousin in Santa Ana. But my cousin kicked me out because I started doing weird things like picking up pay phones and talking to no one. I thought people were following me and that my dad was trying to take my dope. It got so bad that my family wanted to put me in an insane asylum, but they decided not to. Eventually I stole five guns from a guy and started taking one with me everywhere, knowing I'd either end up shooting someone or get shot myself.

Meanwhile, Dad moved to a dope house and I moved in with him. The person who paid the rent was a guy who collected SSI. Six people lived in the apartment, and all we had to do was supply drugs to this guy in exchange for staying there. It was a kickback house, a party house. I had a steady supply of dope to sell from my best friend, whose uncle was a meth cook. But pretty soon I was taking all the profit to do the drugs myself, and I took anything I could get—crack, meth, weed, ecstasy, and heroin. One day a guy and two girls showed up at the drug house, and there was a big confrontation over someone's missing gun. The house got pretty crowded, and that's how I met Crystal, when she was trying to find a place to sit. Finally she made her way to the living room couch and sat down next to me.

Crystal: The first thing Thomas said to me was, "Dang, baby, where have you been all my life?" He had this cheesy smile on his face.

"Oh, come on!" I said, thinking that he was just trying to get with me. Still for some reason I felt attracted to him.

All of sudden a pimp and a prostitute who lived there pushed me into another room and started questioning me. "Where's the gun?" "Did you take it? You have it, right? We're gonna beat you up." They bombarded me with accusations, but I didn't know what they were talking about. I didn't have a gun. So much was going on in that place and people were getting high in every room.

Thomas: When they were done questioning Crystal, she came back out to the couch and I said, "Look, don't worry. No one's going to do anything to you. You can stay here with me and you'll be all right." I wasn't going to let anything happen to her. In my heart, I'd always thought, *Man, if I ever meet a girl that I don't want to just sleep with, I'll know she's the one I've been waiting for, the one God put in my life.* That's how I felt about Crystal and why I leaned over a few minutes later and said I wanted to marry her. Granted, I was strung out and hadn't slept in days, but I still knew she was the one, and I meant it with all my heart.

Crystal stayed for one night and we slept together. I remember asking her if she believed in love at first sight and she said, "No, of course not!" I also asked her if she believed in God and she said yes. I wanted her to stay but she left the next morning.

A DOUBLE LIFE

Crystal: Now I'll tell my story. Both my parents were drug addicts. Dad sold speed, and when I was five, our house was raided and my parents lost custody of my older sister, Vanessa, and me. We moved in with our grandparents, who had worked hard to come to the U.S. from Mexico. My grandparents spoke only Spanish and we answered back in English. They were stubborn that way—they never wanted to learn English and we felt the same about Spanish. But that's how we grew up, and it worked for us.

My grandparents raised us the best they could. They faithfully took us to a Catholic church and to classes for confession and confirmation. Sometimes we'd visit my parents on the weekends—that is, if Dad wasn't locked up. When we were with my grandparents, we did things right and lived the way we should, but when we were with our parents, they'd get high, get drunk, and even let us drink. We lived a double life, and my grandparents didn't have a clue. They didn't even know what it looked like for a person to get high.

Dad's mom, my Grandma Angie, had a house in Santa Ana and every time Dad got out of prison, that's where we'd go and visit my parents. Mom and Dad lived in different apartments sometimes too, but they couldn't hold jobs long enough to stay in one place for long. Mom ended up cheating on Dad and they split up when I was a kid, but they still saw each other until I was eighteen. When Mom first left Dad, he stayed at Grandma Angie's and sold drugs.

I started drinking when I was eight years old, swiping beers from my dad when he wasn't looking. Because he didn't actually raise me, he never disciplined me. One time when I was nine, he was having a party and I grabbed a beer, opened it, and started drinking it right in front of him. Everyone looked at him to see what he'd do, and all he said was, "What am I gonna tell you?" I could get away with so much and that's why I liked spending time with him. After all, how could he correct me when he was doing the same thing?

Vanessa, who was four years older than me, was smoking pot at twelve and I soon joined her. That year my grandparents decided to "take us out of the ghetto" so they moved from Santa Ana to Temecula, California. I hated moving away because I missed my dad. Sometimes Mom and Dad went months without calling or visiting us. Whenever we didn't hear from them, I always thought I wasn't good enough. And then when they finally *did* call or visit, Grandma couldn't say no to seeing our parents. Sometimes we'd stay in Santa Ana over the weekend or even for the summer.

Many relatives on Dad's side of the family were from a notorious gang, and they had big kickbacks (parties) and barbecues at Grandma Angie's. They would put foil on the windows, sell drugs, and jump people in the backyard. In case of a drug raid, Grandma Angie's house had a hallway closet with a secret hole in the ground where everyone could dump their dope to hide it.

SINKING

Some of my new friends in Temecula introduced me to speed when I was twelve, and right away I was hooked. I had no worries, no cares, and no pain, but it took over my life. On the weekends I'd sneak out to an apartment in our complex known as the party house, where a twenty-five-year-old guy and his wife and two babies lived. This couple smoked speed and always provided it for me. One time while I was at their place, I was "jumped in" to a gang. It was like an initiation, with six people punching, kicking, and hitting me for eighteen seconds straight, all of them trying to get their best shot. I felt pretty sore afterwards.

When I was fourteen, I started feeling paranoid and thought I was losing it. As a freshman at Temecula Valley High School, I got mad at people simply for making a face I didn't like. I started fights with other girls and beat them up for any reason. I hated all my teachers so I ditched class and took lines of speed in the school bathroom to get high. At the end of ninth grade, I was kicked out and placed in a continuation school. By this time my grandma and grandpa knew something was up. "You're not listening," they'd say, or "You're grounded!" Finally they gave me an ultimatum to either get right or leave. So I left and stayed with friends, then with a forty-year-old guy in my neighborhood who gave me speed, and later at a Motel 6 with other friends. To help with rent, I worked nights as a waitress at a Mexican restaurant. During the day, I went to continuation school. I tried selling speed as well, but I ended up smoking more than I sold.

With only one class left before graduation, I got into a fight with a girl at continuation school. It was her fault, and she started it simply because she didn't like me. Yet the rules were clear: no fighting in continuation school or you're automatically out. So, knowing I'd have to leave anyway, I got on the bus and never went back.

Next, I went to my Aunt Linda's house in Whittier, where I enrolled at California High School to finish my senior year. I stayed clean for four months, attending school and doing well. Then one afternoon I was walking home from school and met a twenty-three-year-old guy who lived down the street. Just out of prison, he was standing in his driveway getting high on speed, and I stopped to get high along with him. Then I began hanging out with him and his friends, and a few weeks later, he robbed a store and was back in prison.

HOOKED

On speed again, I quit school, left Aunt Linda's, and moved to a Motel 6 in L.A. with my new friends from Whittier. One night we were all getting high in the room when my dad showed up at the door. "Pack your stuff and get out of here," he said. "I'm renting an apartment in Anaheim, and you're coming with me to get clean." I don't know how Dad knew where I was, but I left with him. Then Mom found out that Dad and I were in an apartment together, and she wanted to move in too. Dad, who had always been in love with her, said, "Yeah, okay, come and move in."

So there we were, together in the apartment with my parents getting high behind my back and me getting high behind theirs. We all knew what was going on, but to save face, we didn't get high together. One night as I came back to the apartment after being gone all day, I saw a trail of blood leading to our door. When I walked inside, my parents weren't there but I saw blood everywhere. They had been beating each other up, so I hardly stayed there anymore. But at that moment, I didn't know if they were dead or alive.

It turns out, Mom hit Dad over the head with a crowbar and he was in the hospital. Dad recovered but Mom was on the run. Because she wasn't a U.S. citizen, she was being deported to Mexico for hitting someone else over the head and putting him in a coma. So when I found that out, I left the apartment and went to stay with friends at the Katella Hotel in Anaheim where we all got high together. That's when I went to the drug house and met Thomas. After spending the night together, I woke up the next morning and took a ball of meth that Thomas gave me. Then I went to Walmart and walked out carrying a box of clothes I didn't pay for, planning to sell them. But I got busted instead.

DOING TIME

That was my thing—I'd go into a Walmart, steal a bunch of expensive things, and then go back and say, "I don't want these but I lost my receipt." Then they'd hand me two or three hundred dollars.

I was sentenced to the Musick Jail Facility in Irvine. Thomas came to see me every weekend and he'd say, "When you're out, we'll get off dope and get clean together." He was always higher than a kite when he said it.

Thomas: I had big dreams for us—finding a job, moving into a place, and getting clean. I still had my Honda Accord that I'd bought with only eight miles on it for $30,000. For two years I was late on the payments, but because I'd worked in the financial industry, I knew how to avoid the repo man. Still, every time I saw a tow truck, I was afraid someone was coming after me to take the car.

After Crystal was in jail a couple of weeks, I looked online to see when she'd be released and found out she had only a week left. *That doesn't make sense*, I thought. *How the heck is she getting out so soon? Did she rat me out and tell them I'm a drug dealer?* I knew the charge for theft was at least a few months.

When I picked Crystal up on her release date, we got high on speed together and then had a big fight while I was driving. I started freaking out, thinking her sentence had been reduced because she snitched on me. Suddenly I pulled the car over to the side of the road and took out a knife. Shaking, I faced Crystal and held the knife to her neck. "Look, what are you doing?" I asked. "Are you after my car now too?" All I wanted was for her to give in and confess. But instead she started screaming.

Crystal: I told Thomas, "I don't even have a license. And I don't know how to drive!" Thomas was so high that he just sat there glaring at me. After a while, I asked if I could lay my head on his lap and he said okay. But he kept the knife at my throat for about forty-five minutes. Because I didn't confess anything, Thomas thought I wasn't taking him seriously. But I held my ground, knowing I hadn't done anything wrong and I wasn't after his car. Finally, he set the knife down and started driving again. All I wanted to do was get out.

Thomas: At the next stoplight, Crystal opened the passenger door, jumped out, and started walking. Five minutes later, she called me.

"Can you pick me up at the 7-11?" So I did. That's how it went for us—we'd get into fights, beat each other up, and then call each other back.

Crystal: We fought like cats and dogs. Sometimes when Thomas was driving on the freeway, I'd pull on the steering wheel and almost kill us both. And I'd always change my mind when I broke up with him.

ON THE RUN

Thomas: We stayed together for a year, homeless and mostly living out of my car. Crystal got locked up two more times for drugs. Sometimes we'd get to the place where we had no dope and no money so we'd stay with my mom, who lived in Murrieta. She blessed us a lot. And because she had become a Christian, she had one requirement when we stayed with her: we had to go to church.

Often we went with Mom to Calvary Chapel Menifee, which was my grandma's new church since she'd moved from Pomona to Menifee. Sometimes Crystal and I went to church high, and other times we were coming down off speed, but we'd still go to church. Tired of living on the streets, I tried for months to get sober, but I wasn't able to stay with it on my own.

One Sunday I noticed a glass-covered bookcase in the foyer of my grandma's church. Inside were pictures and testimonies of recovered addicts from a place called U-Turn For Christ. As I read through the testimonies of men and women who had been set free from drugs and alcohol, I wondered if that would ever happen for me.

Then I started breaking out in boils all over my body and I felt "dope sick" for about six months. Grandma looked into rehab programs like Teen Challenge and the Salvation Army, but I always found reasons not to go. She noticed me lingering at the U-Turn display one Sunday and asked, "What about U-Turn For Christ, Thomas? Look, I don't care where you go. Just let me know and I'll pay for it."

Taking a closer look at those U-Turn pictures, I realized all the guys looked pretty old and I thought, *I don't want to go to that old guy place.* Still, I said to Grandma, "All right, let's do it."

I knew Grandma could only afford to pay for me, so I broke the news later to Crystal: "Look, Babe, I'd love for you to go to U-Turn For Christ with me, but it's $800 and Grandma can't pay for both of us. I don't know what you're going to do, but I have to go."

Crystal: I loved Thomas and had tried to take care of him the best I could. Yet even when we stayed clean for a while, we still fought like crazy, even ripping each other's shirts off. It was bad. When Thomas told me he was going to U-Turn, all I could think to do was move in with my sister Vanessa and get clean on my own. Then Thomas' mom offered to pay half the money for me. And Pastor Jim from Calvary Chapel Menifee wanted to sponsor the other half. But first he called Pastor Gerry to ask his advice. "I've got this couple, Thomas and Crystal," Pastor Jim began, "but they're not really a couple."

As Pastor Jim explained our situation over the phone, Pastor Gerry listened and prayed. Then he said, "Tell Crystal that if she's serious about getting clean that you want her to attend three services at your church this weekend." So that's what I did. I stayed with Thomas' grandma and she drove me to all three church services—Saturday night, Sunday morning, and Sunday evening.

ADVENTURES IN PHASE 1

Thomas: Mom and Grandma took me to the men's ranch on a Friday in March 2006, and Crystal arrived on the following Monday. On my ninth day in the program, I went on a "bread run" with another guy in the program named Buddy. We were told to pick up day-old loaves of bread from a few local grocery stores, and we had permission to take the ministry truck. But along the way we stopped for a few other things, like cigarettes.

That evening at Bible study, Pastor Lance had one of his "confess-your-sins services," where he read Scripture and asked if anyone needed to confess anything and get right with the Lord. I looked over at Buddy and saw him squirming in his seat. Pretty soon, Buddy started blurting out everything we did.

"Who's your accountability?" Pastor Lance asked.

"Thomas," Buddy said, as I felt myself slink down in my chair while he went on to explain. "First we went to Thomas' grandma's house to get some silverware because all we have here is plastic, and I really wanted some metal knives and forks. Then we stopped at Carl's Jr., and after that we bought cigarettes. Finally, we picked up the bread in Yorba Linda." I never smoked a day in my life and Buddy smoked up the whole pack while I drove.

Pastor Lance gave us our discipline: dig a hole, write an essay, and restart the program. Upset, I walked back to my room and right in front of the overseers, I started cussing everybody out—all sixty guys in the bunkhouse. "I'll do the hole and the essay," I yelled, "but I won't restart the program because I need to graduate the same day as Crystal. Besides, why should I have to restart? It was all Buddy's thing!"

By then it was after midnight and I decided to leave. I packed my bags and tossed them on the side of the road, over by the women's ranch. Someone must have thought I was trying to get Crystal so they called the cops. But I started walking and got away before they arrived. I walked a long time, and at about 3 a.m. I reached the Wells Fargo Bank in Perris. I found a pay phone, called a taxi, and it showed up an hour later. "This place, man, they kicked me out and I need a ride," I explained. "Look, I only have five dollars and a CD player, but I need to get to my mom's in Murrieta."

"Don't worry about it," the driver said. "Just get in." When the taxi pulled into my mom's driveway at 5 a.m., the dashboard meter read $55. I thanked the guy again and again, then I got out and started knocking on my mom's bedroom window. She peeked through the shade to see who it was and she started crying and then opened the front door for me. "What are you doing?" she said. "Your grandma paid for you and you're supposed to be in Perris. What's going on?"

I felt bad. I didn't want to hurt my mom or my grandma. *Oh, man,* I thought. *What now?* Then, realizing I had forgotten my pillow and sleeping bag, I said, "I need to go back, Mom. I forgot my pillow and sleeping bag." At this point, someone might think, *Really? Who cares about that?* But I had this thing about using my own stuff, and I was determined to go back.

STARTING OVER

Thomas: Mom had to work a shift at Walmart that morning, so when she got off in the afternoon, we rode back together to the ranch. After we pulled in and parked, Mom and I walked toward the front gate where Rudy, one of the overseers, met us. "Hey, Rudy," I said, like nothing had happened.

Rudy stood in front of me so I couldn't get by. "What are you doing?" he asked. "You want to be a man and you want to get clean?"

"Yeah, you know…" I said, listing my excuses for leaving.

Rudy drew a line in the dirt with his shoe and looked straight at me. "You say you want to be a man? Well then, cross this line. Come back and do it right."

Then Mom started crying. "Just go, Thomas, just go!" she said.

"All right, I'll come back." I crossed the line and walked back to my room, ready to start over at day one. Because I had cussed out the bunkhouse at midnight, I had to dig two holes, write a 3,000-word essay, and wear the "word-fast vest" for two weeks. The word-fast vest looks like a safety construction vest, and whoever wears it can't talk to anyone, day or night, unless he needs to speak to a leader or discuss something work-related. I managed to finish all the discipline, and I graduated from Phase 1 two weeks after Crystal.

Crystal: I was nineteen and Thomas was twenty-one when we came to the ranch. At first, all I wanted to do was get the whole thing over with. I did well for most of Phase 1, but I did write a few essays.

For one thing, I thought my overseer, Suzy, had an annoying voice when she prayed, and I didn't like how happy she was. So I plugged my ears whenever she prayed. I tried to be discrete about it and do it underneath my hair. But then one time at Bible study I saw the other girls grinning and staring at me so I turned around and I'm like, "What?" That's when Phyllis, another overseer, noticed what I was doing and said, "Crystal, go to the pantry." The pantry was the counseling room, the place where we got disciplined. That was my first essay.

Another time during a service with Pastor Lance, he gave us the opportunity to confess our sins. "You don't want to go through the ranch experience with anything on your plate," he said. "You want to do it clean."

A girl in the program looked over at me and we both raised our hands at the same time to confess that we'd been smoking. Sometimes we'd confess and still get disciplined but that time we didn't. Pastor Lance prayed for us and we were "graced" out.

LIVING APART

When Thomas left the ranch after nine days, somehow I knew he was gone. Someone lined up all the vans to block off the women's ranch so he couldn't get in, and when I saw those vans, I knew it was because of Thomas. So I ran back to my room and started packing my stuff. Phyllis walked in while I was packing and sat down next to me. "What are you going to do, Crystal?" she asked. "Where will you go? He's got nothing. You'll be homeless."

I knew Phyllis was right, but I still cried. When Thomas returned to the ranch the following day, no one told me he was there. I felt heartbroken for a whole week—looking, hoping, and praying that he would come back. Phyllis watched me like a hawk. And Peggy Brown, Pastor Gerry's wife, told me, "Just trust the Lord, Crystal. He's got Thomas in His hands."

Whenever we had a chapel service with the men, the guys would sit in front of us and I would always search for the back of Thomas' head. Of course, at the time there were nine bald guys in the program and I couldn't tell if one of them was Thomas or not. Then one day Phyllis finally told me he was back. "He's been here several days now," she said. I remember just praising the Lord when I found out; I was so happy.

At the ranch, the men and women are kept separated, and we aren't allowed to have anything to do with each other. When women go to the men's ranch for a Bible study, we sit in the back and we aren't supposed to even look at the guys. Still, some girls gawk at the back of the guys' heads. I know, because I was looking for Thomas! But those were the rules and if you didn't follow them, you were disciplined.

Thomas: Let me tell you the men's perspective. When we sat up in front of the chapel at a service, we were not allowed to look back. We were supposed to keep our eyes forward and focused. We were there for one reason, and that was to hear the Word of God, not to look at women or anything else. And that's why, for a limited period of time, we had no communication with the opposite sex. We were encouraged to remember that the only relationship to worry about was the one we had with the Lord.

While Crystal was looking for me, I was looking for her too. She was assigned to a housekeeping work crew at Murrieta Bible College, and one time I asked someone there in housekeeping, "Does a girl named Crystal come here from the ranch?" Word got to the overseers that I was looking for Crystal, so they took her off the housekeeping crew and transferred her to the Western Eagle food bank. But because I worked as a driver for Western Eagle, they took her off the food bank crew and kept her at the ranch for the remainder of Phase 1. Knowing how much we missed one another, our overseers didn't want us running into each other and getting distracted from the program.

Finally I tried writing Crystal a letter. I was slick about it, using my mom's return address and being careful to mail the letter from the Bible college so it was stamped by the Murrieta post office. I remember thinking, *Sweet, I thought of everything!* But sure enough, when the letter arrived at the ranch, the leaders got suspicious. Someone opened it and read the first few words, "What's up, Baby?" Crystal never got the letter and I was disciplined.

MEETING JESUS

Crystal: God began working in my life as soon as I arrived at the ranch, and He spoke to me especially through the Bible studies. In the second week after Pastor Gerry's Friday night message, I went forward to give my life to the Lord. Feeling broken, I prayed for myself and for Thomas. *Lord, do a work in my life. And do a work in his life too. Break the prideful person that he is. And give him as many holes as he needs to dig.*

Thomas: God answered Crystal's prayer immediately! I dug a lot of holes, at least seven, and a couple more in Phase 2. But more importantly, I rededicated my life on that same Friday night service during the second week, alongside sixty broken men, thirty broken women, and all the families who joined us. Pastor Gerry gave the altar call and told us, "Hey, get right with the Lord, man," while Johnny Reno rocked out and led us in worship. I felt the Lord calling me through it all, so I walked up to the front and prayed, *Lord, I'm sick and tired* *of living this way. Please show me something from You, and I'll serve You for the rest of my life.*

As I walked back to my seat, I noticed the guy sitting in the seat next to mine—a baldheaded, gangster-looking guy from L.A. It was a trip because he was singing and praising the Lord with all his might, and I'd never seen anything like it. *Wow, Lord, look at this guy, just praising You!* That's how God answered my prayer and "showed me something." I surrendered to Him that night and never looked back.

From then on, I just wanted to read God's Word. I remember when I had to memorize a couple of verses from Philippians 4:6-7. Here's what it says:

> "Be anxious for nothing, but in everything by prayer and supplication, with thanksgiving, let your requests be made known to God; and the peace of God, which surpasses all understanding, will guard your hearts and minds through Christ Jesus."

I felt so anxious about learning these verses in only a week, and I thought, *Man, this is going to be too hard!* But I challenged myself, and with God's help, I recited the passage to my overseer the next week. I felt proud, but mostly thankful that God showed me how to be patient, not only in learning His Word, but also applying it.

Crystal: Proverbs 3:5-6 meant a lot to me during this time:

> "Trust in the LORD with all your heart and lean not on your own understanding. In all your ways acknowledge Him, and He shall direct your paths."

Since I was a little girl, I did my own thing and never listened to anyone. So to submit to someone else's authority, I had to keep praying, *Give me strength, Lord!*

A verse that helped me with this new mindset was Philippians 4:13, "I can do all things through Christ who strengthens me." For so much of my life, I had no clue what I was doing and I knew there had to be something better. I didn't know how good it could be, trusting God and His will for my life. His plans were far better than what I could have ever imagined.

After I gave my heart to the Lord, Peggy Brown shared with me later that she recognized "this is one that God wants to use." But because I was only nineteen, Peggy asked God for wisdom and discernment about giving me any kind of leadership position. I'd been in Phase 1 for six weeks when circumstances changed at the women's ranch—Phyllis was getting married, leaders were coming and going, and they needed someone to step in as an assistant overseer.

I think Peggy and the other leaders could see I followed the rules (I got better at it). I had confidence about serving the Lord, and I also had a lot of compassion for the other girls because I knew what they were going through. So I became the assistant overseer at the end of Phase 1. In that position, I began assigning work crew jobs, running set-up crew on Sundays, and just being there for the women.

MOVING TOWARD MARRIAGE

After I finished Phase 1, Pastor Lance called the women's ranch for me. Thomas and I were going to start marriage counseling.

I had no idea that was going to happen, but when I arrived I saw Thomas for the first time in two months. We sat down next to each other outside, both of us were nervous, yet we couldn't stop smiling. I felt so happy, knowing we were about to start the next chapter of our lives together—this time with God in the center. Pastor Lance and his wife, Yvonne, counseled us every week for six months. During those sessions we each wrote an essay. Thomas wrote about why he deserved to marry one of God's daughters, and I wrote why I deserved to marry one of God's sons. We still have those essays.

Thomas: After finishing Phase 1, I moved to the San Jacinto house and found a job doing electrical work for a construction project in Coachella Valley. I worked for a pastor friend who was an electrician and after training and school I became certified. Meanwhile, I visited Crystal every Sunday during visiting hours, from 12 to 5 p.m. During our visits, we took walks, played games, prayed, read the Word, and talked about our future, including how many kids we wanted. Every other week I gave Crystal one hundred dollars and told her to save it. God had convicted me about keeping my repossessed Honda, so we were saving for another vehicle.

Crystal: As we progressed along in our marriage counseling, one day Pastor Gerry finally said, "Let's set this wedding date!" So we chose November 18, 2006. With only weeks to plan our wedding, I wasn't sure where to start. My family wasn't speaking to me at the time, so I didn't have relatives to help me. But my future mother-in-law, Sue, came to visit me often, and I loved that. She was always there for me, and we became very close. I even began calling her Mom.

When Sue and I walked into David's Bridal a few weeks before my wedding, I felt overwhelmed when I saw the rows of bridal gowns, not to mention the price tags. "Just pick one!" Sue said cheerfully.

What's she talking about? She can't afford this! Heading for the clearance rack at the rear of the store, I saw my dress right away, in my size and marked down to $129. I loved everything about it, from the elegant train and dainty shoulder straps to the pearl-and-sequin-covered bodice. In the dressing room, Sue helped me zip up the long white gown, and when I walked out and stood in front of the three-way mirror, I knew it was perfect. Next, we picked out a matching tiara, veil, earrings, necklace, and shoes. Leaving the store, I turned to Sue and said, "You know, that was a total God thing!" I couldn't stop thanking her.

As we were driving back, Sue asked, "What color do you like, Crys?"

"I don't know," I said. "Peach?"

Then as if my dress and accessories weren't enough, Sue stopped at Michael's and bought everything we needed for the reception—plates, napkins, streamers, candles, and a cake topper.

GOD'S PRINCESS

A week before the wedding, my grandparents came to visit me at the ranch, and it was the first time I'd seen them in years. "Are you sure you want to marry this guy?" they asked, thinking I was too young to marry. "How about if you just date him and go to college?" But when they saw how much I loved Thomas, they finally said, "If this is what you want, Crystal, then we'll be there." They both came to the wedding, and God restored our relationship. We talked to each other every day after that.

Thomas: Peggy orchestrated everything for our wedding, and Calvary Chapel Romoland came alongside to help with the details. They even provided a finger food buffet for the reception. Fifty people came to celebrate with us, and it was like a U-Turn For Christ family wedding.

Crystal: We had a simple service at Calvary Chapel Romoland. No bridesmaids or groomsmen, just Thomas and me. Grandpa walked me down the aisle, Pastor Gerry officiated, Pastor Johnny played the worship, Pastor Anthony led us in communion, and Pastor Mario took pictures. All the women from U-Turn attended because they were my girls. Because I was serving at the ranch, I couldn't really get into the wedding planning, but many people helped and it all came together beautifully. Besides my grandparents, my dad also attended the wedding. The Lord's hand was in it all, and we even honeymooned in San Diego for a week.

At the ranch I was often told, "You are the King's daughter," and I actually felt that on my wedding day. I felt like God was blessing His daughter for being faithful and serving Him. My faith was built on knowing that God was my Father, the King, and I was His princess.

Because of that, I realized I was worth more than I ever thought. He was my Father who sent His Son to die for me. And seeing the way He cared for me, I felt very pampered by my King.

MARRIAGE AND MINISTRY

To save money, Thomas and I planned to move in with his mom after the wedding. Pastor Gerry found out about our plan and took me aside. "Do you really want to move in with Thomas' mom, Crystal?" he asked. "Wouldn't you and Thomas rather stay here while you continue working at the women's ranch?" I liked that idea and I said yes.

Thomas: Pastor Gerry talked to me too, and I told him we'd stay with Mom only until we could afford to move. "No, you won't," he said. "In Genesis 2:24, the Bible says to 'leave your father and mother' and be joined to your wife."

Feeling helpless, I said, "Well, that's the best I've got, Pastor. I've been thinking about this for six months and I've got nothing else."

"How about if you move into the small trailer at the women's ranch?" he offered. So that's what we did. Crystal worked with the women, and we started getting plugged in at Calvary Chapel Romoland and at the ranch. I began ushering at the church, teaching youth group, leading a home fellowship, counseling guys in Phase 1, and sometimes teaching on Friday nights. God used all these things to train me for the ministry. Then in November of 2007, we welcomed a son, Thomas Jr. We soon outgrew our trailer and moved to one side of the Marcum House, which was the house used for the guys in Phase 2.

OUT OF THE FIRE

As Thomas Jr. grew, I couldn't help but think about my dad. He still lived on the streets, moving from woman to woman, drinking and getting high. Seeing his lifestyle was difficult for me, especially because I used to do it with him. For years I prayed for him and pleaded, "Dad, you need to come to the ranch."

Finally one day Dad promised, "Okay, I'll go after the holidays." So in 2008, right after New Year's, I called and said, "Dad, I'm coming to get you right now, regardless." As soon as Crystal and I arrived at his place, we started packing his stuff into trash bags to take with us. Then Dad said, "What about my TV and radio?"

"Oh, you won't be needing those," I said, trying not to smile.

If I hadn't pushed him, I don't know if Dad would have gone to U-Turn. He was strong, prideful, and he ran with prison gangs most of his life, even working for the Mexican Mafia. A small man with tattoos all over his body, Dad never flinched at the biggest, toughest guys in prison. Jude 22 says,

> "And on some have compassion, making a distinction; but others save with fear, pulling them out of the fire, hating even the garment defiled by the flesh."

By the time we brought Dad to U-Turn For Christ, I felt like we were pulling him right out from the fire of his hell on earth.

Once when I visited my dad during his Phase 1, I found him at "the three crosses," a place where the guys gather each night to pray and share praises. Dad sat alone in front of one of the six-foot crosses, and as I approached, I saw that he'd been crying. "What's wrong?" I asked, sitting down next to him.

"Man, I'm tired of living this way," he said. "I feel so broken."

I believe my dad knew the Lord but just needed to get back on track with Him. For over thirty years, his life had followed a pattern of getting locked up, finding the Lord in prison, getting out, and then walking away from Him. Dad had never experienced an established relationship with God, but that night by the crosses, he surrendered and the Lord began using him. Dad came into his own as a leader, serving as an assistant head overseer and ministering powerfully to the guys at the ranch. Now both my mom and dad knew Jesus.

FINDING CRYSTAL'S MOM

After being ordained in 2010, I attended a U-Turn For Christ pastors conference in Mexico, and I recruited four other pastors to help me search for Crystal's mom there because we'd lost contact with her. With Pastor Jose Alvarado serving as interpreter, we hit the streets of Ensenada for six hours, inquiring at missions and asking different people if they knew her. We learned she was known there as "la bandida," the bandit, and finally someone pointed out an abandoned industrial building and said, "She's over there."

We found Crystal's mom sleeping on a dirt floor in a back room, on drugs and with a bucket for a bathroom. It was our first meeting, and after telling her who I was and that I was married to her daughter, I offered to help her. At first she hesitated, but then she said yes, she wanted help. Next she climbed into the truck with us and we escorted her to a local women's ministry called the Genesis House, where she came to know the Lord.

Crystal: God restored Mom's life at the Genesis House. She stayed for three years, and then she was hired at the Gabriel House, an orphanage for disabled children. There Mom was trained to stretch and exercise the children's limbs since most of them couldn't move. Mom earned a paycheck, got her own apartment, and learned how to live on her own. She even started learning how to be a mom. We eventually bought Mom a cell phone. She never had one before and had no idea how to use it. One time she called me from Mexico and asked, "How do I text?" It was a little difficult to explain it long distance, but it was a joy knowing my mom was restored.

MOVING ON

Thomas: I continued doing electrical work with Pastor Brad, but then the recession hit and I was laid off. *Lord, what am I going to do? How will I pay the bills?* I prayed. Jumping from job to job, I managed to make ends meet for several months, and then I got a call from the Calvary Chapel Bible College and they hired me as their head electrician. The job came with a two-bedroom condo, utilities, and even meals. We loved living there. But it didn't last for long.

Three months later, Pastor Gerry asked me to pray about pastoring a U-Turn For Christ in Camino, California. At the time, Crystal was pregnant with our second child, Isabel. I visited the Camino facility and prayed, but I didn't feel God's leading. Eight months later, the need resurfaced and Pastor Gerry asked me again. "Okay, Pastor, I'll pray," I said.

The Lord gave me a Scripture, Joshua 1:9: "Do not be afraid nor be dismayed, for the LORD your God is with you wherever you go." I fasted and prayed, *Lord, this is such a huge step! You've got to show me something so I'll know this is from You.* Then He brought me back to the same Scripture in Joshua, "I will be with you wherever you go."

I laid it all out to Crystal. "Look, this is what the Lord's giving me, and you need to make sure He's giving you the same thing. Because if we go, we're going together, and I need to know that you've got my back on this." Crystal prayed about it, and the Lord gave her the same answer. So we packed everything in a U-Haul and in October of 2010 we headed up to Camino in the northeast part of the state. We moved into a 500-square-foot apartment, and it turned out to be one of the worst winters Camino ever had. With sixty feet of snow, we were spinning all over the place when we drove, doing dough-nuts in the middle of the road.

Crystal and I felt devastated that first year and we questioned our move. We missed our families terribly, as well as our family in Christ. Yet we stood on God's promises and prayed, *Lord, we know You gave us this work and called us to this place. So we're going to be faithful.*

HEALING

When I moved to Camino in 2010 I told my dad, "I want you to come with me." But he said no, that the Lord had called him to stay in Perris. Then Dad came up for Christmas a few months later to check things out, and God gave him a heart for Camino. He asked Pastor Gerry if he could join me here in the ministry, and he moved up in 2011. Now he serves as the assistant pastor at the ranch and also manages our thrift store. He's doing such a great job here, especially with the hard-core guys.

Dad's in his mid-sixties, and in his words, "There's no such thing as retirement." He's not only a blessing to the ministry, but he's also making up for lost time with his grandkids.

Crystal: When I lived out on the streets, I didn't even talk to my family, but now God has restored my relationship with each one of them. I visited my mom a couple of years ago, and she said, "You know, I was never able to be a mother to my kids, and there's nothing I can do about that. But I want you to know I'm so sorry for what I did."

Mom's confession meant a lot. "I don't want you to live with that on your back anymore," I told her, "because for me, it's all water under the bridge." There's been a lot of healing in my mom's life, yet she still struggles. Satan robbed her of a lot, but I will never lose hope for her.

SPIRITUAL PARENTS

Peggy Brown became like a mom to me while I lived at the ranch. I never had a mom to take care of me, so Peggy was my spiritual mom, the one I went to about everything. Even after I got married, I'd go to Peggy and say, "I'm going crazy—what do I do?" She was the only one I had, so I asked for her advice about my babies, my marriage, and about the women at the ranch. She spent time with me, prayed for me, and talked to me on the phone almost every day. Sometimes I even spent my days off with her.

To me, Peggy is an example of a woman after God's own heart. All day, every day she lives her life selflessly for the Lord as a strong, supportive wife to Pastor Gerry. She's always there for her kids and for the women at the ranch. Even today if I go to her for counsel, she always takes me to the Word. I love her.

Thomas: I appreciate the way Pastor Gerry cares for his family, loves his wife, disciples his flock, and runs the U-Turn For Christ ministry. His example has been so influential. Pastor Gerry and Peggy are our spiritual parents and today they are still a big part of our lives. We praise the Lord for both of them.

AT HOME IN CAMINO

Crystal: Thomas and I are a strong team! Through the Lord, we have overcome so many obstacles together. Today I'm a stay-at-home, homeschooling mom to our three kids: Thomas Jr., Isabel, and Trinity, our youngest who was born in 2012. Being a mom has brought out the best in me. Moving to the mountains from Southern California was a huge adjustment for us. For one thing, we had to learn how to drive in the snow, but now we love it here. It's been an amazing blessing for us to be used by God through U-Turn For Christ.

Thomas: My marriage to Crystal constantly reminds me of God's grace, and I'm so grateful that He saw fit to bless me with one of His daughters. Crystal is my greatest encourager and critic at the same time. We've both had a lot of adversity in our lives, and when we came to the Lord, we didn't want to solve conflicts in our flesh anymore. We've learned how to come to the Lord with our problems, talk things out, get into God's Word, and pray together. We try to live by Ephesians 4:26: "In your anger do not sin; do not let the sun go down while you are still angry" (NIV). Because of God's work of grace in our lives, He gives peace to our hearts, our marriage, and our family.

Now that I have two daughters of my own, I'm even more conscious of how I treat my wife, because I know that little eyes are watching.

Being a dad has helped me have compassion for the families I deal with at U-Turn For Christ Camino, and it helps me express love to those dads who are hurting.

Camino is a small town, with a population of about 1,750. Our U-Turn For Christ is affiliated with Calvary Chapel Placerville, and with six other guys on staff, our program usually has anywhere from ten to twenty men. The guys serve in work crews at our U-Turn For Christ thrift store located down the street, and they also help out in the community and local churches.

EARS TO HEAR

When I was ten, I felt the Lord calling me, convicting me, and tugging at my heart for the first time. Though I tried to run away, I always knew my life was meant for a specific purpose—that I was meant to serve God. I learned the hard way that I'm only one dumb mistake away from being right where I started. I need the Lord more and more, every second of the day, and I've learned to depend on him for everything.

Here at U-Turn for Christ Camino, I see men's lives changed, just like mine. I see guys come into this ministry completely broken and I watch them leave restored. I see them getting back together with their wives, their children, and their families. This is my motivation to keep pushing ahead and I want to provide the best facility possible, where men are discipled for Jesus Christ.

Sometimes the hardest thing to do for our loved ones is nothing—nothing except give them over to the Lord and pray. Sometimes it means letting them get flat on their back, with absolutely no resources, until they look up and see Jesus Christ. And when that happens, we can welcome them home with open arms.

Izzy, Thomas, Crystal, Trinity Grace and Thomas Jr.

Lord, when You do a work in us, it is so beautiful, but when You do a work in two of us as a couple, it doesn't get any better!

Please be with Thomas and Crystal and their precious family as they continue to reach out to those in their community and lead people to Jesus. Use them like never before and open a new work for the two of them as they give all the glory to You.

In Jesus' name, Amen.

U-TURN FOR CHRIST CAMINO, CALIFORNIA
Pastor Thomas & Crystal Mendez
Physical Address: 5649 Pony Express Trail Camino, CA 95709
Mailing Address: P O Box 626 Camino, CA 95709
(530) 644-1982
email: info@uturnforchristcamino.com
website: www.uturnforchristcamino.com

CHAPTER 11

Let him who thinks he stands take heed lest he fall.

1 CORINTHIANS 10:12

PASTOR STEVE MATTIER
Prodigal Pastor

Weaving through Los Angeles traffic, Steve turned up the oldies station and belted out a song, "I've got sunshine on a cloudy day…" Excited to be back in his hometown, he reminisced about growing up here—bussing tables at his grandma's restaurant, singing gospel music at the neighborhood church, and performing in a Doo Wop band with friends. He remembered the hard times, too, spending sixteen years as a drug addict. Now an influential pastor and overseer at U-Turn For Christ in Lexington, South Carolina, Steve marveled at the new life the Lord had given him in the past few years.

Now on his way to visit family in L.A., Steve reflected upon the sweet fellowship that he had spent reuniting with his fellow pastors at the annual Pig Roast at the U-Turn For Christ ranch in Perris, California, the day before. It was such a blessing sharing all the latest news about the ministry in Lexington to Pastor Gerry. It had been a year since Steve had visited the ranch, where he'd been officially ordained as a pastor in 2002.

Then, a familiar exit on the 110 freeway caught Steve's attention, Century Boulevard, which led to Figueroa Street. Well-known for prostitution and drugs, Figueroa used to be one of Steve's regular hangouts. Feeling curious about the area, he was drawn to check it out, and suddenly he veered his rental car onto the Century Boulevard exit. As he turned onto Figueroa, women in tight skirts and spiked heels sauntered by, looking for customers. Steve pulled his car over and rolled down the window. A woman caught his gaze and ran to his car, opened the passenger door, and let herself in.

This is Steve's story.

"I need to stop here first," the woman said as we approached the next corner. Puzzled, I glanced over at her, noticing her nervous anticipation, and knew exactly what she needed. I waited in the car while she made her transaction. Back a few minutes later, she folded a little bag of white powder and slipped it inside her purse.

We checked into a motel, and with a trembling hand, I turned the key to our room and flipped on the lights. "I'll be right back," the woman announced as she hurried off to the bathroom. Before closing the door, she turned around, holding up the bag of cocaine. "Want some?"

"Absolutely not." I said firmly. "I'm no addict!"

I sat on the bed, flipping TV channels, and a voice in my head began: "So you call yourself a pastor? You just came from a pastors conference? What a joke!" I jumped up, wanting to run, but instead I walked over to the bathroom and knocked on the door. The woman opened it partway.

"What?" she said.

"Can I have some?"

"But I thought you…"

I opened the door the rest of the way and saw her holding the pipe of crack cocaine. Taking a hit, I felt the old familiar rush and knew that I wanted—no, I needed—to feel this way for a long, long time. Whatever it took, I had to stop the guilt, the shame, and the accusing voice inside my head. I needed to block it all out. And that's what I did.

The rest of that night passed in a blur, and we didn't do anything together except take more hits. The next morning I drove the woman back to Figueroa Street, and then I went to her supplier and purchased my own stash. Stopping off at a liquor store, I bought alcohol, and then I holed myself up in the motel, smoking crack cocaine, drinking, and bringing in a couple of prostitutes. When my $2,000 savings account was gone, I pulled out a credit card to buy more. After my card reached its $2,000 limit, I pulled out another card and maxed that one out too. At the end of three weeks, I had spent $6,000 and was penniless.

With no cash or credit left, I felt a dark sense of impending doom, and reality set in quickly. I had brought shame on the ministry, and I experienced deep conviction for letting the Lord down, not to mention all the guys in South Carolina. I'd made such a horrible mess of things. What would I do now?

REMEMBERING

I remembered back to when life had been so simple, so carefree. Growing up in Watts, a neighborhood in South Los Angeles, I was the middle child with two brothers, Ronald and Anthony. We were all close, raised by a single mom, Rosa, and by our grandmother, Ophelia McFashion, who lived next door. I never knew my father, but Mom and Grandma both worked hard to provide for us.

My grandma, the matriarch of the family, stood only 4 feet 11 inches tall, and she had a strong, intense personality—a real firecracker. Her home was the hub for all holidays, birthdays, and family celebrations. My cousin, Jackie, a few years older than me, lived nearby and she was like a sister to me.

Before the Watts riots in the mid-'60s, our neighborhood was a peaceful, safe place. We lived on a dead-end street, and though I was never fast or strong enough to play sports, my sport was socializing and hanging out with friends. We weren't raised Christian, but Mom sent us to Sunday School every week at the church at the end of the road. It's what all parents did in our African-American community, even if they didn't go to church themselves. I was a happy, easygoing kid, but without a father as a role model, I had no real direction in life.

Mom worked as a nursing assistant, and when I was very young, I remember she wore a white uniform. By the time I reached middle school, she had changed jobs and became a waitress in my grandma's newly opened restaurant, McFashion's Café. Grandma served the best soul food I've ever eaten: fried chicken, ham hocks, collard greens, red beans and rice, sweet potato cornbread, and a peach cobbler that was par excellence. My brothers and I worked at the restaurant too, washing dishes, bussing tables, counting money— everything except the cooking. Only Grandma cooked! We had fun helping at the restaurant and the regular customers became like family. Our experience there gave us all a strong work ethic: "If a man doesn't work, he shouldn't eat." The restaurant became so popular that Grandma later opened a second McFashion's Café.

In my last year of middle school, we left our Watts neighborhood and moved to West L.A., where Mom's boyfriend married her and bought us a nice house. My brothers and I changed schools, and because we lived farther away, we worked less hours at the café.

In those days, Motown was all the rage, and like most young boys, I idolized groups like The Temptations and The Four Tops. I dreamed of singing Doo Wop music, and since God had gifted me with a decent voice, I began performing with local bands and appearing in talent shows. Once I joined the music scene, I learned quickly that drugs and alcohol were available wherever we performed. I tried marijuana and alcohol for the first time when I was fourteen and continued using recreationally throughout high school.

According to cousin Jackie, I was the smart kid in the family, the one who got good grades and was considered a nerd in school. And yet, I never felt like I worked to my potential—I wanted to have fun instead. During my senior year at George Washington Preparatory High, I had a friend whose mom was also single and she let her son do whatever he wanted. She had given him the entire third floor of their house as his own personal space, complete with a built-in stereo and black lights. In the final weeks of our senior year, while most classmates prepared for commencement, I stayed at this friend's house with six other guys and we smoked marijuana for two weeks straight. Pooling our money together, we purchased a huge amount of weed, and we rolled joints and smoked continuously. Finally I realized, *Man, I gotta get back to school!*

Meanwhile, my mom knew I was staying with a friend but she didn't know I wasn't going to school, until the office called her two weeks later, asking where I was. Since I was so close to graduating, the school authorities said I needed to write ten essays in one day if I wanted to graduate. Somehow I pulled it off, and I graduated with my class in 1971.

FALLING OFF THE CAREER LADDER

Unprepared for life after high school, I felt aimless for several years. My grandmother had sold her restaurants, and I hadn't applied to any colleges or universities. Then in 1977, Jackie, who worked for

General Telephone, helped me get a job as a telephone operator. I did well in that position, and by 1979 I was promoted to management. But after relocating to Orange County, my drug use escalated when a co-worker introduced me to cocaine. Every two weeks on payday, I'd make my purchase, and my co-worker and I would sit up together all night snorting cocaine, drinking, and smoking pot.

In 1983 I began smoking rock cocaine and I loved it. This type was a pure form and it felt different than ether-based cocaine, which had made me sick when I smoked it. By December of that year, I was promoted to a supervisory position, and I moved back to L.A. to live with my grandmother and help her out. As a supervisor, I made good money and I loved my job. Then I began smoking crack, and by June of 1984, the cocaine had so taken over my life that I voluntarily walked away from my job. For seven years, I had loved working for General Telephone, but my job had gotten in the way of my cocaine.

After losing my job, I disappeared, hiding out at my girlfriend's place and smoking crack. No one in my family knew where I was until I showed up two months later at my grandmother's house. When I arrived, Grandma immediately sat me down at the kitchen table with a family friend who asked, "What's going on, Steve?" Too ashamed to admit my addictions, I told them I'd had a nervous breakdown, and they believed me. This family friend gave me a thousand dollars to catch up on my car payment because, up until that point, I'd been a good kid and held down a steady job. Besides, my cocaine use wasn't visibly evident yet.

LIVING FOR THE NEXT HIGH

Many of the friends I hung out with had made it in Hollywood, either in music, movies, or behind the scenes. I ran with the "in" crowd, where people walked around carrying little vials, and if they spread the cocaine out on a table for their friends, they were considered cool. And if they smoked it, they were even more cool. Not until years later did any of us recognize the long-term effects—how it took away our jobs and destroyed our lives. The very first time I tried cocaine, I was addicted. The high was euphoric, and it entrapped me immediately.

Returning to live with my grandma, I settled into a routine: find a job, make some money, go out and get high, disappear, and eventually go back home. I never used drugs around my family because I felt too ashamed. I wasn't one to go out and get crazy and then come back begging for help. So I'd go off with friends and stay away, sometimes for months at a time. Naturally as a result, all my family relationships became very strained, with lost birthdays, Mother's Days, Thanksgivings, and Christmases. My disappearances took a huge toll on my mother, and grandmother especially, hurting them a lot.

Yet even during those difficult times, I felt loved by them both. They never turned me away or told me to shape up—they were simply glad to have me around. Sometimes, though, it was like having an elephant in the room because we never talked about my drug use. Instead, they'd say things like, "How are you doing, Steve?" or "Hope you're getting better." They knew I was using, but they simply never brought it up. They always held out hope for me.

My disappearances soon became the norm, and I was gone for days, weeks, months, or even a year at a time. Remembering that time, my cousin, Jackie, recalls, "We searched hospitals and went to see every John Doe at the morgue who fit Steve's description. It was awful. Then one day Steve appeared at his grandma's front door, looking like something out of a horror movie. He'd lost a lot of weight and looked like he hadn't bathed in a long time. We were shocked when we saw him, wondering how this could have happened."

For sixteen years, I went through a series of treatment programs—twenty-five of them—trying to find help. The county government offered very accessible rehab programs and gave out "general relief" to single men, which included food stamps and a monthly stipend.

The longest time I stayed sober was eleven months and the shortest time was a few days.

During one season of sobriety in 1990, I reconnected with a woman I'd dated in high school and we got married. Although she was aware of my battles with addiction, I happened to be doing well at the time of our marriage so she thought I was cured and we'd live happily ever after. However, my problems resurfaced and affected our marriage big time.

I made a few unsuccessful attempts at walking with the Lord. In 1994, I entered the Union Rescue Mission in Downtown L.A., and along with the Twelve-Step program, we were required to participate in a Bible study. A chaplain on staff pastored a small church nearby, and my wife and I started attending. One Sunday I went forward at an altar call, but I didn't know what Christians were supposed to do after that because I had no example to follow, no one to disciple me. Our marriage ended two years later in 1996.

FINDING U-TURN

Later I was hired as a volunteer coordinator for a rehab program called Midnight Mission, where I worked for a total of two years, in between staying sober, getting high, and starting over. One night when I didn't show up for work, my supervisor, Carrie, went out looking for me and found me out on the streets, bingeing on drugs. After bringing me back to the mission, Carrie sat me down and said, "What do you want to do now, Steve?"

"I want help," I said.

Carrie told me about U-Turn For Christ, where her friend, Erin, worked. Pastor Erin did my intake assessment over the phone, and a few days later, someone from the mission drove me to the ranch in Perris. I remember that day so clearly, June 22, 2000, a couple of months before my 47th birthday.

Accustomed to the big city, I immediately experienced culture shock in Perris, which was like a desert. Another adjustment was the way U-Turn For Christ did church, which was completely different from the churches I'd attended in the black community. For one thing, I was used to being preached at instead of learning the Bible verse-by-verse. And in our community, we had choirs singing and a soulful instrumental sound. But more than anything else, the thing that stood out to me the most was watching godly men who truly lived out their faith—I'd never seen that up close before.

As the weeks passed, the Holy Spirit started chipping away at my stony heart, and in its place He gave me a softened heart. I had come to the ranch feeling exhausted, so tired of trying to get better. But as I learned the Word of God day after day, the Holy Spirit grabbed hold of me and began making me into a new person.

Ezekiel 11:19-21 reads,

> "'Then I will give them one heart, and I will put a new spirit within them, and take the stony heart out of their flesh, and give them a heart of flesh, that they may walk in My statutes and keep My judgments and do them; and they shall be My people, and I will be their God. But as for those whose hearts follow the desire for their detestable things and their abominations, I will recompense their deeds on their own heads,' says the Lord God."

This Scripture rang true with me.

Being forty-seven years old, I carried myself in a way that showed I was serious. I didn't want any more foolishness, and I viewed U-Turn through the work ethic that my grandmother had taught me. If I was given a task, I simply did it. Because I had studied the Bible at the Union Rescue Mission, I knew my way around it too. I sincerely wanted to change my life—really, for the first time.

My plan was to stay at U-Turn for two months, enough time to finish Phase 1, and then head back to L.A., find a job, and move on with my life. But after six weeks in the program, an overseer took me aside and asked me to pray about staying on to become an assistant overseer. Right away I thought, *No way, I didn't come here for that! I want to get my life together and then leave.*

However, I'd been hearing a lot about obedience and the importance of listening to those in authority. So I began praying about staying on and I went to two trusted friends at the ranch, one at a time, asking what they thought about it. They both agreed it was a good idea. I continued praying and God gave me peace. "Yes, I'll do it!" I finally told my overseer.

As soon as I said yes, doubts flooded my mind: *I can't believe you just did that! Do you even know what you're getting yourself into? You'll be here for months!* and my skepticism continued on and on. Even so, I knew deep down in my heart that it was what the Lord wanted me to do. This was the moment of true surrender for me, when I stopped trying to figure out my own life and said yes to what the Lord was calling me to do.

MOVING TO LEXINGTON

After completing Phase 1 and serving as an assistant overseer for seven months, Pastor Gerry sent me on a new assignment as overseer of the U-Turn For Christ ranch in Lexington, South Carolina. The facility had started the previous year as an outreach of Calvary Chapel Lexington, and John Hoppe, the church's senior pastor, took me under his wing when I arrived in 2001.

Interestingly, several years before, my mom had moved to Augusta, Georgia, and since that time, she'd often asked me to come and live with her there because she and my stepfather had divorced. I always responded with, "Mom, I could never live out in the country!" But

God knew what He was doing because after I moved to Lexington, I was able to jump on the interstate and visit her in less than an hour.

The ministry in Lexington became a labor of love for me, yet I looked forward to returning to U-Turn in Perris the following summer for the annual Pig Roast and pastors conference. Being ordained by Pastor Gerry in 2002 turned out to be a great blessing, and I anticipated another sweet reunion in 2003.

THE TRIP THAT CHANGED EVERYTHING

When I left for California that summer, my church in Lexington happened to be in the middle of a major construction project, erecting a "sprung" building on the church property. It's like a structure resembling a huge tent. The men from U-Turn were providing the labor for this project, and during my absence, my assistant Mike Armor doubled up on his responsibilities to keep the project going. Before I left, Pastor John took me aside to talk. I told him my itinerary after landing at the airport in L.A. "First I'll head out to the ranch in Perris. Then I'm meeting a friend at church in Santa Monica," I said, "and then I'm picking up my brother Ronald in L.A. and we'll visit Grandma at the nursing home."

Pastor John nodded thoughtfully, and then he said. "Make sure you have someone with you when you drive through L.A."

"Of course," I agreed. "I'm planning on it."

At the airport, I rented a car and then drove to Perris for the annual U-Turn For Christ Pig Roast. The next day, I started feeling a little cocky. *I've been gone for two years now,* I reasoned, *so I really don't need anyone with me when I drive through L.A. I'll be fine!*

That's how it all started, driving alone on the freeway and getting caught up in the music, the memories, and the passions of my old life. Breaking my promise for accountability didn't seem like a big deal at the moment. I had grown pretty confident in my abilities as a Bible teacher and leader. I knew the Lord had gifted me, and I also knew I was really good at it. But the scariest part was that when I studied the Bible to prepare for teaching, I no longer saw God's Word as something that applied to me. Instead, I viewed myself only as a "dispenser" of the Word, believing I had arrived and could overcome temptation all by myself.

But when I spent all my money on the drugs, the reality of it punched me in the face. Because of my sin and selfishness, I ended up crying out to God like I never had before. Deep down, I was a coward; I didn't like owning up to my mistakes! My go-to method of dealing with things had always been to run. But this time, realizing the depths of my sin, there was nowhere to hide. I knew I had to find my way back to God—and fast—before I ended up dead on the streets.

STARTING OVER

We have a saying at U-Turn For Christ: "No matter how long you've been there, if you stumble and fall into sin, you go back to Day 1, Phase 1." And on that day when I came to my senses, sitting alone in my motel room feeling guilty and ashamed, I called U-Turn in Perris and confessed what I did. Someone came to get me and drove me to the ranch, and when I arrived, I wept like a baby. The next morning I started Phase I all over again—waking up at 5:30 a.m., going to Bible study, serving on work crew, going to more Bible study, reading Proverbs by the campfire, and memorizing Scripture. The body of Christ surrounded me and loved on me. Then I got alone before the Lord and asked for His forgiveness, and I apologized to my church in Lexington.

During that first week, Pastor Gerry didn't say anything to me because he wanted me to spend time alone with the Lord. After a week had passed, he invited me into his office. Now anyone who knows Pastor Gerry knows that he has a commanding presence, and I was especially aware of it that day! But when I walked into his office, he smiled one of those megawatt smiles, gave me a big hug and said, "I love you, Steve." Then he opened his Bible to John 21:15-17 and read to me.

> "So when they had eaten breakfast, Jesus said to Simon Peter, 'Simon, son of Jonah, do you love Me more than these?'
>
> "He said to Him, 'Yes, Lord; You know that I love You.'
>
> "He said to him, 'Feed My lambs.' He said to him again a second time, 'Simon, son of Jonah, do you love Me?'
>
> "Peter said to Jesus, 'Yes, Lord; You know that I love You.'
>
> "Jesus said to him, 'Tend My sheep.' He said to him the third time, 'Simon, son of Jonah, do you love Me?'
>
> "Peter was grieved because Jesus said to him the third time, 'Do you love Me?'
>
> "And Peter said to Him, 'Lord, You know all things; You know that I love You.'
>
> "Finally Jesus said to him, 'Then feed My sheep.'"

In those moments with Pastor Gerry, I was personally handed a plate loaded full of grace and forgiveness. He not only shared the story of how Jesus restored Peter after he had denied the Lord, but Pastor Gerry and I were actually living it out. I truly experienced the Lord's forgiveness that day. And that's what U-Turn is all about.

I stayed in Perris for nine months. After that, any apprehensions I may have had about returning to Lexington were short-lived, because just like the prodigal son, my church welcomed me back with open arms. I gratefully stepped back into ministry, but this time with a humbled heart.

LOSS AND GAIN

In 2004, two significant events happened. First, my dear grand-mother, Ophelia McFashion, passed away from a stroke. I'll always be grateful for her loving influence and example of integrity, hard work, and character. The second major event was meeting my beau-tiful wife, Merol. I first noticed Merol in church one Sunday morn-ing, and she looked absolutely stunning—there's no other way to put it. Right after the service, I introduced myself and within a few weeks I knew I'd be asking her to be my wife.

Merol has three adopted children: Joshua, who was then eight; Diamond, seven; and Elijah, five. As I got to know the children, I loved their mother even more. We dated for eight months and were married by Pastor John on April 24, 2005. During our wedding cer-emony, I said my vows to both Merol and the children, committing to love and cherish them all to glorify and honor God.

In 2012, I lost my beloved mother, Rosa, to bladder cancer. Mom had been a believer since 1972, and from that time on she had prayed for my brothers and me. During all those years that I was lost and caught up in the world, my mother later told me she had always been praying for me. I believe her prayers changed the course of my life and that she's the reason I'm still here.

Living closer to my mom when I moved back to South Carolina meant that I got to help her when she became sick with cancer—vis-iting her in the hospital, reporting to my brothers, and taking care of her estate. On one occasion, before the Lord took Mom home, it was just the two of us in her hospital room and she said, "Son, I'm so glad the Lord brought you out here because He knew I was going to need you for this time." It was a poignant moment that I'll always treasure.

Mom's cancer brought healing between my brothers and me. Because of my past lifestyle, we had become estranged, and whenever we talked on the phone, I was always the one who called them. But when Mom got sick, they flew out to Lexington, stayed in my home, and even came to hear me preach. After that, they started calling me, and God healed the animosity between us. Now when Ronald calls, sometimes he says, "Steve, I just wanted to hear your voice."

UPDATE

Merol homeschools our three children. Joshua is now eighteen and a senior in high school. In addition to school, he works part-time and operates one of the cameras for our Sunday church services. Diamond is sixteen and plays the drums in the worship team for children's ministry. Elijah is fourteen, likes basketball, and enjoys playing Sonic Hedgehog on the Wii.

Fatherhood has affected me tremendously. I'm normally an analytical, no-nonsense kind of guy, but I've learned that parenting doesn't work that way. I've had to adjust, compromise, and change! Parenting helps me appreciate God's grace, because I need so much of it myself.

The U-Turn For Christ ministry in Lexington continues to grow, averaging forty to fifty male residents per month. We serve in the jails; help with community projects; support an annual Run with the King event (celebrating Martin Luther King); and assist with a local agency called LICS (Lexington Interfaith Community Services), which provides food, clothing and shelter for people in crisis. We've also sent out two missionary teams that have started U-Turn For Christ ministries internationally—in Jacó, Costa Rica and in Trinidad and Tobago.

At the ranch, God is not only helping alcoholics and addicts to stop using, He's also helping them become a productive force in our community. Our desire at U-Turn is to show God's glory and extend His grace and mercy as we reach out to serve and love our neighbors here.

MAKING SENSE OF IT ALL

Being asked to share my story for this book has made me reflect about a lot, and I want to point something out that I've learned.

When Jesus was led into the wilderness to be tempted, Satan presented Him with every enticement the world has to offer. But Jesus answered him, over and over, with "It is written…it is written…it is written" (see Matthew 4:4-11). Our Lord left us the perfect example to know Scripture and hold on to it when we're tempted, because His Word will give us victory over anything that causes us to stumble. Memorizing Scripture has the power to change our hearts and set us free, and that's why it's the basis for the U-Turn ministry.

Seeking the things of God is a daily battle, and 2 Corinthians 10:4-5 has become my life verse:

> "For the weapons of our warfare are not carnal but mighty in God for pulling down strongholds, casting down arguments and every high thing that exalts itself against the knowledge of God, bringing every thought into captivity to the obedience of Christ."

Because of what the Lord allowed me to go through, I'm in a unique position to share His goodness, love, and power with others at U-Turn who have a hard time believing that God is real. Only the Lord could have produced the life that I have now—there's no other explanation! Over the years, I underwent behavior modification, clinical counseling, rehab, AA, NA, and many other therapies. And although they worked for a while, eventually I would return to the drugs and alcohol.

No one ever tried to change my behavior at U-Turn For Christ, but God did a heart change. And when that happened, my behavior was different. The reason I don't take drugs, smoke or drink anymore is because I no longer want to do those things—God has given me new desires.

> "Delight yourself also in the LORD, and He shall give you the desires of your heart. Commit your way to the LORD, trust also in Him, and He shall bring it to pass. He shall bring forth your righteousness as the light, and your justice as the noonday." (Psalm 37:4-6)

Many who come to us at the ranch are prideful and puffed up, and I recognize them! I learned the hard way that "pride goes before destruction, and a haughty spirit before a fall" (Proverbs 16:18). My own pride had me convinced that I didn't need accountability. But we are all accountable to God and to each other. Hebrews 4:13 declares, "There is no creature hidden from His sight, but all things are naked and open to the eyes of Him to whom we must give account." And that's why today I never travel alone.

I continue to warn others about what happened to me. Sometimes they say, "Yeah, yeah, I know, I know," but they still walk through their own experience, like I did, before grabbing onto the lesson God wants to teach them. For me, that lesson had to be seared into my conscience and into my spirit so that He could use it to minister to others and possibly keep them from the same fate.

If you've ever seen a car chase—and there are a lot of them in L.A.—then you know that police officers will throw down spikes onto the road and when the drivers run over them, their tires go flat. However, since the cars still keep going, sparks start flying everywhere, like little explosions on the ground. Well, that's what I used to be like. I kept racing along in my sin, with sparks flying all around me, but I wouldn't stop until the bitter end. Today, because I experienced all of that, there are no more sparks left in me. I'm completely done with the old life—yes, absolutely done.

Jesus summed it up this way, saying "I am the way, the truth, and the life. No one comes to the Father except through Me" (John 14:6).

He said over and over again in the book of Revelation that He is the Alpha and the Omega, which means the first and the last. Having a relationship with Jesus is where it all begins and ends. There's no other way. He's the only one who can change us from the inside out.

Diamond, Elijah, Merol, Steve and Joshua.

From the streets of L.A. to leading the ministry in South Carolina is a long way for man, but a short step for You, Lord, and for that we are forever grateful.

In and out of so many programs until Steve gave way to Your program—surrender. And now, Lord, Steve is helping so many others to just agree with You, and to admit that we are all in need of a Savior.

Bless Pastor Steve, I pray, and pour out Your blessings on him. In Jesus' name, Amen.

U-TURN FOR CHRIST LEXINGTON, SOUTH CAROLINA
Pastor Steve & Merol Mattier
1156 Barr Road, Lexington, SC 29072
(803) 951-2197
email: uturn@cclexington.org
website: www.cclexington.org

He also brought me up out of a horrible pit, out of the miry clay, and set my feet upon a rock, and established my steps. He has put a new song in my mouth—Praise to our God; many will see it and fear, and will trust in the LORD.

PSALM 40:2-3

PASTOR STEVE NORDGREN
Rescued, Redeemed, Restored

Steve stepped outside the bunkhouse into the darkness of early morning. Walking briskly, he circled the U-Turn ranch property, one lap after another. In this treasured hour before the bunkhouse lights came on at 5:30 a.m., Steve prayed and watched the sunrise illuminate the desert sky. It was the only time he would have alone all day before the guys woke up and everything broke loose.

Attempting his second time through Phase 1, Steve wondered if he would ever feel close to God again. He had tried so many times to follow the Lord but always slipped back into drugs. Only two years earlier, he had served as an overseer at the ranch—that is, until that fateful weekend when he went home on a weekend pass and injected meth.

Interrupting Steve's thoughts, the Lord spoke gently to his heart. "You know I love you, Steve," He said. "But you're not obeying Me. And that's why you're having so much trouble!"

Suddenly, it was as if the Lord pulled back the blinders covering his heart and mind, and for the first time Steve saw the depravity of his sin—the stealing, the lies, the drinking, the drugs. Something broke deep inside of him, and tears began to flow. Lifting up his hands to the sky, Steve cried, "Lord, what have I done? I've ruined my life! I'm so sorry. I have nothing left to offer You, but here I am, ready to surrender. I'll do anything You want...I'll go anywhere."

This is Steve's story.

My life of crime began in third grade when I stole fingerpaints from my classroom at Webster Elementary in Ballard, a neighborhood in Seattle, Washington. Not only did I steal them, I also fingerpainted all over one side of my house. Clearly, Mom and Dad weren't happy, but they didn't discipline me for stealing, or for painting the house. Years later when we moved, my artwork on the house remained.

Our school, a tall, red brick structure, was situated directly across the street from our house. A year after the fingerpainting incident, my older brother Gene acquired a BB gun, and one night he and I took turns leaning out of our upstairs bedrooms to shoot the school windows. Unfortunately, the night janitor spied us from across the street and called my dad, who hurried home to make us walk over and apologize. Later, while sitting in class one day, I looked up and noticed lots of little holes in the glass windowpanes and thought, *Holy schmoly, I did that!*

In sixth grade, our school provided roller skates to use at recess, and I thought, *Cool, I think I'll cruise through Ballard on these!* So one day a friend and I skated off campus, spending the afternoon exploring downtown. Eventually I said, "Hey, we better go back!"

We tried sneaking into the school gym to return the skates, but we found out someone had already told on us. This only added to my long and colorful history with the school principal. At the time I thought she was a mean lady, but the truth is, I was a little hellion. And because Dad worked as a custodian for the school district, my antics were not appreciated. I was held back in sixth grade, and I thought it was because of all the trouble I caused, but it was probably due to the fact that I needed glasses and didn't know it.

FAMILY LIFE

Mom and Dad were binge drinkers, and sometimes their binges lasted for weeks. Dad was big on family outings, taking us camping to places like Heller Lake and Snoqualmie, but my parents usually drank while we camped. Other times they wouldn't drink for months and things would seem normal for a while. When Dad finally got caught drinking at work and someone had to drive him home, he was fired. So we left Ballard and moved to Downtown Seattle, just in time for my second year of sixth grade.

In Seattle, my parents managed a motel a few blocks away from the Space Needle. With little supervision at their new job, their drinking was easy to hide. Gene and I shared a motel room, and it was pretty cool because my parents didn't keep close tabs on us. Besides my brother Gene, who was four years older than me, I had three sisters: Marty and Kristina, who were grown and had left home; and my sister, Randi, who was two years older than me.

By the time I started my second year of sixth grade on Seattle's Queen Anne Hill, I was already drinking and smoking pot. Gene sold marijuana so it was always available. On weekdays, I'd ride the bus to meet two friends at the Aurora Bridge, and then we'd hike up a huge staircase to get to school. Along the way, we'd smoke pot that I'd stolen from my brother's stash. It was our little thing we did every morning, and those two friends were the only sixth graders I could find who would smoke weed with me.

To support my habit, I dipped into my brother's cash earnings, and I also stole money from the motel safe. When I would come home with pot pipes from the local head shop, Gene would ask, "How'd you get all this stuff?" I had quite a collection. Gene knew I was ripping off my parents, but he didn't know I was stealing from him too. And whatever else I wasn't allowed to have—whether it was wine, cigarettes or cigars—I'd steal it from stores.

One day my buddies and I got caught smoking weed on the playground, and my bong was confiscated. After getting suspended for three days, we started walking home when I randomly said, "Hey, let's run away!" We made it as far as South Seattle before realizing we were hungry and had no place to sleep. We spent the first night with a family member and the next two nights on an empty houseboat on Lake Union. When I finally returned home, my parents were on a drinking binge, so I didn't get in trouble.

ONE BIG PARTY

Gene always had parties in our room where we drank and smoked pot with our friends. I thought I was in the "in" crowd because all his junior high friends, even the beautiful girls, were nice to me. But that only lasted a little while because my parents' drinking escalated and we had to move again. For the next couple of years, we moved around a lot, first to Denver and then to Los Angeles. Once in L.A., I started dabbling in hard drugs like LSD, speed, coke, black beauties, and hash. To support my habit, my drug career advanced from selling pot to selling other substances.

Just before starting high school, we moved from L.A. to Oceanside, California, where Mom and Dad managed another motel, this time only a block away from the beach. High school was like one big party, and I was the life of the party. By this time Gene had moved out so I even had my own room. My sister, Randi, and my parents lived separate from me, behind the motel office, and every evening we ate dinner together in their living quarters. However,

I'd eat fast because I couldn't wait to get back to my own room and party. Mom kept Randi close by and was very protective of her.

On the other hand, I did whatever I wanted. I lived the California dreamin' thing—listening to loud rock music, having friends over at all hours, and drinking and smoking every day. It seemed like everyone in Oceanside knew about my party room. Besides selling weed to my friends, I had lots of friends from the nearby Marine base who would stay at our motel when they got paid. Then when I was in the eleventh grade, someone brought over a vial of meth. I snorted it and even though I didn't like the jittery feeling, it grabbed hold of me and I was hooked.

Later that year when my parents went to visit Mom's family in Canada, we got word that Dad passed away there from a heart attack. Sadly, because I was into drugs so heavily, I didn't process the loss of my father in a normal way. When Mom came home, she began drinking even more, so Randi took over running the motel. As I sunk deeper into my addictions, I cut so many classes that I was banished to continuation school. I didn't last there either.

A FINAL BINGE

Then I got involved in a big meth operation with Gene, running drugs back and forth from Oceanside to Wyoming. During this time, I lived with a girl at the motel, and before long she got pregnant. Things escalated from there when I got caught twice on drug runs, and my daughter Cassie was born while I served time in jail. After my sentencing, I spent thirteen months at the Chino prison.

While in prison, I asked myself, *What have I done with my life so far? Let's see—well, I've partied and sold drugs.* I always had the feeling that somehow things would work out and that I wouldn't be a drug addict all my life. One good thing happened while I was incarcerated; I finished my schooling and earned my GED.

I worked in the kitchen during my prison term. One evening after the dinner rush, I heard music coming from behind a closed door and thought, *What's going on in there?* Something drew me, and I know now it was the Lord. I walked over to the door, opened it slowly, and peeked inside. Then I took off. This happened three nights in a row, and on the third night, right after I bolted, a Mexican guy who was covered in tattoos opened the door and called after me, "God wants me to tell you to come back tonight for a concert."

I stopped and turned around. "Oh, really?" I said. I'd never heard anyone say that God told him something. I didn't know what he meant, and I thought he was being witty. But because I had always been a music lover, I said, "All right, cool, man. I'll come back later. That would be awesome!"

That night in 1987, I heard the gospel preached like I'd never heard it before, and I gave my life to the Lord. I realized I was going to be in prison for a long time and wanted to do anything I could to stay out of trouble. After the service, I hurried back to my bunk and started reading the Bible. I felt hungry for God's Word and as I read, I thought, *Wow, man, it's the Bible!* Even though I'd read the New Testament before, honestly, I couldn't tell you who Jesus was or what salvation meant because I hadn't understood it.

I always kind of believed there was a God—kind of. I knew there was something out there bigger than me, even though drugs might have enlightened the idea. But that day when I read the Bible on my bunk, the Scriptures came alive and I thought, *Whoa, so this is what life's all about!* The Lord started answering my questions, and I began having a relationship with Him. Soon after that, I signed up for Bible correspondence courses and learned my first memory verse, 2 Timothy 2:15:

> "Be diligent to present yourself approved to God, a worker who does not need to be ashamed, rightly dividing the word of truth."

Over the next year, I read through the Bible and got grounded in my faith. There was no doubt about it—I had an encounter with the Lord Jesus Christ and my life changed.

OCEANSIDE REVISITED

By the time I was released from prison, Randi and Mom had already left the motel. Mom moved to her own apartment in Oceanside and I lived with her. I did well for a little while, but without accountability I slowly gravitated back to the drugs. Over the next ten years, I bounced in and out of prison, and in and out of my daughter's life. My MO was to work in construction for a while and then get strung out. Finally I switched from construction to moving furniture, because I didn't have to think when I moved furniture. I tried getting clean by going through different secular programs, but I always violated with dirty tests. I lacked the power to get off drugs, and deep down I knew I needed Jesus, that He was the only One who could help me. I kept going back to the world and I wasn't able to stay clean and sober, go to church, or submit to Him.

In 1992, a friend from my apartment complex introduced me to "the riverbed." Located behind a drive-in theater in Oceanside, the riverbed was its own little city, where people sat in tents and sold drugs cheaper than anywhere else, kind of like a swap meet. The first time I saw the riverbed I thought, *This is crazy, this is nuts!*

Oceanside was a military party town, with lots of drugs, prostitutes, and homeless people. In 1995 some believers from Calvary Chapel Vista came to Oceanside because they had a heart for the city and its outcasts. They started a church called Calvary Chapel Mission Avenue, later renaming it Living Hope Calvary Chapel. I stumbled upon their gathering one Sunday morning when a fellow addict said, "I know where we can get free donuts!" I went for the donuts, but I'll tell you, when I walked in, I saw such beautiful worship. The service was casual, with people of all ages who came just as they were. After worship, Pastor Brad Lambert opened up the Bible and started teaching. *This is incredible!* I thought. Years later, I realized that God had sent these loving and kind Christian believers to Oceanside just for me.

I was strung out on drugs and I hadn't slept for about a week. I tried to leave right after the service, but all these men surrounded me, wanting to find out who I was and wanted to talk to me. It had been a while since I'd showered or shaved, and I looked like a skinny, long-haired, crazy guy. Yet I could tell they sincerely cared about me, and it blew my mind. God used these same men in my life for many years. They would find me and ask, "Want to go to church?" Even though I received the Lord in 1987, I'd never been discipled and I didn't know how to keep walking with God. I remember looking at those men and thinking, *These guys are living a life that's a dream to me.*

But the Lord clearly spoke to my heart: "It's not them, Steve, it's Me. They're people just like you, and they're only vessels."

I drifted in and out of church after that, showing up in between taking drugs. As I got to know the men there, they began sharing their stories with me. "No way, you did drugs?" I'd say. I realized, *Wow, this guy was on alcohol, and this one was on drugs.* God eventually showed me that they were indeed no different than me. They had all been rescued, redeemed, and restored, and now they were being a conduit of love to me. Through their example, God was painting me a picture of how much He loved me personally and had a plan for me too.

Later some of the guys told me that Pastor Brad would say, "If we don't see Steve for six months or so, we know it's bad."

Whenever I came back to church, I'd walk in thinking, *They're going to be so mad at me!* But it never happened. They always gave me big hugs, loved on me, and showed compassion.

Once when I had been gone a long time, a brother named Fred called me up and said, "Have you ever heard of U-Turn For Christ?" In my heart, I wanted out of this mess, but honestly, church had never been enough. I'd go to church and then leave thinking, *There's got to be more to this. What am I missing?* But when Fred told me about U-Turn, I sensed it was what I needed—a place away from Oceanside, a place to learn and grow and trust the Lord. Yet, as much as I wanted that, I wasn't willing to commit and make the decision to go.

There's a psalm that is heavy, but it's exactly how I felt and in the same way, my very own heart cried out,

> "For innumerable evils have surrounded me; my iniquities have overtaken me, so that I am not able to look up; they are more than the hairs of my head; therefore my heart fails me. Be pleased, O LORD, to deliver me; O LORD, make haste to help me!" (Psalm 40:12-13)

GETTING OUT OF GOD'S WAY

Six months later, I showed up at Living Hope Calvary Chapel, crying and feeling emotional. A brother named Luke sat behind me and put his hand on my shoulder. "Steve, have you heard of U-Turn For Christ?" he said.

I turned around. "Yes, and that's where I need to go!"

After the service, Luke took me up front to talk to Pastor Brad. "Steve wants to talk to you about U-Turn For Christ," he said.

"Are you willing to go right now?" Pastor Brad asked.

"What, today? Wait a minute," I said, stalling. "I've got things to take care of first. Yeah, I want to go, but come on—right now?"

"If you'll go tonight," he said, "we'll take care of the donation and get you there."

I knew Pastor Brad was checking my heart to see if I really meant what I said. He gave me an extra day to pack, and one of the guys drove me to the ranch the next day.

When I got to the ranch, right away I knew something was different. In other programs I had attended, people told me what was wrong with my mind or tried to dig into my past. But U-Turn had a different approach: the solid teaching of God's Word. Every morning we woke up to devotions in the book of Proverbs, and it cleansed me.

> "How can a young man cleanse his way? By taking heed according to Your Word. With my whole heart I have sought You; oh, let me not wander from Your commandments!" (Psalm 119:9-10)

Then we would go out in the community to do service work applying Matthew 20:26-28,

> "Whoever desires to become great among you, let him be your servant. And whoever desires to be first among you, let him be your slave—just as the Son of Man did not come to be served, but to serve, and to give His life a ransom for many."

Up until this time, I felt like I'd been living in the trinity of stupidity—just me, myself, and I. I lived such a selfish life not caring about my family, my daughter, or anyone else. But by helping people and getting involved in ministry, I learned how to be "other" centered to get the focus off me and my circumstances and onto Jesus. He's the "author and finisher of my faith," according to Hebrews 12:2, and He was the only One who could truly make me into a man of God.

SATELLITES AND CONSPIRACY THEORIES

Years of drug use had messed me up, but God's Word transformed my mind, like it says in Romans 12:2, "Be transformed by the renewing of your mind." While under the influence of meth, I thought satellites were watching me and I tried to run away from them. Little conspiracy theories consumed my mind, and I spoke in riddles that people didn't understand. Sometimes I couldn't speak at all! But Hebrews 4:12 says God's Word is powerful:

> "For the word of God is living and powerful, and sharper than any two-edged sword, piercing even to the division of soul and spirit, and of joints and marrow, and is a discerner of the thoughts and intents of the heart."

Reading God's Word changed me. To be able to sit down, talk normally with people, and have my mind back was truly a miracle.

After Phase 1, I planned to return to Oceanside, go to church, and start my life over. Then my overseer, Steve Mallipudi, said, "Steve, do you want to stay here at the ranch and help out? Pray about it." I realized the Lord was giving me an opportunity to avoid Oceanside and its temptations, and that felt right. So for the next year, I served as an overseer of a work crew at Calvary Chapel Bible College in Murrieta Hot Springs. Later I worked as an overseer of a property in Hemet called the Complex, a huge warehouse donated to the ministry. Along with Mark Rich and another brother, we scrapped the place, hooked up electricity, sorted donations, and provided security. After eight months, the Complex was renovated.

BLESSED OUT?

Things were going great in the ministry, but then I went home to Oceanside on a weekend pass and injected meth. When I returned to the ranch on Sunday, I was still coming down off the drug and I thought everyone was looking at me. But no one even noticed. I didn't want to tell the truth, yet I couldn't look anyone in the eye. I had opened the door to sin, and it was hard to hear the Lord's voice. I started losing my effectiveness for ministry and the enemy whispered, "You've failed now, but you don't want to go back to Phase 1, do you? You know where you're going if they find out—right back to the top bunk! So go ahead and leave. You need to take care of your daughter because she doesn't even have a dad. You need to go back and take care of your elderly mom…leave!"

When a person leaves the ministry at U-Turn, there are two ways it can happen. You can either walk out against your commitment or get a blessing from your pastors. We call it "being blessed out." When someone leaves, Pastor Gerry wants to make sure that he or she is being guided by God, so he always asks, "Do you have a Scripture confirmation?" He may also ask, "How is God speaking to you?" So I knew I needed to be ready for Pastor Gerry with convincing answers.

As I chewed over what to say, I remembered sorting through some recent donations to the ministry and seeing a wooden plaque with the verse, "He guides them to their desired haven" (Psalm 107:30). Grabbing for anything to get me home, I thought, *That's my verse! That's what I'll tell Pastor Gerry and then I'm outta here.*

I met with Pastor Gerry in his office. "Hey Pas," I said, "I feel like the Lord's calling me back to Oceanside to take care of my mom and my daughter. I think it's time to move on."

Pastor Gerry didn't ask for a verse. Instead, he blessed me. First he gave me money, and then he gave me a 1978 Datsun Pickup, that had a little front-end damage. I had asked Pastor Gerry, "Man, could I get that truck?" and he just gave it to me, along with his blessing.

I moved back to Oceanside and did very well for the first few months, landing a construction job with great wages. I bought a brand new truck—I'd never owned a new one—and started making payments. On the weekends, I took meth, figuring it was fine because I could still function. *No big deal!* I thought. God's still blessing me with a good job, good money—I've got the whole thing! I lived with my mom in her apartment, but in time I began hanging out at the riverbed, and before long I stopped going home. Meth became a full-blown day-in-day-out kind of thing. And then one Monday morning—when I did wake up—I couldn't make it in to work. After that

I started missing days during the week and was given the worst jobs that no one wanted. Everyone knew I was a backslidden Christian, and they started making fun of me. Like the double-minded man in James 1:8, I was unstable in all my ways. I couldn't get along with people and my life went downhill quickly. Soon I walked off a job and was fired. I spent the next two years slamming meth, and things never got better.

My sister Randi says, "Steve was supposed to be taking care of Mom and helping her. Mom knew he was on drugs but she didn't know the extent of it. Steve had a lot of head knowledge about God—I mean, he could quote the Bible backwards and forwards, and he'd always tell us, 'You should be doing this! You should be doing that!' I'd say, 'Are you kidding me? You're going to tell me how I'm supposed to live while you're doing this stuff?'"

DUMPSTER DIVING

I let a homeless girl live in my bedroom, and together we went out to dig in the dumpsters at night. I stacked junk up to the ceiling and we had cockroaches everywhere. Even though we had a brand-new apartment, it looked terrible. One day Randi showed up unannounced to do an intervention. She brought my niece and nephew, both young teenagers, and also Dave Duran, an assistant pastor from Living Hope. *How dare my sister do this,* I thought, *bringing my niece and nephew to see how bad I'm living.* I was upset.

Pastor Dave came in and kicked the girl out. Then he said, "Steve, if you don't change, something bad is going to happen."

Around that time, my fifteen-year-od daughter Cassie had come to live with me. Her grandmother couldn't handle her because she kept running away, so I was given the opportunity of a lifetime. For the first time Cassie and I lived together, but sadly, it was also the first time my daughter saw me on meth. I felt like she was probably looking at me in a negative way so I tried to be her friend, like a really cool dad, but in reality, I wasn't a good dad at all.

Cassie had never been part of my life before. She lived with her grandmother right down the street from me, and I'm not kidding, I never went to see her, even on Christmas. Because I had always been in and out of prison, I didn't have a real relationship with her.

There at the apartment, Cassie hung out with all the teenage kids at the complex, who weren't the best influence. At one point, a kid there scratched up my truck, and then I found out he tried to kiss my daughter. I walked outside ready to strangle the guy, but fortunately I never got my hands on him. Cassie saw a very angry side of me, a side she had never seen, and she hightailed it out of there, back to her grandmother's. I cried when she left, feeling like a huge failure. I thought, *Now my daughter's gone and she'll probably never talk to me again.* Then I remembered Pastor Dave's words: "If you don't change, something bad is going to happen."

SINKING DEEPER

I was using all the time, ripping people off and figuring I'd be stuck as a drug addict for the rest of my life. *I'm never going to be able to walk with the Lord,* I thought. I've tried and I can't pull it off. I was in a dark place like a hellhole. I hated meth and what it did to me, but I couldn't give it up. I had no hope. I stopped reading my Bible and going to church. I was open game for the Devil to speak into my life and he did. "You're always gonna be on this stuff," he said. "You might as well give up." I wasn't brave enough to take my own life, but I felt desperate.

I had always been able to look back on a situation and say, "The Lord was trying to give me a detour sign here." In the moment, I couldn't see it—I'd get locked up in jail or put into a program. But since I'd already lived a year-and-a-half at U-Turn For Christ and walked with the Lord, I believe God was giving me a sign. Even in my state of being under the influence, I recognized God's love for me and had enough belief to say, "I need to do something better!"

Randi and Pastor Dave came to visit me one more time at my apartment. "Steve, you need to go back to U-Turn For Christ," Pastor Dave said.

Then Randi tried. "Either you go back to U-Turn or you go to the riverbed, one or the other. It's your choice." I remember wanting to choose the riverbed. It would have been so easy just to live down there with the others, make myself a little hooch, and collect cans to sell. Then my sister mentioned my fourteen-year-old nephew, Joey. "He used to look up to you, Steve. Remember when the two of you would ride bikes together down to the beach?"

When I heard how Joey once felt, my heart broke. What have I become that my niece and nephew don't even want to come over anymore? Right then, I knew I needed to get back to U-Turn, and the next day, Randi drove me to the ranch. She said I literally rolled out of the car into the arms of my friends. And as soon as I arrived, I knew I was home, back where I needed to be. That was in the fall of 2001. Sadly, the same day I left Oceanside, my mother was admitted to the hospital. She'd been sick for a while, laid up in the back room of the apartment, and we didn't know what was wrong with her. I'd only been at the ranch for a week when one of the pastors walked up to me and said, "Your mom isn't doing well and you need to go home."

SAYING GOODBYE

I spent one night with my mom at the hospital, and she went to be with the Lord the next morning. I regret that I didn't stay up all night with her. I was coming off meth so I slept in a chair next to her bed. But I'm thankful my mom was able to see me go back to U-Turn, and she went to be with the Lord knowing I was okay.

In 1998, after coming home from U-Turn the first time, I had shared the Lord with my mom and told her how important it was to read her Bible. Mom was Catholic and after we would talk, she'd go talk to a priest at St. Mary's Catholic Church in Oceanside. She said he gave her permission to attend church with me at Calvary Chapel, as long as she still went to mass.

Mom didn't go to church regularly, but she got to know my friends and really liked them all, to the point that she said she wanted them to do her memorial service. I believe my mom had a relationship with the Lord. She embraced the work of Christ on the cross and recognized the changes in my life. When I backslid, she ministered to me and tried to help me. She gave me so much comfort and stood by me all those years. Even though she enabled me, I know she did the best she could. My mom was a very sweet person and she loved me unconditionally to the very end.

When Mom passed away, I thought, *I don't want any more family members to die without me being right with Christ!* I made a commitment to be there for my family and since then, the Lord has allowed me to share Him with many of them.

I stayed in Oceanside a few more days. Randi took me to the apartment and said, "I need to downsize, and you're going to help me." It was no easy task! I loved my junk and I had accumulated a lot. By the time we were done, we filled ten dumpsters, and it was just like watching an episode of the TV show, "Hoarders." Randi kept telling me, "Trash it, Steve! You don't need it. I'm only paying for a small storage unit."

DOING BUSINESS WITH THE LORD

Back at the ranch again, I started waking up at 4:30 every morning to walk and pray. One morning I prayed, *Lord, where did I go wrong? What did I do? How did I get so off track?*

248

STEVE NORDGREN: *Rescued, Redeemed, Restored*

The Lord started laying everything out, revealing each step into sin along the way. "Remember, you got a home pass, and you didn't tell the truth. Remember when you grabbed that Scripture off the plaque?" and on and on. Finally He said, "You don't have to live like that anymore, Steve."

I'm so grateful for what the Lord showed me that morning and for the lessons I learned, especially the lesson that God never blesses disobedience. He never condones our sin or winks at it in any way. Under the influence of drugs, I walked in lies and deception. As I believed those lies, I began manipulating others and I was manipulated by the enemy himself. Drugs opened up a whole different spiritual realm.

James 4:1-10 says,

> "Where do wars and fights come from among you? Do they not come from your desires for pleasure that war in your members? You lust and do not have. You murder and covet and cannot obtain. You fight and war. Yet you do not have because you do not ask. You ask and do not receive, because you ask amiss, that you may spend it on your pleasures. Adulterers and adulteresses! Do you not know that friendship with the world is enmity with God? Whoever therefore wants to be a friend of the world makes himself an enemy of God. Or do you think that the Scripture says in vain, 'The Spirit who dwells in us yearns jealously'? But He gives more grace. Therefore He says: 'God resists the proud, but gives grace to the humble.' Therefore submit to God. Resist the devil and he will flee from you. Draw near to God and He will draw near to you. Cleanse your hands, you sinners; and purify your hearts, you double-minded. Lament and mourn and weep! Let your laughter be turned to mourning and your joy to gloom. Humble yourselves in the sight of the Lord, and He will lift you up."

I realized that I had never totally submitted my life to God because I'd always tried to resist the Devil in my own strength. When God showed me the depths of my sin that morning, I raised my hands and surrendered it all. I realized, *I've got to go back to Pastor Gerry and make it right!*

I had to work up the guts to tell him the whole truth. I imagined that after confessing, I'd be in big trouble—minimum, digging a 5 x 5 hole.

"Pastor Gerry," I began, "I need to tell you something. I've failed tremendously. I weaseled my way out of the ministry when I was here before, and I lied to you when I said I needed to leave."

Somehow, Pastor Gerry had known all along. And instead of knocking me down, I received grace and mercy. "Steve, we need more men like you who are willing to tell the truth when they fail."

What? I thought. I was flabbergasted. Then I told him what had happened in Oceanside and what the Lord taught me through it all.

"Think about the calling you have on your life, Steve," Pastor Gerry said, "and pray specifically about that." And like a good father, he embraced me as a son and offered restoration. That time with Pastor Gerry was one of the most beautiful experiences I ever had. Before our meeting, I had felt so nervous, but I walked out with victory saying, "Yes! Thank you, Lord!"

A couple of weeks later, I was asked to serve as an overseer at the Western Eagle food bank. *Wow, God,* I thought, *You actually want to use me again?* With a crew of fifteen guys, we all rode the ministry bus from Monday through Friday to unload trailers, sort food, store it in the warehouse, pack it into boxes, and then load the boxes into people's vehicles. After working at Western Eagle for several months, other overseers at the ranch started telling me, "Hey Steve, I heard you're going to Tennessee to start a new ranch."

"No way!" I said. "There's no chance of that." Then I was officially told the plan: "Steve, you are going to start a ranch in Tennessee. So be praying about it and seeking the Lord."

But there was one major problem. Just before leaving Oceanside and returning to U-Turn, I had been arrested and put on probation for having paraphernalia and syringes. Knowing I needed to make things right before leaving for Tennessee, I went to visit the probation department.

"Hi, I'm Stephen Nordgren," I said to the probation officer at the counter, "and I'm getting ready to start a drug rehab in Tennessee called U-Turn For Christ."

The officer pulled out a long drawer and looked up my file. "Mr. Nordgren, you're on probation," she said. "You can't leave the state."

"Yes, I know but will you please go tell your boss that I've been clean for a few months now, and I feel very strongly that I'm supposed to start this ranch in Tennessee?"

The officer left the room with my file and then returned with her boss. "Mr. Nordgren," she repeated, "you can't leave the state."

"But I believe God is calling me to Tennessee," I explained. "It's an opportunity He's placed in my life, and it has everything to do with me staying clean and sober."

The two women went to a back room for a few minutes and then returned. "Mr. Nordgren," the officer said, "if you'll stay out of trouble, you won't hear from us. And we hope to never see you in this courthouse again." Then she added, "Have a nice life!"

TENNESSEE

A few days later, on February 28, 2002, I boarded a bus headed for my new home in Greeneville, Tennessee. I remember praying, *This is crazy! You want to use me, Lord?* Finally it made sense why my birthday was on April Fool's Day! Because if it were my choosing, I wouldn't have chosen the guy on that bus to go to Tennessee.

I knew that "God uses the foolish things of this world to put to shame the wise," (1 Corinthians 1:27) and now I felt like He was confirming His plan. I'd always hated my birthday before, but after reading this Scripture, it became my life verse! What a blessing to be born on April Fool's Day and to realize that God was willing to use me, a foolish person. On that bus trip, I clearly heard from the Lord and felt excited as I anticipated my new ministry. When I arrived, Pastor Gary Hall from Greeneville Calvary Chapel welcomed me warmly, and he's now a close friend and dear brother.

During my first two years in Greeneville, I didn't hear a word from Cassie. *What am I going to do?* I thought. *She's still mad at me.* I prayed and handed her over to God's care, knowing He was able to do something even though I couldn't. I didn't even know where to find her. Then one day I called an old number and Cassie answered. "Dad?" she said, "good to talk to you! Wow, how are you doing?" It was as if nothing had ever happened, and the Lord restored us, right over the phone. She told me she was dating a guy named Jesús Venegas and asked if they could come to Tennessee for a visit. I put them up in separate rooms and we had a wonderful time, going to the mountains and just having fun together.

While she was here, Cassie and I talked about the time she lived with me in Oceanside. "Did you know I was on drugs?" I asked.

"Well, I was wondering why you'd sleep for a couple of days and then be awake for a long time and then go back down," she said. "My friends thought you were super cool, though."

I used to think she had found my needles and taken pot from me, so I asked her about that too. "No, that's not true," she said. "I kind of suspected you were on something, but I didn't really know."

I developed a great love for Cassie's boyfriend and later, when I went to a U-Turn Pig Roast in California with Cassie and Jesús, I asked them, "Hey, when are you guys getting married?"

"Dad, we'd love to get married," Cassie said. "Will you officiate?"

Cassie caught me off guard. "You're kidding me, really?" I said. Then I went to see Pastor Gerry and said, "Hey, man, can we do a wedding?"

"Sure," he said. "Let's get some counseling going and do this!"

So on July 7, 2007, Cassie and Jesús became man and wife. It was my first time to officiate at a wedding and I felt nervous, but it was beautiful. For so much of Cassie's life, I'd never been there for her, so having that special restored relationship with her now has been a huge blessing. I'm baffled at how God had His hand on my daughter and kept her sheltered from all the stuff I did. It was only His grace.

MY BEST FRIENDS TODAY

For thirty-nine years, I was single and essentially pretty lonely. I knew that if I ever did marry, I would need to hear from the Lord. In 2009 a woman named Christine came through the women's ranch, and while she was here, I thought there might be something between us, but I wasn't sure. After finishing Phase 2 she returned home to Boston, and we kept in touch with very short phone calls. I continued seeking the Lord about our relationship and went to Pastor Gerry for counsel. Our courtship lasted a long time, a few years actually, and we finally went from phone calls to Skype. By then, we were sure the Lord had brought us together, and Pastor Gerry encouraged me to ask Christine's dad for her hand in marriage. On February 24, 2012, Pastor Gary Hall married us during a small ceremony in Tennessee.

I assumed that pouring myself out for others in the ministry would be great prep for marriage, but nothing could have prepared me except walking through it. Learning how to love my wife and be self-less didn't come naturally, and being married is probably the number one reason I'm still being changed and rearranged. But it's also the greatest blessing because my wife is my best friend, and having someone to be with all the time is very nice.

Christine is a stay-at-home mom to our two kids—Brad, fourteen, and Ann Marie, eleven. Brad and Ann Marie are beautiful, amazing children, and they are our first ministry. They're both an answer to prayer because I always wanted more kids. I consider them both my own and have a close, special relationship with each one. In addition to being a mom, Christine also helps out at our U-Turn thrift stores and mentors the gals and leaders at the women's ranch, which began in 2004.

Today both my older brother, Gene, and my sister, Randi, are walking with the Lord. And as Randi has reflected on how I've changed since coming to U-Turn, she says: "Steve used to be such a selfish, self-centered, spoiled brat. Believe me, that's hard to say because today he's my best friend! But he has softened, and the Lord has poured an inner strength into him—you can just see it. Now Steve thinks of others before himself, he loves and forgives people, and he gives everything over to God. Family is very important to Steve, and he especially loves being around the kids because to this day, he's like a big kid himself."

THANKFUL

Serving as director of U-Turn For Christ in Greeneville since 2002 has been the most awesome job in the world. I see men and women come here beaten and broken, not knowing what tomorrow holds. They've burned bridges, done rotten things, and felt bad about themselves. I talk to them a few days after they arrive, noticing a little bit of hope when their mouth turns up slightly into a smile, and I say, "Yeah, God!"

Later I'll hear, "Man, you wouldn't believe what God's doing in my life!" I watch the process of Him working, and I detect a little joy as they start to realize, *Wow, God, You've got a plan for me. You can restore my marriage. You can get my children back. You've rescued me!*

I watch women come out from under abusive relationships, abortions, and the sad lifestyle of drugs and alcohol. I rejoice when they find healing and forgiveness from the Lord, and I think, *This is the most exciting ministry!*

Here in Tennessee, we do the same thing I learned at U-Turn For Christ in Perris, California—disciple men and women. People come to get away from the cares of this world. We don't talk about all our problems; instead we focus on the solution. We all have similar pasts, but what's the remedy? The remedy is a relationship with Jesus Christ. One of my favorite verses, James 1:22, says it all: "Be doers of the word and not hearers only, deceiving yourselves." We provide an opportunity to take hold of God's living and powerful Word, which is able to change us. U-Turn For Christ offers nothing else but Jesus Christ and Him crucified. That's it, plain and simple.

Men and women rescued, redeemed, and restored—that's my vision for U-Turn For Christ Tennessee. Yet it's so much bigger than that. People may change here, but it's only the beginning—what they do when they go back home is what matters. Our desire is that they would be a shining light and make an impact on their families and churches, allowing the Lord to do what He wants to do. And then the ripple effect will spread out into the community and God will get all the glory.

In this ministry, I see restoration all around me, over and over again. I just sit back and say, "Wow, God, You are doing miracles! Thank you for allowing me to be a part of what You're doing."

Brad, Steve, Ann Marie and Christine

Father, may Your hand remain on Pastor Steve and his family. Dear Lord, he has seen what it's like to walk with You and be so blessed, and also what it's like to live in spiritual poverty without You.

I pray that You will show him Your goodness. Use him to bless others all the days of his life, just as he has been blessed. In Jesus' name, Amen!

U-TURN FOR CHRIST GREENEVILLE, TENNESEE
Men's and Women's Ranch
Pastor Steve & Christine Nordgren
1186 Black Road
Greeneville, TN 37743
(423) 639-3720
email: info@uturn4christtn.com
website: www.uturn4christtn.com

CHAPTER 13

"I am the vine, you are the branches. He who abides in Me, and I in him, bears much fruit; for without Me you can do nothing."

JOHN 15:5

MARK RICH
God's Full Circle

"Leave me alone!" Mark growled under his breath, "I don't know what you're talking about."

The demonic voices in his head were back, recounting every shameful thing he'd ever done. Following him to work on the graveyard shift, the voices taunted Mark as he stocked shelves on the pet supplies aisle at a discount department store.

"Stop talking to me," Mark told the voices, "or I'll lose my job!"

Mark had tried to make an agreement with the voices, begging them to quit bothering him at work. But that night, they came in full force, spewing accusations and refusing to leave. Mark felt like he was in a courtroom answering their incessant questions, and soon he became convinced that the store manager was coming after him too.

Leaving piles of merchandise in the aisle, Mark hurried to the row of registers and picked up one of the store intercom receivers. Calling for his manager, he announced: "Michael Hunt, Michael Hunt, get to register 3—now!" Then he added, "And quit playing around. These games have got to stop."

Mark hung up the receiver and waited. Moments later, his boss came sprinting down the detergent aisle, clearly upset. "Mark, what do you think you're doing?" he asked, catching his breath. "What's going on here?"

Mark rambled, "Stop blaming me! I…I…didn't do nothin'…it's not my fault…" Imagining that his manager was accusing him, just like the voices, Mark suddenly demanded, "Now unlock the doors because I'm leaving."

Michael exchanged a knowing look with the night security guard, and they both escorted Mark outside. Before the door slammed shut, Mark heard his boss yell, "You're fired!"

This is Mark's story.

My sister Marta watched over me like a little mother, carrying me around the orphanage where we lived in Zacatecas, Mexico. Just babies ourselves, Marta and I were given up by our biological parents when I was two and she was three-and-a-half. With nine older children still at home, and another baby on the way, our parents in Mexico could no longer take care of us.

Situated out in the middle of nowhere, our humble Mexican orphanage was run by Catholic nuns. The poor, ranch-style home had lots of bunk beds, and whenever it got overcrowded, we'd double up and sleep two in a bed. All the children helped with cooking and cleaning, and we all looked out for each other. I was a quiet, happy little boy, and was always playing with a ball. One of my favorite memories from the orphanage is when missionaries visited us because they always brought toys, clothes—and best of all—peanut butter and bread. At Christmas they brought walnuts and oranges, a special treat that tasted like candy to us.

After living there for two years, Marta and I were both adopted by Clarence and Serafina Rich, a Christian couple from Southern California. Our new mom took us to church every Sunday and I loved it, especially the arts and crafts. A godly woman, Mom was the spiritual leader of our family. She prayed for us, read the Bible to us, and taught us to trust God for everything. Dad owned a barbershop and worked most Sundays, but he came to church with us on Christmas and Easter.

Mom talked to my school friends about Jesus and always invited them to church. As I got older, I felt more and more embarrassed when she did this. If my friends walked by while Mom was outside watering the grass, she'd say, "Jesus loves you!" Some of my friends didn't mind, but when she talked to the dopers and gang members, I'd tell her afterwards, "Mom, stop doing that or they'll come back looking for me!"

At age fourteen, I took my first drink when a friend snuck a bottle of tequila to a football game. Then I began smoking marijuana and lost all interest in going to church. I told Mom I wasn't going anymore because I wanted a weekend job, but it was only an excuse. She never forced me to go back.

Mom had some type of lung problem, as well as a bad heart, so she was in and out of the hospital a lot. Sometimes she would hemorrhage and cough up so much blood that Dad would have to call an ambulance to take her to the hospital. Her absences left me with a lot of unsupervised time on my hands. If Dad was working, Marta and I took a bus to visit Mom. Lying there in the hospital bed, Mom often looked at me with eyes of love and said, "Marquitos, one of these days the Lord is going to reach you, and you're going to answer Him."

My drinking and smoking gradually led to other things—hallucinogenics, acid, LSD, and PCP. After a few years of sneaking out of the house and partying, I came home one night and found my pot pipes and bong smashed on top of my bed. It was Dad's way of saying, "You've been found out!" The next day he told me, "Son, if you're not going to obey the rules, you need to go. It's too much of a strain on your mother." And with that, Dad kicked me out of the house.

HOMELESS

As a junior in high school, I suddenly found myself with nowhere to go. Friends fed me, and I slept curled up outside the school gym for the first few nights. Then I stayed in a friend's camper and later at another friend's home. I began failing my high school classes and attended school less and less. My school counselor called me in and told me I'd have to quit baseball since I wasn't going to school. That got my attention—I grew up playing baseball, playing left and center field on a league team. I enjoyed the game and it meant a lot to me. "If I can't play baseball," I told the counselor, "I'll just quit school."

"If you quit, what are you going to do with your life?" he asked. "You have options. You could go to continuation school, night school—"

"What about the army?" I interrupted.

"Well, since you're under seventeen, you would need your parents' signatures."

"Then I'll go get them." I ran home and asked my parents to sign the papers, and they did.

BIG PLANS

For the first time in a long time, I felt excited about the future. *Now I'll finally get my life straightened out and pursue a career,* I thought. But my excitement was short-lived because the drugs followed me right into the military.

I worked as an army cook, and once when I barbecued a meal outside for the platoon, my sergeant had the crazy idea to use wood and gasoline to ignite the barbecue. Although I was stoned at the time, I realized the imminent danger so I took two steps back when he poured gasoline on the grill. After the fire ignited, my sergeant threw the gas container over his shoulder, hitting me and dousing me with gas. My arms and chest caught fire immediately and I fell to the ground, but not before the skin was burned off my right arm. I spent the next ten days in the burn unit at the University of California Irvine Medical Center, where I endured excruciating treatments.

Three months after enlisting I got pulled over by the Military Police for selling marijuana and acid to some guys in my barracks. I was given an Article 15, which meant I was demoted in rank, thrown in jail, and kicked out of regular service into the reserves.

After the MPs put me in the brig, they said, "We have your mom on the phone and we want you to tell her what you've done." That was one of the hardest things I've ever done. When I told Mom I'd been arrested, she cried. Then she told me not to worry. I felt so ashamed, knowing I'd failed again, especially after telling my parents I was going to change my life and start over. After serving time in jail, my parents allowed me to come home while I finished my schooling in the reserves.

Back at my parents' house, I resumed my old ways of sneaking out at night in my dad's car and partying. Now eighteen, I drove to my girlfriend's house one night to drink, and on my way home I fell asleep at the wheel and crashed my dad's 1978 Ford Granada into a parked car. Sadly, I totaled his car—the only nice one he'd ever had. To make it worse, Dad had just finished paying it off.

My head went into the windshield when I crashed, so the ER doctors had to remove glass from my face and stitch up my chin. I called Marta from the hospital and she picked me up. She told me Dad was pretty upset, and I felt really bad. Since the Ford Granada was the only vehicle my father owned, Marta gave him her car so he could drive to work. Dad and I never talked about it afterwards.

Just before completing my three-year enlistment, I stopped showing up for my monthly weekend in the reserves, and I received a dishonorable discharge. I went to live with a friend, who asked me if I wanted to break in to a house that belonged to some people on vacation. We didn't plan to do anything except use it as a place to party. But after we got drunk, one thing led to another, and partygoers started pilfering through the house, taking whatever they wanted. I took two shotguns and shoved them down my fatigues, intending to sell them later on. Then I wandered outside in the dark and stopped to shoot at some old cars in a ditch. What a rush I felt!

After returning to the house, I joined my friends on a joyride to the beach in the homeowner's vehicle. We wrecked the car, abandoned it, and then fled. Five days later the owners returned from vacation, and someone tipped them off about our party. The next thing I knew, I heard helicopters flying overhead as I sat watching TV and drinking with my friends. When a bright light shone inside through a window, we scattered like cockroaches.

I hid in the closet while my friends jumped out the window. The cops nabbed them all, and they soon found me too. For the next three to four years, I spent time in and out of jail. After every release, it seemed like Satan was waiting for me at the gate. One time after being let out, I actually found a tiny bag of meth on the sidewalk, as if the Devil himself left it there for me.

At the age of twenty-one, crystal meth became my drug of choice. Meth was cheaper than cocaine, it lasted longer, and it helped me stay awake at my new job as the nighttime baker at a donut shop. It was a good job and I was able to move into my own apartment.

LOSING MOM, LOSING MY MIND

Mom's health worsened, so Marta got in touch with me to visit her at the hospital. When we walked into her room, Mom greeted us with a big smile. She always had a smile on her face, even when she was sick, and now I know it was because of Jesus. Mom was a very kind and gentle woman who loved me unconditionally, even when she knew I was doing drugs. Because of her deep sense of peace I believe her prayers for me reached the very throne room of God. As I sat on the side of her bed, holding her hand, she turned to look at me. "I won't be around much longer, Marquitos," she said softly, "and even though I may not live to see it, I know someday you'll surrender your life to God." That was the last time I saw my mom, and those were her last words to me.

Reflecting back, I see my mom's great wisdom because she knew how to apply God's Word with a prodigal like me.

> "But the wisdom that is from above is first pure, then peaceable, gentle, willing to yield, full of mercy and good fruits, without partiality and without hypocrisy. Now the fruit of righteousness is sown in peace by those who make peace." (James 3:17-18)

My drug use worsened and paranoia set in. After working ten years at the donut shop, I got another job working the graveyard shift at a department store stocking their shelves. During this time, I started hearing voices and I even talked back to them. They waited for me after work, asking question after question and convincing me that they knew everything about me. When the voices came, I felt like I was in the middle of an argument, and I couldn't concentrate on anything except their accusations. Their voices sounded magnified to me, kind of like I had a microphone in my ear. The moment I left work and stepped out the door, they were there, ready to interrogate me about all the bad things I had ever done. I tried to prepare for the exchange beforehand by thinking up excuses and lies for their mind games on my way home, but they always overpowered me and I felt like I was going crazy.

Then one night the voices showed up at work to torment me. When my manager heard me yelling on the loudspeaker, he thought I was a mental case, and he was right—I had truly lost my mind. Still on drugs, this was my last real job. Now without an income, I stuffed a backpack full of clothes, left my apartment, and I just started walking. I never went back.

LIVING ON THE STREETS

Because of the voices in my head, I was one of those homeless guys you see walking down the street and talking to himself, yelling at the sky, and cussing people out. For eight months I slept on park benches and ate out of garbage cans. I waited until people finished their picnics or birthday parties at the park, and then I searched through their leftovers. I still heard the voices, and I also started seeing words written out on the sidewalks and street signs. I felt like someone was following me, and when I got a day job in construction, the voices came to taunt me, forcing me to leave the work site.

After doing meth for eleven years, my brain was fried and I couldn't take it anymore. The voice that told me to leave my last construction job sounded like the voice of my sister Marta.

It had been years since I'd seen Marta, and in my confused state I thought she was playing games with me and forcing me to admit I was crazy. So one day I called her on a pay phone.

"Marta," I said, "I've had enough. You've got to leave me alone and let me go on with my life. I'm tired of you following me around. You need to stop it. I can't deal with it anymore."

"Mark, what are you talking about?" Marta asked. "You're scaring me. What's wrong?"

"You know what I'm talking about," I insisted. "I know you've been putting things in my ear."

"Listen to me. I'm not following you. In fact, I don't even know where you are. But if you're ready to get off drugs, I'll help you. Meet me after work today at five o'clock and we'll talk."

I hung up the phone and rode a bus to Marta's workplace at The Word For Today (the radio and publishing ministry of Pastor Chuck Smith at Calvary Chapel Costa Mesa). I sat down outside on the grass and waited there, hidden behind some trees. At five o'clock I watched Marta walk out of her building, get into her truck, and drive right past me.

When I saw her looking in her rearview mirror, I waved my arms and her brake lights flashed. Then she turned the truck around and pulled up next to me. "Mark, is that you?" she asked, leaning out the window.

"Yeah, it's me," I said. Then she started crying.

No wonder Marta didn't recognize me—I hadn't showered for days and my long, black, messy hair hung down in my face. Standing there in my filthy clothes, I felt like a dirt clod.

Marta recalls, "Mark would come and go every couple of years. He'd either have long hair or shave it all off, and often he'd grow a different kind of beard. I was always shocked by his appearance. This time he looked pretty down and out, like a homeless stoner. I was sad but not surprised.

"I used to give Mark money because I felt sorry for him, but then I realized I was enabling him so I stopped. It got to the point where I couldn't let him stay with us because he got violent and angry. He would wake up in the middle of night screaming that someone was trying to strangle him, like he was demon-possessed. I believe demons *were* around Mark and that they wanted to kill him, like it says in John 10:10: 'The thief comes to steal, kill, and destroy.' The thief is Satan, and he was out to destroy my brother. Sometimes Mark would just have this blank stare, and I knew it wasn't him."

TOUGH LOVE

Once Marta realized it was me standing there on the grass, she said, "Get in right now." I threw my backpack in the rear of her truck and climbed in. She drove me to her house, where I was reunited with my nephew, Halston, and my brother-in-law, Ephraim.

Marta remembers, "Halston loved his uncle so much, but my husband and I had to protect our son. Because of Mark's drug use, Halston didn't even meet his uncle until he turned three. Yet Mark was always loving and kind to his nephew. One time Mark gave him a little stuffed animal, and Halston treasured that gift, knowing it was all he had from his Uncle Mark."

When we arrived at the house, Marta told me to get in the shower. Then she put my old clothes in a plastic bag, threw them away, and brought me some new ones. I got dressed and came downstairs, where a big plate of hot pasta was set on the table for me. It tasted delicious, and as I ate, it dawned on me that I hadn't eaten food on a plate or used a fork in a long time. After dinner, Marta, Ephraim, and Halston waited for me in the living room. "We need to talk" Ephraim said, and he invited me to sit down.

Ephraim looked at me solemnly and asked, "Are you done now, Mark? Are you through with all of this?"

"Yes," I answered, meeting his gaze. "I'm tired of what's going on."

"Well, if that's how you feel, then Marta and I have an answer for you."

Now they're going to tell me to start going to church, I thought. *They'll say I need to stay with them and get back on my feet.*

"We've been talking to Marta's boss, Jeff Smith, about a place called U-Turn For Christ," Ephraim explained. "If you're really serious about changing and letting the Lord work in your life, we think it would be a good place for you." Then they prayed for me and I went to bed.

NOT WHAT I THOUGHT

At six o'clock the next morning, on July 9, 1997, Marta and Ephraim woke me from a deep sleep. "We're leaving for U-Turn For Christ now," Ephraim announced.

"What do you mean we're leaving now?" I mumbled, still half asleep.

"You said you wanted a change, remember? So we're taking you right now," Ephraim repeated.

I rolled over, thinking, *I didn't mean I'd go this early!* Then not wanting to disappoint Marta and Ephraim, I finally said, "Okay… all right."

When I think about it now, I'm glad Marta and Ephraim made me go to the ranch so soon. At thirty-four years old I was stuck in my addictions and I needed to be taken right away! Otherwise, I would have made up excuses like, "Give me a week or two, and then I'll go." Ephraim called it like it was, as it says in Hebrews 3:12-13:

> "Beware, brethren, lest there be in any of you an evil heart of unbelief in departing from the living God; but exhort one another daily, while it is called 'Today,' lest any of you be hardened through the deceitfulness of sin."

We all piled into the car and before I knew it, we were driving off the freeway and turning down a dusty road. *Where are they taking me?* I wondered. *Am I under observation?* I imagined people following me, doctors observing me, and the FBI coming to get me. That's what the drugs did to my mind.

As we approached the ranch, I looked around and thought, *This isn't a rehab! I mean, where's the horseback riding, the shady trees, the swimming pool, and the counseling center?* The ranch property didn't look anything like the lush, peaceful setting I'd pictured.

As we pulled up to the entrance, I noticed a man carving a wooden cross near a large grapevine, and I could see smoke rising from an outdoor kitchen in the distance. No resort facilities were in sight. Then a gentleman named Mario Rocha came out to greet me. He took me inside the U-Turn office and offered me a chair.

"Okay, Mark," he said, "you'll have a couple of weeks to detox and come down,"

Even though I wasn't coming down off hard drugs, I still wasn't all there. That first week at U-Turn, I felt standoffish and I didn't want to talk to anyone. Sometimes I walked around the ranch in circles and snuck out to the back of the property to smoke. I thought I could be strong but I wasn't.

NIGHT OF TRANSFORMATION

Every day we'd go out on work crews and then come back to the ranch to eat dinner together. After our physical food, a guest speaker came to serve us spiritual food. Romans 10:17 tells us that faith comes when we hear God's Word, and I learned that in order to grow spiritually, I needed His Word every day.

After living at the ranch a couple of weeks, I was especially drawn in by a particular evening speaker. That night as some men shared how God was restoring their lives, I realized, *Hey, everybody here needs to change, not just me!* When the speaker gave an altar call, I stood up and prayed. I didn't have a dramatic conversion experience, but I had one burning thought: *I want to put God first in everything from now on, in every decision I make.* In my heart, I knew God had transformed me. After so many years of drug use, I finally understood that I needed to do all the things my mother had taught me: go to church, read the Bible, and put my trust in God. That night I decided I wanted to live the rest of my life for the will of God.

> "So then, since Christ suffered physical pain, you must arm yourselves with the same attitude he had, and be ready to suffer, too. For if you have suffered physically for Christ, you have finished with sin. You won't spend the rest of your lives chasing your own desires, but you will be anxious to do the will of God. You have had enough in the past of the evil things that godless people enjoy—their immorality and lust, their feasting and drunkenness and wild parties, and their terrible worship of idols." (1 Peter 4:1-3 NLT)

From that moment on, I wanted to have the mind of Christ, and do things His way, not mine.

A few days later I thought, *I need to start paying attention to what's being said around here!* In those first Bible studies with Pastor

Gerry, I had a hard time focusing, and I suddenly realized that if I was serious about understanding God's Word, I needed to start taking notes. Afterwards, every time Pastor Gerry or anyone else taught, I'd listen intently with pen to paper. Later I'd read through what I wrote and think more about the message and Scriptures. I still have a backpack full of the notes I kept, and I believe this was God's way of reaching me and sanctifying me. As the Word of God cleansed my mind, the Lord began healing me and delivering me from my addictions and all that went with them, just like it says in 1 Corinthians 6:11:

> "And such were some of you. But you were washed, but you were sanctified, but you were justified in the name of the Lord Jesus and by the Spirit of our God."

One day I went out on a work crew to clean carpets at a church, and my job was to vacuum all the carpets first. As I ran the vacuum back and forth, I glanced up at a white board on the wall and read these words:

> "He who abides in Me and I in him, bears much fruit; for without Me you can do nothing." (John 15:5)

I remembered how Pastor Gerry had been telling us the value of memorizing Scripture, and I couldn't get that verse out of my mind. Quickly I found a piece of paper and wrote it down. Then I read it over and over until I memorized it. To this day, John 15:5 is imprinted on my heart and foundational in my life. Whenever I counsel men who need to be strengthened in their walk with Jesus, I share this truth, that without the Lord we can do nothing.

READY OR NOT

Just before Phase 1 ended, I received a phone call from Marta. "Mark," she said excitedly, "can you believe your graduation day is next Friday? Are you ready?"

I didn't know how to answer. Part of me wanted to leave yet part of me didn't. When I looked at others who were graduating, I could see they were happy. But whether they were happy about going home or about having a new foundation in Christ, I wasn't sure.

Then Marta said, "Never mind—don't tell me anything yet. I'll see you Friday and then we'll talk."

Before Friday arrived, Pastor Gerry took me aside. "How's it going, Mark?" he asked. "Do you have plans after graduation?"

"I guess I'm waiting to see what the Lord has next for me."

He noticed a lot of growth in me over the past two months. "Would you consider staying on as an assistant overseer?" he asked. "I believe that you could minister to the men coming through here."

Right away I thought, *How can I minister to anyone when I'm still in need of being ministered to?*

Pastor Gerry continued, "We'll meet together every Friday, and if there's ever a situation you're unsure of, my door will always be open." I felt hesitant, and my expression must have shown it. "Just pray about it, Mark, and let me know."

I did pray. *Lord, what do You want me to do? Which direction should I go? Is this where You want me?* I didn't hear an audible voice, but in my heart I felt led to give more time to the Lord at the ranch. I'd already spent so many years living for Satan, but God had given my life back and given me hope. So I stayed.

As assistant overseer, one of my jobs was to take a crew to Murrieta Hot Springs Conference Center and oversee their work. We did painting, weeding, cleaning, and anything they needed. Sometimes my crew struggled to get along and work together. One guy would get mad because he worked more than another guy and someone else got aggravated about doing a job he didn't want to do.

The Lord showed me how to bring peace between the men and help them deal with their frustrations by speaking softly and sharing Scripture with them. With every conflict we resolved, God was preparing me for the work I'd do at a later time. Ephesians 2:10 says we were created for these good works:

> "We are His workmanship, created in Christ Jesus for good works, which God prepared beforehand that we should walk in them."

Sometimes I'd ride along with Art Gonzales and Johnny Reno for coffee house concerts at a shopping center near the ranch. Art and Johnny played music while I handed out gospel tracts. One time I met some troubled kids there who were open to talking about the Lord. I felt nervous at first and didn't know what to say, but God gave me the words. Then I prayed with them and I felt so excited to offer them hope.

MORE TO LEARN

After serving at U-Turn for a year, Marta asked, "What do you think about going to Bible college?"

"Well, I've thought about it, but I don't think so."

"Ephraim and I want to pay your tuition," Marta continued. "We'll take care of everything. All you have to do is go there and study." What a wonderful opportunity it was. However, after completing one semester, my dad, who had been a smoker all his life, was diagnosed with cancer. He had moved in with Marta's family, so I left Bible college to help take care of him.

Before this time, my relationship with Dad was strained because I had been so rebellious, disrespectful, and dishonorable in the past. But when I came to help, I was able to lovingly bathe him, feed him, and pray for him. This opened up opportunities for my dad and I to talk about the Lord, and I was able to share with him what I'd learned from studying the Bible at U-Turn and Bible college. Before Dad died eight months later, he was able to witness with his own eyes the words of truth my mother had spoken: "One day Mark will surrender his heart to Jesus." God is so good.

After Dad died, Marta called me from work and said, "Jeff Smith wants to offer you a job in the radio room."

I was surprised and thought, *That's nice of my sister to get me the interview.* Out of respect, I went in and talked with Jeff, but I felt unqualified and told him, "I don't know anything about radio, and I've never worked for a Christian ministry."

"Don't worry about it, Mark," Jeff assured me. "We'll train you."

Still feeling unworthy, I asked, "But do you know my background? Do you know my past?"

Jeff chuckled. "Yes, Mark, I know everything about you. We've prayed for you for years, even before you went to the ranch. Just come on board and we'll show you what to do."

And that's how I started working at The Word for Today in 1999. Only by God's grace! My first job there was to duplicate radio productions of Pastor Chuck Smith's teachings through the Bible. As part of my work, I listened to his teachings all day long, making sure they didn't have any errors. Then I'd send the teachings to different domestic and international radio stations that aired them.

Although I wasn't able to continue my education at Bible college, God was faithful to honor my heart's desire to study His Word. As I listened to Pastor Chuck's Bible teaching of the Word each day, I realized He was providing my education in a way that was much better than anything I could have imagined!

MEETING CATHY

In 2000 a new employee named Cathy joined The Word For Today publishing department. A widow with three children, Cathy wrote radio promotions for Pastor Chuck's books and resources. She turned her work in to me, and our jobs required us to work closely together. Yet, because Cathy and I were both very shy, we barely spoke to each other.

Much later, I found out Cathy had been a widow for nine years, and during that time she had one simple prayer, just between her and the Lord. She prayed that if God wanted her to marry again, He would bring someone who was her age since her first husband was ten years older. She didn't want to worry about raising her children alone again, and she wanted to be at peace about that.

Cathy belonged to a widow's group at Calvary Chapel Costa Mesa, and one day the ladies took her out to celebrate her thirty-seventh birthday. While they were out, Cathy confessed that she liked me, but as soon as she said it, she felt nervous. One of Cathy's beloved mentors sat next to her and softly whispered, "I have a birthday scripture for you, Cathy—it's Psalm 37:37. Read it when you get home and then thank God for it." As soon as she got home, Cathy couldn't wait to look up the verse. She opened her Bible and read, "Mark the perfect man, and behold the upright, for the end of that man is peace."

Even though Cathy understood that the word "Mark" in this verse was a verb, in this case she read it to mean me! The Lord also revealed to Cathy that the chapter and verse, both thirty-seven, were significant because we were both thirty-seven years old. This was exactly what she had prayed for. But after being a widow for so long, Cathy still wasn't convinced. She fervently prayed for God to show her His perfect will without a doubt, for her and her children.

During this time, The Word For Today ministry moved to a different building, and I helped Cathy transport the publishing archives. One box we moved was filled with newspapers, and we noticed that the paper on top featured a picture of Pastor Chuck on the front page, smiling from ear to ear. In the picture, he was standing in front of a rainbow that was painted on a wall, and the caption read, "God keeps His promises." Cathy picked up the newspaper and showed me the date, July 8, 1997. "How neat," she said. "God keeps His promises! In July of 1997, I asked Jesus into my life and was born again."

I smiled and said, "That's when I gave my life to the Lord too, in July of 1997." Cathy gasped. She looked at me and then quickly looked away and said she had to leave. Eventually she told me this was when the Lord confirmed to her that we would someday be married. We were not only the same age physically, but also the same age spiritually! I would be a husband and father that would bring her family peace. God had answered her prayer, and as we continued to serve alongside each other in ministry, there was no doubt in our minds that the Lord had brought us together.

Cathy's fourteen year-old son, Jesse, worked part time after school in The Word For Today radio room, and one day he asked me, "Do you like my mom?" His question took me by surprise, and all I could say was that I honored Cathy and thought she was a godly woman.

Jesse grinned and said, "It's okay with me if you want to date her." After that, I talked to Cathy's daughters, Sterling, age thirteen, and Toni, ten, and they also agreed that I could see their mom.

Cathy and I were married on August 15, 2001, by a justice of the peace. We didn't have money for a wedding because we had to save up to move into a three-bedroom apartment where we could all live.

After the ceremony, Cathy and I said our vows again before the Lord, making a commitment to honor and serve Him first in everything.

A year later we worked together at a pastors conference in Hawaii and it was like a honeymoon for us, with all expenses paid.

GROWING ON THE VINE

When Cathy and I married, Jesse, Sterling, and Toni became my children and I became their dad in every respect. Because their father died when they were all under the age of five, I adopted them as my own, and they all wanted to change their last name to mine. Matthew 6:33 says, "Seek first the kingdom of God and His right-eousness, and all these things will be added to you." He really *did* add to me! Not only did He bless me with a beautiful wife, He also gave me three great kids who clearly love me and call me Dad. It's more than I ever could have imagined.

For six years our family served together in children's ministry, and then when our son Jesse turned twenty-one, he was arrested for a previous offense of underage drinking and committing a burglary. He got in with the wrong crowd, drinking and using meth, but God busted him. When Jesse went to jail, we stepped down from chil-dren's ministry to support him. After his release, Jesse started attend-ing an addiction recovery Bible study called One Step to Freedom, and Cathy and I went with him. It was a difficult time watching Jesse make the same mistakes I once made, but through this hardship we bonded and grew closer.

Following Jesse's commitment to attend the One Step Bible study, Cathy and I began helping in the ministry by counseling and leading small groups. We've stayed involved since 2007, and over the years, Jesse has led worship and given his testimony at the study, sharing what the Lord has done in his life. In 2014, I was asked to teach and oversee the One Step ministry at Calvary Chapel Costa Mesa.

Additionally, Cathy and I serve with U-Turn For Christ when we can, teaching the men's and women's Bible studies. At one of their annual Pig Roast events, Pastor Gerry asked me to share my testimony. God also allowed me to serve on a mission trip to Mexico with U-Turn, and we recently traveled with Pastor Gerry and his wife, Peggy, to Israel. While there, I taught a Bible study at Gideon Springs, where Gideon chose the army that defeated the Midianites in Judges 7:1-7. After I taught, Peggy whispered in Cathy's ear, "Mark is U-Turn's Gideon to us, God's mighty man of valor." That was humbling for me.

The Lord continues to bless our family with many opportunities to serve. Today I assist in overseeing the various departments at The Word For Today, including the publishing and radio departments and the warehouse. Cathy still works in publishing, now with our twenty-four-year-old daughter, Toni, who is Cathy's publishing assistant. Sterling is twenty-six and happily married to her husband, Gabriel. They attend Calvary Chapel Refuge and she serves in children's ministry, just like she did with us years ago. And Jesse, now twenty-eight, works in the IT department at Calvary Chapel Costa Mesa. He also serves in the high school ministry, encouraging kids not to compromise but give their all to Jesus. Because of God's faithfulness, all of us as a family, are involved in ministry.

Recently the local sheriff's department asked Cathy and I to train as chaplains to counsel incarcerated men and women in the jail system. We're presently training with a program that will support inmates with a job, family counseling, education, and most importantly, a relationship with Jesus Christ. Cathy and I will offer spiritual support and help men and women get plugged in with Bible studies and other opportunities that teach God's grace and forgiveness, with the goal to avoid future arrests.

CLOSING THE CIRCLE

Since marrying Cathy and becoming a dad, I can see how God has orchestrated my life and brought me full circle. First, He allowed me to be in an orphanage, where Christian parents adopted me, loved me, and gave me their name. Later He gave *me* the opportunity to adopt, just like my parents, and I adopted Jesse, Sterling, and Toni as my own children. He enabled me to give them the same compassion, understanding, and love that I received from my parents. Even with my sin of addiction to alcohol and drugs, my dad loved me. God allowed me to love Jesse through his addictions too and to see my son restored. I'm in awe of the Lord's powerful work in us all! He not only gave back what I lost, but He gave me more than I ever had before.

I want to thank Pastor Gerry for his ministry to reach the homeless, the outcasts, and the lost. Thank you for the opportunity I was given to be at the ranch, where God gave me a second chance to get my life back. U-Turn For Christ grounded me in God's Word and enabled me to build a foundation on the solid rock of Jesus Christ. Some people may think the ranch is too strict, but I believe it was good for me. I *needed* to restructure my life and learn how to put the Lord first in everything.

When men and women graduate from U-Turn For Christ, or from any drug and alcohol ministry, they need accountability. They need family and friends who come alongside to ask how it's going and what they're doing. They need others to be a part of their growth and get educated on what temptations will bring them down and draw them back into sin. With men, this type of accountability may seem impossible, but with God's help, it is possible.

The way to reach out to those who are hurting and in bondage to sin is with love, the Word of God, and the peace of God.

I was fortunate to have that accountability from Marta and Ephraim. My relationship with them has been fully restored, and I am blessed to have a sister who always loved me and a brother-in-law and nephew who adored me to pieces. Marta says she's proud of me, and she's especially thankful that I can serve the Lord now in many different ways. God has done so much for me.

For anyone who may be struggling, going through trials, or is tempted to get back into drugs, there is hope! There's hope because God loves you so much, and He has a plan for you. I encourage you to be like Daniel in the Bible, and don't make compromises that limit the work God wants to do in your life. Keep yourself in fellowship. Find Christian friends who will hold you accountable. Continue praying. God promises that He will complete the work He started in you and in me (Philippians 1:6).

To all the mothers who have sons or daughters going through difficult times—keep praying! It's that fervent prayer of a righteous *mother* that avails much (James 5:16, emphasis mine). Though you may not see the difference your prayers are making, or notice any change in your lifetime, keep believing in God. Believe in His promises, just like my mom believed that someday I'd answer the Lord's knock on the door of my heart. Though your children may look at you and laugh, though they may not receive what you're saying, be assured that God's promises are true. And He will keep each one.

> "Yet He sets the poor on high, far from affliction, and makes their families like a flock.
>
> The righteous see it and rejoice, and all iniquity stops its mouth. Whoever is wise will observe these things, and they will understand the lovingkindness of the LORD." (Psalm 107:41-43)

Mark, Cathy, Jesse, Toni, Sterling, and Gabriel

Lord, You are a God of miracles! From a humble Mexican orphanage to the height of leading in ministry at The Word For Today, You have had Your hand upon Mark completely. The many ways that he blesses others is greater than what Mark knows, but You see it all.

Thank you for Your amazing grace. You have poured it out on Mark's life and are using him in such special ways. Please continue to open doors for Mark and his family as they keep their eyes on You. In Jesus' name, Amen!

ONE STEP TO FREEDOM • Friday Nights @ 7 pm
Calvary Chapel Costa Mesa
3800 South Fairview, Santa Ana, CA 92704

Office: (714) 825-9673 ext. 5011
Mobile: (714) 697-6058
website: www.handsofhope.cccm.com
email: markr@twft.com

EPILOGUE

I can do all things through Christ who strengthens me.

PHILIPPIANS 4:13

THE RIPPLE EFFECT CONTINUES

We often sing about the amazing grace of God, but to experience God's grace is to simply stop for a moment and think about every breath He gives. Because with each breath we take, we're reminded that He has a plan and a desire to use us for His glory.

Jesus said,

> "The thief does not come except to steal, and to kill, and to destroy. I have come that they may have life, and that they may have it more abundantly." (John 10:10)

I believe that the abundant life Jesus spoke about includes the blessing of waking up in the morning, knowing we are saved and we belong to Him. There's an excitement in this day, realizing God wants us to represent Him and look expectantly for opportunities to bring Him glory.

In *U-Turn For Christ 2*, you've read about some men and women who have demonstrated their belief that God has a plan for the expansion of His kingdom, using lives that are fully surrendered to Him. And they share His truth and grace with everyone they serve.

When the ministry of U-Turn For Christ began in Perris in 1993, our vision was to help others who found themselves in the same bondage of addiction that we had known. But God had a much bigger plan! Today, at the printing of this book, there are thirty-six U-Turn For Christ facilities worldwide, and the ministry keeps growing. Just as in Mark Rich's story, many men and women take what they've learned at U-Turn For Christ and use it to extend God's kingdom in other ministries around the world. Do we have the makings of another book? You bet we do!

> "But as it is written: 'Eye has not seen, nor ear heard, nor have entered into the heart of man the things which God has prepared for those who love Him.'" (1 Corinthians 2:9)

We look forward to watching His amazing grace continue its work, allowing the ripple effect to spread to families, communities, states, nations, and the whole world. As we keep our eyes on Jesus, may all our lives have this redeeming influence.

I invite you to be part of the ripple effect that God wants to do in your life. It starts by simply admitting you are a sinner and then asking Jesus to come into your life and be your Lord and Savior. If you would like to do that now, just bow your head and heart before the Lord and pray with me:

Dear Jesus, I know I'm a sinner in need of a Savior. I believe You are the Savior of the world and You came to die on a cross and forgive my sins. Please forgive me and come into my life. Be the One who directs me, now and forever. I can't do this on my own, so please fill me with Your Spirit and help me live my life to please You. Thank you for allowing me to be part of the family of God! In Jesus' name I pray, Amen.

If you just prayed this prayer, welcome to the family of God! Now find a Bible-teaching church, such as a Calvary Chapel, where you can continue to grow in the grace and knowledge of the Lord Jesus Christ. Please contact us if you need help with that endeavor! In the meantime, open your Bible to the gospel of John and start reading there.

Come and visit us at U-Turn For Christ when you have the opportunity, or write to us. We'd love to hear from you, and we look forward to meeting you.

God Bless! Pastor Gerry Brown

> "And let us not grow weary while doing good, for in due season we shall reap if we do not lose heart. Therefore, as we have opportunity, let us do good to all, especially to those who are of the household of faith." (Galatians 6:9-10)

U-TURN FOR CHRIST

U-TURN FOR CHRIST U.S. LOCATIONS

CORPORATE HEADQUARTERS

°CALIFORNIA
Pastor Gerry & Peggy Brown
U-Turn For Christ Perris, CA
20170 Patterson Ave
Perris, CA 92570
(951) 943-7097 or (951) 943-2233
(951) 940-1575 fax
info@uturnforchrist.com
www.uturnforchrist.com

U.S. RANCHES

ARIZONA
Pastor Jimmy Esther
U-Turn For Christ Payson
509 W. Frontier Street
Payson, AZ 85541
(928) 468-6336
uturnforchristaz@gmail.com
www.uturnforchrist.com

CALIFORNIA
Pastor Thomas & Crystal Mendez
U-Turn For Christ Camino
5649 Pony Express Trail
Camino, CA 95709
(530) 644-1982
info@uturnforchristcamino.com
www.uturnforchristcamino.com

COLORADO
Pastor Jeff Hill
U-Turn For Christ Colorado
514 North Wahsatch Ave.
Colorado Springs, CO 80903
(719) 473-6285
connect@uturncs.com
www.uturncs.com

HAWAII
Pastor Alex & Jen Young
U-Turn For Christ Kauai
1781 Ioane Road
Anahola, HI 96703
Mailing Address: PO Box 1781
Kapaa, HI 96746
(808) 820-8014 office
(808) 651-2081 cell
uturnforchristkauai@gmail.com
www.uturnforchristkauai.com

MAINE
Seven Oaks Training Facility
154 River Rd.
Orrington, ME 04474
(207) 991-9555
sotc@ccbangor.org
www.ccbangor.org

NEW JERSEY
Pastor Kevin & Noreen Hay
U-Turn For Christ New Jersey
123 White Oak Lane
Old Bridge, NJ 08857
(732) 757-5525
elisha@ccob.org
www.ccob.org

NEVADA
Pastor John & Mary Anne Jimenez
U-Turn For Christ Pahrump
PO Box 5344, Pahrump, NV 89041
(951) 541-8087
pastorbigjohn@aol.com

NEW MEXICO
Pastor Mike & Evangelyn Gomez
U-Turn For Christ New Mexico
205 Camino Cuatro
Albuquerque, NM 87105
(505) 903-8194
uturnforchristnewmexico@gmail.com
www.calvarysouthwest.com

*Men's and Women's Ranches

OREGON
Pastor Kevin & Linda Darr
U-Turn For Christ Oregon
100 Lampman Rd.
Gold Hill, OR 97525
(541) 291-3040
uturn4christ@gmail.com
www.uturnforchristoregon.com

°PENNSYLVANIA
Pastor Ethan & Karli Mullen
U-Turn For Christ Pennsylvania
515 S. 6th Street
Lebanon, PA 17042
(717) 304-9514
info@uturnforchristpa.org
www.uturnforchristpa.org

SOUTH CAROLINA
Pastor Steve & Merol Mattier
U-Turn For Christ South Carolina
1154 Barr Road
Lexington, SC 29072
(803) 951-2197
uturn@cclexington.org
www.cclexington.org

°TENNESSEE
Pastor Steve & Christine Nordgren
U-Turn For Christ Tennessee
1186 Black Rd.
Greeneville, TN 37743
(423) 639-3720
info@uturn4christtn.com
www.uturn4christtn.com

TEXAS
Pastor Ray Todd
U-Turn For Christ Texas
1542 Villareal, TX 76905
(325) 227-1646
uturntexas@gmail.com
www.uturnforchristtexas.com

INTERNATIONAL RANCHES

COSTA RICA
Pastor David & Eva Daniel
U-Turn For Christ Costa Rica
PO Box 148-4023
61101 Jaco, Costa Rica
01150687921155
mightytosave.costarica@gmail.com

GUATEMALA
Tu Vuelta A Cristo
La Bomba, Chiquimulilla
Santa Rosa, Guatemala
(951) 943-2233

INDONESIA
Pastor Symroni Zebua
U-Turn For Christ Indonesia
Jalan Tanah Kongsi No. 73
Padang, Sumatera Barat
25119 Indonesia
085274126630
ronnieindo@uturnforchrist.com

KENYA
Pastor Duncan & Susan Muya
U-Turn For Christ Kenya
PO Box 51164
00200 Nairobi, Kenya
011254738451385 office
011254729861738 cell
dm@uturnforchristkenya.com
www.uturnforchristkenya.com

MEXICO
Pastor Martin Guevara Nunez
Tu Vuelta A Cristo
Playa Dorado No. 22-B
FRACC. Punta Banda
Ensenada, B.CFA 22791
0115216461212422
tvcristo.ens.mx@gmail.com

PHILIPPINES
Pastor Ron & Tess Brown
U-Turn For Christ San Joaquin
Brgy. San Joaquin, Tinambacan Dist.
Calbayog City, W. Samar 6710
011639162241400
pbwy92506@yahoo.com

Pastor Jerry & Edhna Timagos
U-Turn For Christ Bantian
Brgy. Bantian, Tinambacan Dist.
Calbayog City, W. Samar 6710
jeady18mission@yahoo.com

Romualdo "Wads" & Luming Guerrera
U-Turn For Christ Catbalogan
Brgy. Mercedes
Catbalogan City, W. Samar 6700
wadsboy2004@yahoo.com

Pastor Lemuel & Belen Yabor
U-Turn For Christ Lalawigan
Brgy. Lalawigan
Borongan, E. Samar 6800
lemuelyabor@yahoo.com

Pastor Angel "Bong" & JoMarie Ambel
U-Turn For Christ Carayman
Brgy. Carayman
Calbayog City, W. Samar 6710
bongsk2005@yahoo.com

Pastor Mark Glenn Pintor
U-Turn For Christ San Julian
Brgy. Lunang
San Julian, E. Samar 6814
pintorglenn@yahoo.com

Pastor Emil Santiago
U-Turn For Christ Tacloban
Brgy. Anabong
Tacloban City, Leyte 6500
emilsantiago28@ymail.com

PHILIPPINES *CONTINUED*
Pastor Joshua Bajado
U-Turn For Christ School Of Ministry
Brgy. Locsoon
Borongan, E. Samar 6800
joshuabb@hotmail.com

Pastor Jerome & Belen Belarmino
U-Turn For Christ Hernani
Hernani, Eastern Samar
belarminojerome55@yahoo.com

THAILAND
Pastor Joe & Sarah Nelson
U-Turn For Christ
Ban Patong
Phuket, Thailand
01166850293717
joe.nelson27@yahoo.com

Pastor Eric and MJ Johansen
Calvary Bible Training Center
PO Box 67
Mae Sariang, Mae Hong Son58110
Thailand
01166869653286
eric@centralthaimissions.com
www.centralthaimissions.com

TRINIDAD & TOBAGO
Pastor Francis & Adina Celestine
U-Turn For Christ Trinidad & Tobago
330 Bacchus Trace
Valencia, Trinidad & Tobago
(757) 221-0551
calvary.valencia@yahoo.com